THE ENLARGEMENT OF THE EUROPEAN COMMUNITY

Admission to the European Community involves major challenges for the new members: Greece, Portugal and Spain. This book opens with an overview by Juan Antonio Payno of the Banco Exterior de España. This is followed by a historical perspective by the well-known Spanish historian, Josep Fontana. After that, each new member is examined in turn – first a description of its economic characteristics and motives for joining the Community, then chapters on its agriculture and on its industry, bringing out both the problems and the opportunities posed by Community membership.

Each chapter is written by a specialist. The analysis shows that the productive sectors of all three economies, especially Portugal, are backward in comparison with the Nine which joined first – more so than the Commission in Brussels seems to realise.

Some small farmers will have difficulty surviving after entry and major changes in the Community's Common Agricultural Policy will be needed to accommodate products such as olives, fruit and tomatoes.

In industry, import liberalisation has already gone a long way, at least in Greece and Portugal, but this study points to the problems raised for both the entrants and the Community's first Nine members in industries already in trouble, for example steel, shipbuilding, textiles and clothing.

This is a companion volume to *The Second Enlargement of the EEC: The Integration of Unequal Partners*, edited by Dudley Seers and Constantine Vaitsos, which discusses issues of Community policy from the viewpoint of the Nine.

STUDIES IN THE INTEGRATION OF WESTERN EUROPE

General Editors: Dudley Seers, Professorial Fellow, University of Sussex, and Constantine Vaitsos, Professor of Political Economy, University of Athens

Edited by Dudley Seers and Constantine Vaitsos with the assistance of Marja-Liisa Kiljunen — INTEGRATION AND UNEQUAL DEVELOPMENT
The Experience of the EEC

Edited by Dudley Seers and Constantine Vaitsos with the assistance of Marja-Liisa Kiljunen — THE SECOND ENLARGEMENT OF THE EEC
The Integration of Unequal Partners

Edited by José Luis Sampedro and Juan Antonio Payno with the assistance of Fuencisla Rico Martín and Emma Rodríguez Pinar — THE ENLARGEMENT OF THE EUROPEAN COMMUNITY
Case-Studies of Greece, Portugal and Spain

The Enlargement of the European Community

Case-Studies of Greece, Portugal and Spain

Spanish original edited by
José Luis Sampedro and Juan Antonio Payno
with the assistance of Fuencisla Rico Martín
and Emma Rodríguez Pinar

English version edited by
Lyn Gorman and Marja-Liisa Kiljunen

First published 1983 by
THE MACMILLAN PRESS LTD
London and Basingstoke
Companies and representatives throughout the world

ISBN 0 333 34464 2

Printed in Hong Kong

Contents

List of Tables

Preface to the Series

DUDLEY SEERS
CONSTANTINE VAITSOS

This series is designed to explore the implications of integration in Western Europe, specifically the issues raised by the planned (second) enlargement of the European Economic Community to include three new Mediterranean countries - Greece, Portugal and Spain - all somewhat poorer than the existing members.

The series originated in the Institute of Development Studies at the University of Sussex. Work there on Ireland, Italy and Portugal had shown some similarities between the structural problems of countries on the periphery of Europe and those of countries in the 'Third World'. A workshop to explore these similarities was convened at the IDS in November 1977, and its proceedings led to the publication of Underdeveloped Europe: Studies in Core-Periphery Relations.

The next step was the formation of a working group on the European Periphery under the aegis of the European Association of Development Institutes (EADI). The enlargement of the EEC was identified as a focus for further work. Restructuring the economies of the new members, especially their agricultural and industrial sectors, to enable them to survive in competition with the powerful countries that form the core of Western Europe, raises issues familiar to those working in the development field.

Secondly, the enlargement raises questions about EEC policy towards other 'underdeveloped' countries, especially those with exports that compete in West European markets with the products of the new members of the Community.

The series starts with a volume that reviews the experience of the EEC so far on the development of its countries and regions, and its impact on countries of the 'Third World'. The other volumes look at the structure of the new members and the policy issues raised by the enlargement, both for them and the existing Community.

Preface

The Banco Exterior de España, in collaboration with both the Institute of Development Studies (IDS) at the University of Sussex and the Instituto de Cooperación Iberoamericana (Madrid), held the Second Conference on 'Integration and Unequal Development: The Enlargement of the EEC' from 15 to 20 October 1979 in Madrid as part of a series of international conferences in this field. The papers discussed at this meeting are published in two volumes. The first was The Second Enlargement of the EEC: The Integration of Unequal Partners, London, Macmillan, 1982.

Besides the authors of the papers collected here, the following took part in the discussions:

Friedrich W. Albrecht (Commission of the European Communities, Brussels)
Guido Ashoff (Deutsches Institut für Entwicklungspolitik, Berlin)
Manfred Bienefeld (IDS, University of Sussex)
Walter R. Böhning (ILO, Geneva)
Manuela da Silva (Instituto Superior de Economía, Lisbon)
Christian Deubner (Stiftung Wissenschaft und Politik, Ebenhausen)
Amalia Fernández Navarro (Servicio de Estudios Económicos, Banco Exterior de España, Madrid)
Paule Gentot (Commissariat Général du Plan, Paris)
João Guimaraes (Institute of Social Studies, The Hague)
Gabriel Guzmán (Instituto de Cooperación Iberoamericana, Madrid)
Louka T. Katseli-Papaefstratiou (Yale University)
Marja-Liisa Kiljunen (IDS, University of Sussex)
Nikolas P. Kyriazidis (Barclays Bank International, Athens)
Alfonso Lasso de la Vega (Departamento Central de Comercio y Relaciones Exteriores, Banco Exterior de

España, Madrid)
Ramón López Suevos (Universidad de Santiago de Compostela)
Dermot McAleese (Bank of Ireland, Dublin)
Rafael Martinez Cortiña (Banco Exterior de España, Madrid)
José Angel Moreno Izquierdo (Servicio de Estudios Económicos, Banco Exterior de España, Madrid)
Juan Muñoz García (Instituto de Cooperación Iberoamericana, Madrid)
Aurora Murteira (Ministerio da Industria e Tecnologia, Lisbon)
Marios Nikolinakos (Athens)
Peter O'Brien (UNIDO, Vienna)
Jaime Requeijo (Universidad Complutense de Madrid)
Annette Robert (Institute of Social Studies, The Hague)
Matias Rodríguez Inciarte (Secretario General para las Relaciones con las Communidades Europeas, Madrid)
Gonzalo Sáenz de Buruaga (Ministerio de Economía y Comercio, Madrid)
Philippe de la Saussay (IDS, University of Sussex)
Pedro Solbes Mira (Ministerio de Economía y Comercio, Madrid)
Ernesto Tironi (CIEPLAN, Santiago)
Robert Triffin (Université Catholique de Louvain, Brussels)(1)
Loukas Tsoukalis (St Catherine's College, Oxford)
Angel Viñas (Universidad de Alcalá de Henares, Madrid)
Julio Viñuelas (Ministerio de Economía y Comercio, Madrid)
Pedro Vuskovic (CIDE, Mexico)
George N. Yannopoulos (National Bank of Greece, Athens
Bernard Ybars (Institut Economique Régional du Sud-Ouest, Burdeos)

The Servicio de Estudios of the Banco Exterior de España contributed significantly to this volume, which was originally prepared in Spanish by Fuencisla Rico Martín with the assistance of Emma Rodríguez Pinar, under the direction of J. A. Payno. Data for the Statistical Appendix were compiled in the Data Bank Section of the Servicio de Estudios, Banco Exterior de España, by Fernando García Díez in collaboration with Hilario Moyano Campos, under the supervision of J. A. Payno.

The English edition was edited by Lyn Gorman and Marja-Liisa Kiljunen under the direction of the series editors. Helena Mann's meticulous work in preparing the camera-ready copy is greatly appreciated.

NOTE

1. Robert Triffin's paper appears in the first volume of this series, Integration and Unequal Development: The Experience of the EEC, London, Macmillan, 1980.

List of Abbreviations and Symbols

CAP	Common Agricultural Policy
CET	Common external tariff
DC	Developed country
EAGGF	European Agricultural Guidance and Guarantee Fund (also FEOGA)
ECSC	European Coal and Steel Community
ECU	European Currency Unit
EEC	European Economic Community (also referred to as 'the Community')
EFTA	European Free Trade Association
EMS	European Monetary System
EMU	European Monetary Union
ERDF	European Regional Development Fund
EUA	European Unit of Account
GATT	General Agreement on Tariffs and Trade
GDP	Gross Domestic Product
GNP	Gross National Product
GSP	Generalised System of Preferences
GVA	Gross value added
IMF	International Monetary Fund
LAFTA	Latin American Free Trade Association
LDC	Less developed country
MCA	Monetary Compensatory Amount
NIC	Newly industrialising country
OECD	Organisation for Economic Cooperation and Development
PASOK	Pan-Hellenic Socialist Movement
SDR	Special Drawing Right
SITC	Standard International Trade Classification
TNC	Transnational corporation (also 'transnational enterprise'/'multinational enterprise'/'multinational corporation')
UK	United Kingdom
UN	United Nations
USSR	Union of Soviet Socialist Republics
VAT	Value Added Tax
( )	not applicable

n.a. not available
- zero or negligible

NOTE
Abbreviations used only once or very rarely are not included in this list which incorporates those used frequently or in several places in the text.

Notes on the Editors and Contributors

JOSÉ LUIS SAMPEDRO was Professor of Economic Structures at the Universidad Complutense, Madrid, from 1955 to 1972, Consultant for the World Bank in the Dominican Republic in 1972, and Adviser in Spanish ministries and economic institutions. He is author of Efectos de la Unidad Económica Europea (1957), El Futuro Europeo de España (1960), Perfiles Económicos de las Regiones Españolas (1964), Las Fuerzas Económicas de Nuestro Tiempo (1967), and other books.

JUAN ANTONIO PAYNO, Deputy Director of the Servicio de Estudios Económicos, Banco Exterior de España and Professor of Economic Structures at the Universidad de Valladolid, has also been Associate Professor at the Universidad Complutense, Madrid, and previously in the Basque region. He has worked on production structures, economic methodology and regional analysis Among others, he has supervised the following studies: La Crisis de los 70 (1978) and Informe a la Junta de Canarias sobre la posible adhesión de las Islas a la CEE (1980).

FUENCISLA RICO MARTÍN is an Economist with the Servicio de Estudios Económicos, Banco Exterior de España.

EMMA RODRÍGUEZ PINAR is a Bachelor of Economic Sciences.

LYN GORMAN, previously Assistant Secretary (Research and Publications) at IDS, is a member of the Faculty of Education Studies, Brighton Polytechnic. Her publications include articles on trends in development research, information dissemination and the funding of development research.

MARJA-LIISA KILJUNEN was previously a Research Officer

at IDS. She is co-editor of Underdeveloped Europe: Studies in Core-Periphery Relations, and assisted in editing previous volumes in this series.

VASCO CAL is a representative of 'CGTP (Intersindical)' on the Comité de Precios e Ingresos, Junta Nacional de Planificación Nacional, Portugal. He is a Member of the Consultant Committee of the European Free Trade Association (EFTA).

JOÃO CRAVINHO has been responsible for the Industrial Planning and Project Studies at the Central Planning Office, Lisbon; he was Director of the Planning Cabinet in the Ministry of Industry; Supervisor of Industrial Economic Courses at the Universidad de Lisboa; and Minister of Industry in the Fourth Provisional Government. He is now Director of the Basic Studies Group on Industrial Economy, Ministry of Planning, Lisbon; Director of Economic Coordination; and Fellow at the Institute of Development Studies (IDS) at the University of Sussex. He is a member of the Directive Committee of the Socialist Party. He is also co-author of Un Obstaculo ao Desenvolvimento Industrial: o Excessivo Volume de Capital Circulante, Lisbon, 1968.

LUIS CARLOS CROISSIER is Professor of Economic Policy at the Universidad Complutense, Madrid; Chairman of the International Relations Section at the General Technical Secretariat, Ministerio de Industria y Energia, Madrid; and, since 1979, Programme Director in the same Ministry.

SOPHIA EFSTRATOGLOU-TODOULOU is Senior Research Fellow at the Centre of Planning and Economic Research, Athens, and part-time Lecturer in the Department of Economics, University of Athens.

JOSEP FONTANA is Professor of Economic History at the Universidad Autónoma de Barcelona. His publications include La Quiebra de la Monarquía Absoluta, Barcelona, 1978; Cambio Económico y Actitudes Políticas en la España del Siglo XIX, Barcelona, 1978; and La Crisis del Antiguo Régimen, Barcelona, 1978.

ACHILLES G. J. MITSOS holds a DPhil (Economics) from the University of Pittsburgh. He has been Chairman of the EEC Affairs Department, Research Division, Bank of Greece, since 1976.

ADMANTIOS PEPELASIS has been Professor of Economics in several universities in the United States and Athens; Economic Adviser to FAO; member of the Greek Delegation to the UN (Geneva) and OECD (Paris); Director of the Planning and Economic Research Centre, Athens; Governor of the Agricultural Bank of Greece. His publications include *Surplus Labour in Greek Agriculture 1953-1960*, Athens; *Les Problèmes de la Main d'Oeuvre en Greece dans le Cadre du Marché Commun*, Athens; *Rural Issues*, Athens.

JOSÉ J. ROMERO RODRÍGUEZ is Emeritus Professor of Economic Structure and Operational Research, and Chairman of Studies, at the Escuela Superior Tecnis Empresarial Agricola, Cordoba; and Chairman of Studies in the Colegio Universitario de Ciencias Empresariales, Cordoba. He is author of *Colonizacion Agraria en Andalucía*, Seville.

JEAN SIOTIS has been Vice-director of UNRISD (Geneva) since 1975. He was a consultant to the Carnegie Foundation for International Peace, 1960-75; Adviser to the UN Association of Switzerland; Professor at the Postgraduate Institute of International Studies, Geneva. He is the author of *Economic Commission for Europe in the Emerging European System*, 1967; *Permanent Missions to International Organizations*, 1973, and other works.

ARMANDO TRIGO DE ABREU is Associate Researcher in the Agricultural Economic Research Centre, Instituto Gulbenkian de Ciencias, Lisbon; member of the National Planning Council of Portugal; and member of the Executive Committee of EADI. He is author of *Crecimento Regional no Portugal*, 1969; *Movimento Social, Reforma Agraria, Autonomia e Estabilidade do Setor Social*, 1976.

Introduction: The Second Enlargement from the Perspective of the New Members

JUAN ANTONIO PAYNO

The 'second enlargement' of the EEC is considered a single process even though it involves the independent accession of three different countries at different times. The Community talks of a 'global Mediterranean policy' and published a 'fresco' on the enlargement (1). There has been a tendency in Brussels to 'globalise' the enlargement, to generalise the problems of any one of the new members to the others. Yet the Commission has in fact reacted in different ways to the three applications (2) and 'globalisation' has not corresponded to the reality of the separate negotiations, nor to the different approaches of each applicant, based on their different domestic policies. This insistence on a single process may have distorted the negotiations and led to the problems of each member being generalised as if they had common problems.

There is also a tendency to treat the first and the second enlargements as implicitly comparable although in fact there are substantial contrasts. Table I.1 provides data on the two enlargements. Whereas the first brought increases of similar magnitudes in both population and area, the second implies an increase in population which is half as great as the increase in territory and less than the previous enlargement. The contrast between the two extensions is even greater with respect to GDP, which would only rise by some 11 per cent this time.

The three countries of the first enlargement (Britain, Denmark and Ireland) together presented characteristics similar to those of the Six: they were weaker only in some industries such as steel, automobiles and textiles. They made no contribution as regards olive oil and oranges and very little as regards other fruit. On the other hand, they were important shipbuilders. Greece, Portugal and Spain, the countries of the second

TABLE I.1 The first and second enlargements of the EEC: relative size of the enlarged Community

(percentages)

	EEC (the Nine)/EEC (the Six) 1973	EEC (the Nine)/EEC (the Six) 1979	EEC (the Twelve)/EEC (the Nine) 1979	Shares of the Three		
				Greece	Portugal	Spain
Area	130	130	148	9	6	33
Population	133	133	122	4(a)	4(a)	14(a)
Population of working age	135	136	119	4	3	12
Density of population	102	102(a)	83	42	64	43
Gross Domestic Product	125	125	111	2	1	8
Export of goods	123	124	104	-	-	3
Import of goods	130	128	107	2	1	4
Export of goods extra EEC (the Twelve)	133	130	105	1	1	3
Import of goods extra EEC (the Twelve)	143	132	109	2	1	6
Automobile production	122	133(b)	109(b)	-(b)	-(b)	9(b)
Launched ships	146	158(b)	127(b)	1(b)	6(b)	21(b)
Textile production	126	129(b)	121(b)	4(b)	5(b)	13(b)
Pig iron production	122	119	110	1	0	9
Cereal production	131	130	117	4	1	12
Milk production	133	132(c)	107(c)	1	1	5
Meat production	132	130	115	2	2	11
Orange production	100	100	235	24	6	105
Olive oil production	100	100	250	48	8	94
Fruit production, except melons	-	102	139	6	4	28
Energy deficit	134	110	114	2	2	10
Energy consumption per capita	104	102(b)	90(b)	40	21	50
Naval fleet	n.a.	187	164	51	2	11
Fishing catch	201	n.a.	140(b)	2(b)	6(b)	32(b)

SOURCES
Area: OECD, _Etudes Economiques_;
Population: IMF, _International Financial Statistics_, February, 1981;
Estimated population for 2000: _World Development Indicators_, World Bank, 1980;
Population of working age: The Economist Intelligence Unit (EIU), April, 1981;
Density of population: OECD, _Etudes Economiques_ and EIU, April, 1981;
Gross National Product: EIU, April, 1981;
Exports and imports: OECD, _Microtables_ 1979 and _Statistics of Foreign Trade_, (_Trade by Commodities_);
Production of automobiles, ships and textiles: UN, _Yearbook of Industrial Statistics_, 1978 Edition;
Production of crude iron: UNESID, _Informacion siderurgica_ (monthly), several numbers of 1980;
Agricultural production: FAO, _Production Yearbook_, 1979;
Energy deficit: _UN Yearbook of International Trade Statistics_, 1976 and OECD _Microtables_ 1979;
Energy consumption per capita: _UN Statistical Yearbook_, 1978; EIU, April 1981, and World Bank, _World Development Indicators_;
Naval fleet: Construnaves, _Boletin de Información sectorial_ (several numbers);
Fishing catches: FAO, _Anuario Estadistico de pesca_, 1978.

NOTES

(-):	less than 1
- :	nil
(a):	1980
(b):	1978
(c):	whole fresh cow's milk
n.a. :	not available

enlargement, show relatively low figures in GDP, exports and imports, automobile production and steel, cereals, milk and meat; against this, they will add considerably to Community output of ships, textiles, olive oil, oranges and other fruits. Their energy consumption per capita is much below the Community level, especially in Portugal (where it is only 21 per cent of that of the Nine).

Whereas the first enlargement brought overall increases in magnitudes, but involved homogeneous structures and did not require much global change in EEC policies, the second enlargement is presented as an accession of three countries essentially different from the Nine, implying that Community policies will no longer be so applicable (3). Here is where many of the difficulties lie, rather than in a change in the international economic environment.

The comparison with the first enlargement has also encouraged the excessive generalisation already mentioned about the new members. It is true that Britain obviously dominated this first set of three, but there were also many common problems because of its trade links with Ireland and Denmark. One cannot call the weight of the Spanish economy decisive in aggregate terms (see Table I.1) representing approximately three-quarters of the total economic weight of the Three. Greece, Portugal and Spain have only minimal commercial connections (see Table I.2).

There are problems in Greece and Portugal whose dimensions would not be excessively serious for the EEC but may be so in the case of Spain. Some specific problems in one of the Three are so important for the EEC that they affect its policies toward the trio.

There are three main aspects: (a) the historic need for incorporation, among other reasons because of the search for national identity; (b) the choice of a social and political, and therefore economic, model and the dynamics of the national economy as a determinant of the future; and (c) the degree to which those in each national economy can think of long-term development within the international context and in terms of relations with more industrialised countries, particularly the EEC. There are divergencies of viewpoint on these issues in the Three, reflecting perhaps not only the different capacities of each economy, but also different social and political relations which are linked in part with the level of development and in part with the immediate social and political history of each country. But in all three these questions are more decisive - judging from the contributions in this volume - than more or less mechanical calculations about each product (or range of products). Before examining these issues, it may be useful to establish the comparative features of the three economies.

TABLE I.2 Commercial links between Greece, Portugal and Spain

Country of origin	Percentage share in the total imports of each country according to origin		
	Greece	Portugal	Spain
Greece	-	0.3	0.2
Portugal	0.1	-	0.5
Spain	1.4	5.7	-

Country of destination	Percentage share in the total exports of each country according to destination		
	Greece	Portugal	Spain
Greece	-	0.4	0.8
Portugal	0.3	-	2.3
Spain	0.5	2.9	-

SOURCE
OECD, Trade by Commodities, Paris,1979, *seriatim*, and author's calculations.

The point is not to dismiss the problems of the Nine. Rather it is perhaps convenient to consider the difference in approach (reflected in different reasons for joining the Community). This stems from a perspective on history and on the world which does not entirely coincide with those that are, say, Germanic in origin. It is true that the European Community is going to become more heterogeneous. (Today it is heterogeneous, but regions and countries lagging behind the rest have relatively little weight.) It is important to take account of the point made by Josep Fontana (see Chapter 1) that perhaps the internal constraints in each country have been underestimated, since commercial relations alone cannot explain underdevelopment. Then the question is whether inequalities could be aggravated rather than diminished by integration, and it is obvious that the answer depends on the way they are analysed.

Neo-classical analysis, which dominates official documents, is not necessarily appropriate since it takes no account of combined effects, in spite of trying to analyse an essentially total process. In any case, there are two classical prejudices to be overcome: (a) generalisations about nations; and (b) the linked tendency to assume that increasing dependence of the countries concerned implies an aggravation of the situation for each part or group of them. One must be alert to the difference which different levels of analysis will produce.

Institutional Differences

There are noteworthy coincidences in the recent political history of Greece, Portugal and Spain: in the space of two years all three escaped from dictatorial regimes and they have all set up parliamentary systems. Nonetheless, there were substantial differences, especially as regards the Greek dictatorship of the colonels, with a duration (1967-74) and a philosophy far removed from those of the Iberian dictatorships. And, although the distributions of political forces in the parliaments of the three countries are more or less similar, the positions of the parties are substantially different, in particular concerning the EEC.

Undoubtedly, Spain has been least open to the outside world: even the proportion of foreign trade with respect to GDP is lower, and isolation has been decisive in social terms, with limitations on contacts abroad and representation in international organisations.

With regard to economic features, although it has been said that the Three are protectionist, this is an over-simplification. Portugal has lived traditionally in a free trade regime with an economy based on its colonies (see Chapter 5), and has belonged to the EFTA since its foundation; Greece was the first country to ask for special relations with the EEC in 1958, and from 1962 it had an Association Agreement, although this was interrupted by the EEC during the seven years of dictatorship; Spain, on the contrary, has had a strong protectionist tradition and even a long period of economic autarchy (1940-53). Its commercial Agreement with the EEC in 1970 was important, but it has not entailed trade liberalisation.

From another point of view, Spain has had the longest and most global policy of attracting foreign investment and tourism; these factors do not have the same significance in Portugal or Greece as in Spain. For example, in 1979 (see Table I.3) the balance of services represented 39 per cent of the trade deficit in Greece, 4 per cent in Portugal and 94 per cent in Spain; the inflow of long-term capital was respectively 27, 37 and 56 per cent of the trade deficit.

This has helped to shape different economic regimes: while in Greece big foreign firms tend to form an enclave, in Portugal they dominated (before nationalisation) sectors with dual characteristics (large companies together with a multitude of very small firms), and in Spain their presence is much more general throughout the economy.

While these characteristics derive from the different histories of the Three, there are also other problems of identity. For Greece there was the dilemma of being Eastern or Western (see Chapter 2); for Spain the problem is fundamentally one of internal identity (see Chapter 8); for Portugal following the Revolution, the main option was originally seen as one of different ways to socialism and the choice of EEC membership implied choosing the Western way.

TABLE I.3 Balance of payments of Greece, Portugal and Spain, 1979 and 1972

(US $ millions)

	1979			1972		
	Greece	Portugal	Spain	Greece	Portugal	Spain
Exports	3,931	3,593	18,311	835	1,307	3,920
Imports	-8,944	-6,015	-24,023	-2,161	-2,041	-6,236
Trade balance	-5,013	-2,422	-5,712	-1,326	-734	-2,316
Services	1,957	98	5,370	354	208	2,028
Transfers	1,163	2,472	1,789	580	881	868
Current account balance	-1,893	148	1,447	-392	355	580
Long-term capital	1,329	904	3,196	647	-96	231
Basic balance	-564	1,052	4,643	255	259	811
Short-term capital	39	-990	1,525	249	-10	101
Charges on reserves	-2	-99	-3,646	-512	-356	-1,492

SOURCE
IMF, *International Financial Statistics*, Washington, *seriatim*.

Structural Differences

The Three have levels of labour force participation which are lower than the European average. This is due mainly, especially in Spain and Portugal, to the fact that they have younger populations (therefore a higher dependency rate), as a consequence of faster demographic growth, which also means relatively fewer old people. Mortality is highest in Portugal which reflects its lower level of development, but a lowering of mortality is foreseen which may stimulate population growth.

Projections show an increase of two points in the share of the population of the Three in the EEC total in the year 2000, when it would be almost 20 per cent of the EEC (the Twelve). However, the greater proportion of young people would mean that if the working population in 1980 was 21 per cent of the EEC (the Nine), then in 2000 it would be 23 per cent, bringing a net increase of more than a third. This would entail a shift in the demographic and political centre of gravity. But it would also mean a population 'more capable of adjusting to political changes and to the rapidly shifting pattern of the demand for labour'(4).

Thus the Three are still going to have a higher share in the work force than in output. Whether this is good or bad will obviously depend upon whether labour demand in the European economy will stagnate, and if not, upon its geographical distribution.

The labour surplus which exists in these countries (resulting from their economic weakness and fast demographic growth) has been moving into the EEC. Estimates indicate that in 1976 this migration accounted for 1.2 million, compared with 1.6 million international migrations within the EEC (the Nine) and 3.2 million immigrants from other countries (5). There may be a short-term problem regarding the capacity of the Community to absorb this labour surplus if integration should increase its attraction as a destination. It would provoke great social tension and strong pressure groups. This is the reason why the Greek Treaty of Adhesion fixes a period of seven years until free circulation of Greek workers in the Community. However, it also acknowledges important rights for Greek workers already in the Community. An increase in the movement in the EEC (limited periods of residence without work contracts, etc.) would not open the way to an avalanche of immigrants (6), unless many were to work illegally.

In the long run, the EEC would have the capacity to absorb this work force, but the tendency to save jobs in response to crisis situations limits this possibility, since it would imply an increase in unemployment rates which are already very high. In any case, the new members must create employment in their own territory. The important question is whether integration will facilitate the spread of industrial activity or whether, on the contrary, it will stimulate its further concentration in the core countries.

In terms of wage-earning population, both Spain and Portugal are in a similar position to the Nine. (The wage-earning population in Spain represents 70 per cent of the working population and in Portugal 77 per cent against a minimum of 71 per cent in Ireland and a maximum of 92 per cent in the United Kingdom within the Nine.) In Greece a large part of the working population is not wage-earning (many small farmers and small firms). Wages and salaries represented 56 per cent of GDP in Spain (1976) and in Portugal 49 per cent (1975), against a minimum and maximum within the Community of 54 per cent in France and 71 per cent in Luxembourg; in Greece the percentage was low, only 32 per cent. Although in Spain the proportion of self-employed in the working population is slightly higher than in the EEC or in Portugal, wage levels in Spain bear much the same relation to average per capita income as in the Community.

Agriculture

In Greece, Portugal and Spain a high proportion of the working population is engaged in agriculture and this sector accounts for a relatively high proportion of GDP. However, there are distinct differences (see Tables I.4 and I.5). Although no recent figures exist on the active agricultural population in Greece, and those for 1975 are controversial (see Chapters 2 and 3)(7), agriculture employs a greater proportion of the labour force in Greece and Portugal than in Spain. At the same time, industrial employment in Spain is greater (although Portugal comes quite close) and, above all, services are more developed in Spain.

Comparing figures on arable land (although this is not indicative of all agricultural activity) and working population in relation to the EEC (see Table I.5), the higher labour/land ratio is evident in Greece and, to a lesser extent, in Portugal. This corresponds to the lack of large land holdings in Greece: these are characteristic of southern Portugal and southern Spain (8).

TABLE I.4 Working population by sectors in Greece, Portugal and Spain

		(percentages)	
	Greece	Portugal	Spain
1971-5			
Agriculture	38.9	27.8	24.8
Industry	26.3	33.7	37.2
Services	34.8	38.5	38.1
1978			
Agriculture	n.a.	29.2	19.9
Industry	n.a.	35.1	36.9
Services	n.a.	33.7	43.2

NOTE
n.a. - not available

SOURCES
ILO, Yearbook of Statistics 1978 and 1979, Geneva, 1979; Bank of Greece, Monthly Bulletin of Statistics.

Portuguese agriculture is characterised by Trigo de Abreu as stagnant (see Chapter 6). Consequently, net imports of agricultural products had reached 12 per cent of the total trade deficit in 1978. In Greece the agricultural balance is positive and in Spain almost zero (it varies from year to year as a result of imports of maize and soya beans, mainly). As Table I.6 shows, Greek agriculture plays a greater role in total exports with Portuguese agriculture lagging behind. However, agricultural balances of the Three with the Nine are positive, and again of much greater importance for Greece and Spain than for Portugal.

These facts can be looked at in several ways, bearing in mind that in the Three agricultural exports to the Nine represent something like 50 per cent of total agricultural exports, while their agricultural imports from the EEC are far lower. So an important potential market will be opened to the EEC (except for some tropical products).

TABLE I.5 Relative shares of agriculture of the Three and of France and Italy in the total of the EEC (the Twelve), 1978

(percentages)

	(1) Arable Land	(2) Active agricultural population	(1)/(2)
Greece	4.8	12.2	2.5
Portugal	4.5	8.2	1.8
Spain	25.8	19.3	0.7
subtotal	35.1	39.7	1.1
France	23.7	17.3	0.7
Italy	15.6	21.0	1.3
subtotal	39.3	38.3	1.0
total	74.9	78.0	1.0
Other countries	25.1	22.0	0.9
Total EEC (the Twelve)	100.0	100.0	1.0

SOURCES
FAO, FAO Production Yearbook 1979, Rome, 1980, and author's calculations.

The figures for agriculture's share in GDP (Table I.7), compared with the active agricultural population, show the industrial backwardness of the Three, which Pepelasis (see Chapter 3(a)) attributes to rigidity of structures.

ABLE I.6 Agricultural trade indicators in the Three, 1978

(US $ millions)

	Greece	Portugal	Spain
otal imports	645	678	2,306
gricultural imports including mports of EEC origin	205	92	352
otal exports	3,354	2,426	13,103
gricultural exports including	1,019	350	2,290
xports to the Nine	466	173	1,371
otal trade balance	-4,294	-2,716	-5,527
gricultural trade balance	374	-328	-16
gricultural balance (the Nine)	261	81	1,019
ercentage relations:			
gricultural imports/ otal imports	8	13	12
gricultural exports/ otal exports	30	14	17
gricultural imports/ gricultural exports	63	194	101
gricultural imports from the Nine/ otal agricultural imports	32	14	15
gricultural exports to the Nine/ otal agricultural exports	46	49	60

OURCES
ECD, Trade by Commodities, Paris, 1979, and calculations by Economic esearch Department, Banco Exterior de España.

TABLE I.7 Agriculture as a percentage of GDP in the Three, France and Italy, 1978

Greece	17
Portugal	13
Spain	9
France	5
Italy	7

SOURCE
World Bank, World Development Report, 1980, Washington, 1980.

Regional Disparities
A problem which is closely related with the agricultural character of these economies is regional imbalance. As can be seen in Table I.8 (leaving aside differences in the definition of regions and other smaller differences in units), the biggest discrepancy between lowest and highest income is in Portugal; Spain and Greece have a degree of inequality which is closer to that in Italy. However, if attention is focussed on structural inequalities, the worst case is Spain and the best Greece. At this level the regional maximum is related to industrial concentration and the minimum to the predominance of agricultural activity. Thus the most industrialised of the Three, Spain, has the greatest degree of industrial concentration and most advanced agriculture, with Greece coming second in both respects.

Evidently, the Commission was right to be alarmed, since even in the most advanced province of Spain (Madrid) average income is only 85 per cent of the Nine, while the less advanced provinces reach a mere 36 per cent. For Greece, these percentages are 53 and 23 respectively, and for Portugal 37 and 13. Although all Three have important regional imbalances, the most advanced Spanish regions are closest to EEC levels, and it is likely that they might enter more easily into an economic dialogue with regions of the Nine; at the other extreme are the poorest Portuguese regions. While Greece and

Spain have per capita incomes approximately 50 per cent of the EEC average, per capita income in Portugal is in turn only 50 per cent that of Greece or Spain, that is,only 25 per cent of the Community's average.

TABLE I.8 Range of regional income per capita in the Three, 1972

Country	(Domestic product per head as percentage of national average) Region of maximum income	Region of minimum income
Greece	136	57
Portugal	147	52
Spain*	181	80

NOTE
* Disposable family income

SOURCES
EEC Commission,'Reports on the entry of Greece and Portugal'; Banco de Bilbao, 'La Renta Nacional de Espana y su distribucion provincial', Madrid, 1977.

Opening to Foreign Countries
The Portuguese economy is the most open of the Three: total exports and imports of goods and services in 1979 represented 61 per cent of GDP, while in Greece they were only 42 per cent and in Spain 29 per cent. While Greece has opened her economy since 1970, multiplying by 1.5 the share of foreign trade in GDP, Spain remains practically the same and Portugal, although it started with a much higher share, increased this by 13 per cent. However, the greater openness of Greece and Portugal means that their trade deficits of goods and services are 9 per cent of GDP, while Spain's was practically zero in 1979.

Since the services sector in Spain is more important in absolute and relative terms, the country's commercial openness is less advanced than that of Portugal. The dependence on energy imports is similar in the three cases with respect to GDP and, in turn, equivalent to the average of the Nine. However, because of less commercial openness, they represent a very high proportion of total imports in Spain and in all Three they absorb more export earnings than the average of the EEC (see Table I.9).

Differences between the Three arise in another dimension with the rapid expansion of the Greek economy during the 1970s. Its rate of investment has been much higher than those of Spain and Portugal and the capital intensity of output of the economy - insofar as it results from expenditure on fixed capital - has advanced notably in the past few years, approaching the Spanish level (see Table I.10). In fact Spain has reduced investment and maintenance, which means a decline in the capital intensity of production, perhaps an actual decline in the quantity of fixed capital, allowing for depreciation. In Portugal too it would seem that the investment effort (see Chapter 7) has not been sufficient to avert a similar fate.

As can be seen in Table I.11, Spain still has a much more advanced industrial structure, reflected in the greater weight of the chemical sector, and, above all, the iron and steel sector, whereas food products and other consumer goods represent nearly 45 per cent of industrial production both in Greece and in Portugal. According to Vaitsos (9), Greece presents 'a limited vertical industrial integration and non-diversified manufacturing infrastructure', which results in the electromechanical part of its exports to the Nine being 'less than one-ninth of the Spanish equivalent.' Musto (10) attributed to Portugal and to Greece the lack 'of a cohesive and well-structured production apparatus' vertically and horizontally. Portugal is characterised by the predominance of traditional industries based on low wages. On the other hand, in Spain there has been a certain modernisation (for the limits to this, see Chapter 8).

Spain's industrial sectors account for more than 80 per cent of the output of the Three, although in textiles it is only 62 per cent; Portugal produces 20 per cent. It is also predominant in agricultural output, more than 70 per cent as against 20 per cent for Greece, 10 per cent for Portugal, a main exception being olive oil (Greece produces 32 per cent).

TABLE I.9 Structure of foreign trade in Greece, Portugal and Spain, 1979

	Greece		Portugal		Spain	
	Exports	Imports	Exports	Imports	Exports	Imports
Food products	22.4	8.8	6.6	12.9	15.4	10.0
Drinks and tobacco	6.3	0.3	6.1	0.8	2.7	1.3
Raw materials	9.0	6.1	10.1	11.4	2.7	14.3
Fuels	11.8	21.0	0.1	19.5	1.9	30.3
Oils	1.1	0.2	0.9	0.5	2.2	0.5
Chemical products	3.4	8.3	6.0	12.2	7.6	10.1
Manufactures	31.6	12.9	35.6	14.3	29.4	9.4
Machinery and transport material	3.4	39.0	12.3	25.0	26.5	18.9
Miscellaneous manufactures	10.9	3.3	20.5	3.3	11.6	5.3
N.E.P.	0.1	0.1	1.8	0.1	0.1	0.0
Total	100	100	100	100	100	100

SOURCES
OECD, Trade by Commodities, Paris, 1979, and author's calculations.

TABLE I.10 Macro-economic structure of Greece, Portugal and Spain, 1970 and 1979

	1970			1979		
	Greece	Portugal	Spain	Greece	Portugal	Spain
Private consumption	69.1	69.0	67.2	64.2	72.4	68.8
Public consumption	12.6	14.2	8.9	16.2	14.8	10.9
GFCF	23.6	17.6	23.2	25.2	19.9	19.0
Export of goods and services	10.0	23.5	13.2	16.5	25.8	14.5
Import of goods and services	-18.4	-30.4	-14.3	-25.5	-35.0	- 14.6
GDP at market prices	100	100	100	100	100	100
Factors of foreign commerce (balance)	1.8	0.5	- 0.4	3.0	- 1.0(a)	- 0.6
Consumption of fixed capital	5.5	5.3	9.2	7.9	4.5(a)	8.9
National income at market prices	95.1	95.2	90.4	9.3	94.4(a)	90.5
Per capita income	1,091	649	990	2,801(a)	1,519(a)	2,708(a)
Trade balance	-8.4	-6.9	-1.1	-9.0	-9.2	-0.1

SOURCES
OECD, National Accounts of OECD Countries, 1952-1977, Vol. 1, Main Aggregates, Paris, 1979;
UN, Yearbook of National Accounts Statistics 1977 and 1978, New York; and author's calculations.

NOTE
(a) 1977

TABLE I.11 Structure of industrial output, 1975

(percentages)

	Spain	Greece	Portugal
Food products	15.7	26.1	26.2
Textiles and clothing	10.0	19.2	18.7
Chemicals	10.8	7.2	9.5
Coal and steel	17.3	7.4	3.4
Electromechanics	15.4	9.5	12.1
Others	30.8	30.6	30.1
Total	100.0	100.0	100.0

SOURCES
UN, Yearbook of Industrial Statistics 1978, New York, 1980, and author's calculations.

With respect to the second enlargement, the Spanish economy is much more heavily involved in trade: it represents 71 per cent of total exports of the Three and 62 per cent of the imports (the figures for imports of Greece and Portugal are 23 and 15 per cent respectively). Over the period 1972-9, both in Greece and Spain, there was a notable increase in commercial transactions (see Table I.12), more related to exports than to imports; the opposite happened in Portugal, both regarding overall pace of change and because imports increased faster than exports. At the same time, the Three continue to have a negative trade balance and increasing deficit, although the relative increase is less important in Spain.

The structure of the balance of payments presents other significant differences, since the current account balance is negative in Greece and positive in Portugal and Spain. Even in Portugal transfers are much more important than services, while in Spain the opposite is the case. Finally, the inflow of long-term capital represents only 27 per cent of the Greek commercial balance, 37 per cent of the Portuguese and 56 per cent of the Spanish.

This indicates that the Spanish and Greek economies are more dynamic, while external relations are linked more closely with interior economic activity in Spain than in the other two cases, which contrasts with its relatively less open economic situation and its greater protectionism. And at the same time, the Greek economy does not obtain comparable compensation from migrant remittances or from tourism or freight. For Portugal the role of emigrants is much more important than for Spain, which reflects the latter's higher degree of development.

TABLE I.12 Trade development of Greece, Portugal and Spain, 1972-9

(percentage increase)

	Greece	Portugal	Spain
Increase in exports	471	275	467
Increase in imports	414	295	385
Trade deficit	379	330	247

SOURCE
IMF, International Financial Statistics, Washington, several years.

Finally, considering the trade structure by products (see Table I.9), the expansion of Greek exports has been achieved with a growing proportion of exports of manufactured goods; the Spanish expansion is also due to the growing importance of chemical products, machinery and transport material (matched by the decline in the importance of food, raw materials and oils); for Portugal, too, exports of food products and oils have declined in importance, while raw materials, machinery and transport material and miscellaneous manufactured goods have increased. Fuel imports have increased in all cases representing an increase of ten points for Greece, seven for Portugal and thirteen for Spain as a share in total imports. There has been an increase in imports of food in Portugal and of raw materials in Spain.

These data confirm that Spain is more advanced industrially than Greece - in spite of similar per capita income. Agriculture predominates in Greece, while Portugal is agriculturally insufficient. Raw material exports are important for Greece and Portugal, but not Spain. Machinery and transport materials dominate Spanish exports, but are a feature of Greek and Portuguese imports.

In summary, the economies of the Three have varying characteristics and their structures, both agricultural and industrial, present marked differences, as does their recent evolution. Greece has a more dynamic economy, but her industrial structure is not integrated and is less predominant in economic activity than in Spain, whereas its agriculture is more important than in either of the other two countries. In Portugal problems of dualism are serious: agriculture is stagnant and the overall level of production is low, while industry, although not predominant, is partially modernised. The Spanish economy is more developed, more integrated, more dependent upon foreign countries, but less open commercially.

Finally, the three countries are very vulnerable to energy problems, since fuel imports represented around 20 per cent of total imports in Greece and Portugal and 30 per cent in Spain (see Table I.9). (This difference is due not so much to differences in energy sources as in consumption, corresponding to Spain's higher industrial level.) Undoubtedly, the price rises in 1979-80 will have increased these figures for all Three.

To conclude this section, it is important to emphasise how the connections of the Three with the EEC also differ. They are linked in their exports in similar proportions: around 50 per cent of the exports of each country go to the Nine, although somewhat more in Greece, somewhat less in Spain. (However, the Three together represent only 2 per cent of EEC imports: 1.3 per cent Spain, 0.4 per cent Portugal and 0.3 per cent Greece.) But the links in each case are with different countries: Portuguese exports are concentrated on the United Kingdom, those of Greece on West Germany and of Spain on Italy. However, West Germany, France, Italy and the United Kingdom, the main countries of the EEC, are all important buyers of the products of the Three (with the significant exception that the United Kingdom is not a main client of Greece). It emerges that, paradoxically, in the Three the two Mediterranean countries of the EEC - France and

Italy - are principal clients. Of course, the connections with the United Kingdom, West Germany and Holland, and partially with France, show the complementarity among these more industrial economies and less industrialised Mediterranean countries. However, the presence of France and Italy in all cases (even in Portugal which is traditionally Anglophile) indicates a complementarity also between the Mediterranean economies of the EEC and those of the new members, although this does not exclude rivalry in certain products.

THE CONSEQUENCES OF ENTRY

In analysing the likely effects of the second enlargement on the Nine, on the Three or on the foreign relations of either group, one is confronted with many approaches, different presumptions and intuitions. Many analyses are imprecise, not only with regard to the level of detail but also with respect to vague assessments of the situation in which changes are expected to occur. This is not usually the fault of the analyst, but rather the consequence of the limitations of economics, and the complexity of the situation being analysed. This complexity refers not only to the fact that there are many economic sectors and regions with networks of interactions among them, but also that these complex relationships are affected by other economic variables such as the rate of exchange or national monetary policy or the international climate, etc. In short, the number of variables which would have to be considered is so great, and their interactions so numerous, that there is a real problem of indeterminacy regarding present analytical instruments. We do not even know, generally, which are the most appropriate variables for each country.

The problem of indeterminacy is serious and refers to many different influences. Although the process of EEC integration is still partial and is proceeding in very different ways and to varying degrees in each field, such a process embraces not only trade or foreign relations reflected in the balance of payments, as well as international or national policies on production and distribution. These are all determinate, but, on top of this, many other variables are involved. Essentially integration entails a substantial change on the economic horizon and, therefore, fluctuation in the variables for any plan, whether public or private. A major difficulty is guessing these fluctuations and how the different decision-making units can adapt their plans.

These kinds of effects are often referred to under the heading 'dynamics of integration'. However, our ignorance and analytic incapacity are such that either they remain unknown, or, at best, certain assumptions are made which involve taking current trends as given. Often the analysis is limited, basically, to seeing whether present trends (for example, in the production of wine) are compatible with the new situation.

There are other problems, for example, the evaluation of what has taken place or of what one supposes could take place. One frequently forgets that in any process of change there is a group of instruments (capital, people, skills, techniques, etc.) and of relations between them (for example, productivity, market size, prices, costs, choice of products, volume of production, demand, etc.) which are given within a certain economic environment (constituted by its rules, by how these relations have functioned and their results, by the expectations of all of the economic agents, etc.). All these elements are affected by partial or general changes in the environment (which may change rules, results, performance, and always expectations, either in a more or less autonomous way or as an induced result of other changes, and often not even as a result of other changes, but simply of how people perceive them). To summarise, there are certain relations or results which were possible previously but which now in some way are not, so that any statistical analysis which compares the previous situation with the new one can only be useful if constraints are treated as desirable (which makes the corresponding analysis susceptible to being labelled ideological). This problem arises when a changing situation is analysed in a static way. On the other hand, a dynamic analysis takes into account new possibilities which the new environment permits, since change in any form, while ruling out something which was possible hitherto, normally allows something which was impossible previously.

However, it is clear that there is a fundamental difference: while what is ruled out is a definite loss, the new possibilities which are opened up are only potential. There is no assurance that economic agents are ready to go into a new field of activity or even that they perceive it. And in any case, such changes also imply costs, since one must become used to a new panorama with different data, with greater uncertainty and normally requiring changes in long-established mental or organisational customs. In other words, in dynamic analysis a key variable is the will to take advantage of the new circumstances, and this is practically impossible to estimate. It depends essentially upon information, as well as the ability, once having decided to act, to modify the available instruments or the relations among them. For this reason, dynamic analysis is often confused with normative, and in any case is inherently very uncertain.

Changes in the EEC

In the analysis of EEC integration and the second enlargement, the history of the EEC itself has an enormous influence. Three overlapping tendencies can be identified. In the first place, the strategy foreseen in the Treaties of Rome assumed a progressive advance from dealing with issues of direct interest to the Common Market to others which were of less immediate concern. Another more profound process of adaptation was added to this: fundamental changes in member countries' economies, so that what had been achieved would have a certain stability. Yet this very process has led to a degree of instability, and sectoral and national tensions. Thirdly, deepening of this process revealed problems initially unforeseen, which obliged the EEC to pay attention to matters which did not correspond with its original brief. One of these is regional imbalance, and with it, the whole problem of redistributive transfers within the Community. These problems grew out of an erroneous economic conception which maintained that progress of the whole implied progress of all the parts; that is, that an increase in national income would result in a decrease in inequalities between regional incomes. Of course, this has not been so. Another contradiction which has become apparent is that between industrial liberalism in the Community and agricultural protection.

Above all, crises in the international economy have accentuated the problems. One consequence is that the Community is on the verge of finding itself obliged to define explicitly an industrial policy opposed to industrial liberalism, which would change its functioning profoundly.

Within the framework outlined above, we should note that authors in this volume place an unusually great emphasis on the will and the ability for adaptation to new and changed circumstances. Thus, Romero Rodríguez (see Chapter 9) considers that a national effort may well be the greatest benefit of Spain's accession to the EEC. Croissier (see Chapter 10) concludes that the extent to which Spain takes advantage of the opportunities offered by membership will depend on industry's capacity to respond, and my own opinion on Spanish needs has been expressed in Chapter 8.

If the chapters of this book reflect in some way the perspective of the Three, it seems reasonable to say that, while in the EEC emphasis is given to the difficulties of enlargement (reflected in many of the chapters of Volume II in this series), in Greece, Portugal and Spain the fundamental concern is the policies to assure the changes required to deal with the new situation.

It is easy to mistake this contrast of attitudes and to brand the new countries as optimists or well intentioned (which leads one to think that the Community point of view is more realistic) or, as someone once said, to think that the new countries are looking for a _mariage d'amour_ in contrast with the supposed _mariage de raison_ of those which entered with the first enlargement. But this is not the case. It is a problem of the will on both sides. That will seems to be missing on the part of Community negotiators, who are very attentive to the defence of immediate interests, without perceiving that these can be the root of much greater problems in the long run. (See the _Introduction_ and _Conclusions_ of Volume I in this series.)

The Options for Greece, Portugal and Spain

The main question for the prospective members is not whether they will win or lose by entry into the EEC. They will clearly confront real problems (for example, over the 'sensitive' sectors and over markets). However, as Croissier and Mitsos point out, many problems of the Three - at least in the long run - do not result so much from competition with the Nine as from competition with countries at a relatively lower level of development, with lower labour costs and yet, occasionally, more modern plant.

Without joining the EEC, the Three would be faced with uncertainties regarding TNC behaviour and the world market in a period of crisis and transformation of production and the international division of labour; inside the Community, they have an opportunity to influence decisions instead of simply being affected by them.

One important question is what directions the economies of the Three will have to take in the future, and in this respect they are in very different situations. In Greece, 'European' management of the economy was adopted apparently from the signature of the Association Agreement in 1962, and was reinforced with political experience (see Chapter 2). In Portugal opinion initially was against the EEC as Cravinho indicates (see Chapter 5). Only the entry of Britain in 1973 (a country whose economy is linked with that of Portugal), and the ruin of the colonial base of the economy changed opinion in favour of accession. In Spain, in spite of the initial application for entry in 1962 (not accepted by the Community), there might be doubts, from a purely economic point of view, for many years as to whether the EEC or the EFTA would be preferable, though it needed to choose one of these, since it was relatively more isolated from European processes than were Greece or Portugal (see Chapter 8). The first enlargement carried serious implications for Spanish exports to Great Britain, and the treaties with North Africa damaged exports of Spanish agricultural products into the EEC (see Chapter 8), as happened with the Greeks (see Chapter 4).

The option for the EEC among Spanish Europeanists came from the conviction that working under rules which were fundamentally incompatible with the structure of Spanish economic and political power was the only way out of the situation of the country at that time (see Chapter 8).

The parliamentary parties have supported the EEC because it represents the possibility of breaking the stranglehold on the Spanish political process by power groups, which also prevent any transformation of the economy. In Greece the different positions taken by Karamanlis' party (Europeanist) and Papandreou's PASOK (Third-World oriented) are above all related to political and cultural options. In Portugal the opposition of the PCP and the left wing of the PSP reflects their preference for a socialist rather than a social democratic regime. If in Spain there are fewer options, this is not because there are no differences of opinion or interests but because of the social and political structure of the country, whose only way out lies in accession to the Community.

To sum up, it is necessary to sort out the following questions at least: (a) what are the changes which will be imposed on the rules and economic environment of each of the Three by entry into the EEC? (b) what will be the impact of these changes? (c) what technical and institutional relationships and methods of operation will become impossible, with what consequences? and (d) what possibilities will be opened up and what is the probability of their being used to the full (particularly in relation to availability of information, the perception of opportunities, the capacity for exploiting these, organisation and available technology)?

The main difficulty in the analysis is that a comparison is called for between the situation in the case of entry and that which could exist in the case of non-entry, a comparison affected by numerous uncertainties. Nonetheless, particular aspects can be studied and these are the concern of this volume.

Customs Union

While it is tempting to consider the Agreement with Greece as the likely model for those with Portugal and Spain, this is probably misleading. An example is the customs union. The general conditions of the Treaty with Greece establish a five-year transitional period, both for the removal of Greek tariffs against the Community and for the establishment by Greece of the Common External Tariff and integration in the Coal and Steel Community. There are some exceptions normally for seven years but in the removal of current quotas fourteen products are exempt for five years; and for the adaptation of cash payment systems and exports guarantee, three years are normally allowed.

This means that the schedule for the dismantling of Greek tariffs is prolonged by practically two years since, as a consequence of the Association Agreement, the final date for the application and reduction of duties will be 1984. Since 1975 Greek exports to the Community have been exempt from tariffs (except for the _prelevements_ and agricultural compensatory taxes), as have two-thirds of exports from the Community to Greece (the other third constituted then 56 per cent of Customs duties)(11). Greece, on the other hand, has been applying Common External Tariff rights to third countries for all products which are already duty exempt when they come from the EEC.

In the case of Portugal, quantitative restrictions were abolished in 1973. Exemption from duties was granted to 40 per cent of industrial exports from the EEC, which rose to 77 per cent in 1980, with the remaining 23 per cent to be covered by 1985; import taxes were abolished in 1980 (12) (see Chapter 5), although import surcharges of approximately 30 per cent exist for almost another 30 per cent of Portuguese imports; furthermore, the average Portuguese tariff is slightly higher than the Common External Tariff. According to Cal's estimates (see Chapter 7), it was 3.2 per cent in 1978, plus another 3.7 per cent in surcharges.

The tariff gap is greater for Spain. In 1970 Spain received in taxes 14.6 per cent of the value of imports, against 9.8 per cent in Italy for extra-EEC trade (13). Spanish tariffs were ten points higher than those of the Community. According to the Community, it applies an average tariff of 3 per cent on Spanish products (excluding agriculture)(14). Finally, although the Three represent jointly a very small proportion of international EEC trade (2 per cent), Spanish trade represents more than three times that of each of the other two countries and almost double that of the others put together.

Consequently, a transition period of five years is unrealistic in the Spanish case; the Commission itself proposed ten. In the Portuguese case, although tariffs could be removed in a period similar to that in the Greek agreement, the weaknesses and problems of the Portuguese economy may make the Community decide on a longer transitional period. It could even be nearer the limit of twelve years under the Treaty of Rome.

In the case of Spain, it is an open question whether there will be single period (Spanish thesis) or a shorter period for industrial products and a longer one for agricultural products (Community thesis). The EEC, in its 'opinion' on Spain, emphasises the agricultural difficulties of the EEC and the 'sensitive' manufactures and to some extent minimises the general industrial problems for Spain.

The EEC, like the English government, relies heavily on attacking the relevance of the Commercial Agreement with Spain of 1970, alleging that: (a) it was signed when the Spanish economy was weaker and (b) that its application is harmful for the EEC, because the reduction of tariffs applied under it (57 per cent) is greater than applied by Spain (26 per cent). In this sense, it seems to be in agreement with Cravinho's view (see Chapter 5) that the 1972 EEC-Portugal Agreement conveyed the usual message that the rich and strong must be defended from the poor and weak. The EEC forgets that the same EEC-Spanish Agreement of 1970 declared as one of its objectives the strengthening of the economic progress of both parties. Furthermore, it overlooks the fact that the 57 per cent Community reduction of the Common External Tariff was on duty levels which were much lower than those of Spain, so that the effective reduction, measured in the lowering of prices, is much more symmetrical. In any case the fundamental problem of the 1970 Agreement is that it was signed before the first enlargement and the Community did not agree to adapt it later, in spite of the fact that the entry of Britain meant a very great loss in the market for Spanish agricultural products. Furthermore, the growing share of TNCs in Spanish exports (a matter to which we shall return) means that one cannot attribute to the agreement the improvement in Spanish trade balances with the Nine; in any case, the balance of Spanish trade with the EEC is recent, after many years of chronic deficit.

The main problem of the transitional period for

Spain, insofar as the customs union is concerned, is that some positive effects are foreseen in the agricultural sector and much more negative ones in the industrial. For Portugal, the main problem is having enough time to establish a policy to cope with the impact of accession.

The effects of tariff removal will be greater and more negative for Spain because of its higher level of tariff protection. It is difficult to say more, since, as Croissier says, we do not know the motives underlying the present structure of the customs tariff and there has not been any adequate analysis of the effects of the mutual reductions introduced under the 1970 Agreement. In this connection, Cravinho, quoting GEBEI data, attributes the increase of 41 per cent in Spanish exports to competitive power, against a 64 per cent expansion of markets of the EEC.

In general, the effects will depend on commercial flows, and thus on competitive power, elasticities of demand and market size; in addition, all industrial relations are linked with commercial possibilities, which are in turn affected by the presence and strategies of TNCs (15).

The thesis that enlargement will increase the market, thus explaining increases in exports from the EEC to the new members and of exports from the Three, assumes that income elasticities of exports are low, and that there will not be a notable increase in sales in the EEC. At the same time, particularly in the case of Spain, it is estimated that the high income elasticity of demand for imports will provoke a great increase in these, with greater deficits in commercial balances. This may be so, but certain factors are often forgotten which at least alter these considerations. For example, the econometric analysis presented by Mitsos (see Chapter 4) shows, on one hand, that it is possible that the Greek Association Agreement will positively influence exports. On the other hand, the greatest part of this increase would be due to structural transformation: the sectors responsible for growth are not the traditional Greek industries, and this greater presence of new, more elaborate products corresponds to a growing concentration of exports in a smaller number of large companies. Cravinho (see Chapter 5) considers that the EFTA provided a stimulus to Portuguese exports, although in this case concentrated in more traditional industries, such as textiles and clothing. According to Musto (16), these sectors, together with footwear, still represented 28 per cent of Portuguese exports, 19 of Greek exports and 11 of Spanish exports. Yet it is precisely these products of low income elasticity, as well as agricultural exports, which will benefit little from enlargement. In addition, there are other issues such as trade diversion and sensitive products to be considered.

If the argument of income elasticity cannot explain the stagnation of exports from some countries which have shown great dynamism in recent years, it seems logical to think that the opening of a market such as the Spanish, which has been quite protected and has unsatisfied demand for some products, may provoke an invasion of imports, and in this sense it is one of the main gains for the Nine. It seems very likely that an increase in trade and in competition will be produced in the Spanish domestic market.

However, as Vaitsos acknowledges (17), the protection of the South European countries is a reflection not of theory but of structure of economic power. In this sense the loss of national control over the market can be beneficial for the population in some cases. For Spain (see Chapter 8) there are sufficient arguments that tariff liberalisation, by breaking certain situations of privilege, might be favourable for the economy, and might have a great influence in reducing general costs, and removing burdens from competitive sectors which have been paying for the inefficiency of others. On the other hand, although the Commission in its report on Spain points to the persistently high import elasticity, this is due simply to the great technological dependence of the country, a consequence of its model of dependent capitalism, further aggravated by TNCs and technical assistance agreements.

One cannot accept the Commission's argument that regional imbalances in new members will increase as a result of export promotion, because of the weak competitive position of food processing industries. Evidently, this is not so for Portugal or Greece, which are to a large extent already open to industrial competition.

The EMS

With regard to joining the European Monetary System (for which Greece has been given a term of five years), the main issue is efficiency of devaluation as a means of protection and adjustment. Briefly, for Portugal, with lower labour costs, and also for Greece for a certain period, devaluation may continue to be a partially efficient instrument. However, in the case of Spain, there exis serious doubts: comparison of the effects of export increases and rises in import prices still shows certain advantages of a devaluation policy, but less than previously.

We cannot use the low income elasticity of exports argument in connection with the trade balance and forget it when the problem of flexibility of exchange rates is analysed. The difficulties to be faced by Spain and Greece may resemble those which confronted Britain and Italy. Portugal is different, since its deficient agricultural balance would lead to very negative effects on prices. Cravinho also points to the particular danger of Spanish competition, both in the Portuguese market and with Portuguese products abroad (see Chapter 5).

TNCs

The most serious doubts regarding commercial effects relate to the behaviour of TNCs, where there exists, according to Vaitsos, a conflict of interests among present and new members. Penetration of these companies in the Three has been demonstrated, and at least in Spain and Greece, figures show a growing TNC participation in exports (although in Spain they originally invested in order to satisfy the home market). Recent data indicate that the role of transnationals in Spanish exports has intensified (18). They play a similar role in Portugal according to Cal (see Chapter 7).

One important question is whether TNCs, which have become necessary to these economies, will increase, maintain or reduce their presence. This has been dealt with in full elsewhere (19); here, it is sufficient to note the most influential factors (a) on the one hand, a market of a certain size is necessary for the maintenance of profitable manufacturing activities, so when tariff protection is reduced transnationals (as well as national companies may close plants in Spain, Greece and Portugal;

(b) on the other hand, the disappearance of frontier barriers and the recent tendency of TNCs toward international specialisation may lead to a remodelling of their manufacturing activities - in this sense Spain is better protected because of a greater degree of technological specialisation; (c) the Three may be used by TNCs based in Japan or the USA as a way of entering the EEC; (d) above all, tendencies in the international division of labour will be of great importance.

Industry

The main problem for the Three is that a great part (almost all in Portugal) of their industrial bases is facing growing competition from countries of a lower level of development. This may lead to the cessation of exports from many sectors: even their continuation as suppliers of the domestic market would be achieved only at the price of greater protection and, therefore, lower overall economic efficiency. While traditional industries have a low share in the value of industrial production in the Three, the most competitive sectors appear to be metals, transport, machinery, certain electrical domestic goods and the 'sensitive' sectors (coal and steel, shipbuilding, textiles and clothing)(20).

The CAP

As regards agriculture, there are not only important potential benefits but also very serious problems for new members. The problem of increasing surpluses in the Twelve does not seem insoluble (although more than complete self-sufficiency will be reached in wine and oil, which are two really 'sensitive' products for the Three). The problem of supply relates particularly to displacing North African countries which previously enjoyed some advantages of access to Community markets.

Greece has begun to harmonise its agricultural policy with that of the Community (and this should be complete by 1984), and Spain has established an agricultural policy which is compatible with the CAP. On the part of the Community, new treatment is foreseen for relevant products, such as lamb, early potatoes, alcohol and cotton wool. From the point of view of regulation, the adaptation of these two countries should not be extremely difficult.

The agricultural balance of the Three will worsen

because of the increase of imports from the EEC, which will replace other cheaper sources of 'Northern' products. The effect on the Portuguese trade balance may be very important, according to the figures available, and not negligible in the case of Spain. Furthermore, this will produce an increase in prices and foster inflation.

The effects on agriculture are likely to be favourable in general: in the case of Spain, for example, it is estimated that the CAP would benefit 50 per cent of agricultural output, would not affect another 19 per cent, and would damage another 26 per cent. This kind of analysis, based on official prices (guarantee, intervention or support) at a given exchange rate is merely indicative, since it would vary seasonally and with changes in exchange rates. More important problems lie in the different patterns of crops and the technical requirements for their industrial use in conformity with EEC regulations.

While Mediterranean agriculture in general may benefit from accession (at the cost of North Africa), it does not seem that this is true for all such products. As stated by Romero Rodríguez (see Chapter 9), it is probable that big farms are capable of adapting easily to new conditions, but in small farms possible price increases may slightly increase incomes without bringing farmers out of poverty. The adaptation of big farms will mean, without doubt, a reduction in labour and an increase in unemployment in regions which are already suffering. On the other hand, in all probability, it will mean a change in the structure of volumes of production, with adaptation to European demand. This could have repercussions on the structure of relative prices of agricultural products and could even affect negatively small farmers and marginal lands. In the case of Portugal, everything depends on whether the agricultural sector becomes modernised, as has been occurring in Spain.

However, the damage attributed to Northern products is purely statistical. One of the main faults of agriculture in the Three is marketing. The introduction of active marketing systems, with quality standardisation and avoidance of fraud, is essential and critical to the effect of the CAP on agriculture in these Mediterranean countries. Technological training, technical research on local varieties and adequate information on markets are three areas for inclusion in regional development plans. This must be accompanied, as Musto reminds us, by using price policy to affect output rather than income.

Other Problems

The fishery problem, which affects Spain and to a lesser extent Portugal, has international dimensions which can be resolved only within the EEC, in spite of the difficulty the Community has in reaching agreement on this.

The implementation of Value Added Tax will provoke a unique inflationary stimulus as a consequence of the inflexibility of prices. Greece and Portugal, with less advanced tax systems, may have more difficulties here than Spain. As regards transfers, the least that can be hoped for is what has been agreed in the Greek Treaty of Accession, in which a partial reimbursement of VAT paid by Greece to the EEC is foreseen (70 per cent in 1981, decreasing from year to year to 10 per cent in 1985, the last year of the transition period) and three years for its implementation after entry, since it will entail an administrative cost to companies and the government and a change in relative prices. For Portugal, capital transfers are indispensable (see Chapter 5).

The Future

In summary, there are positive prospects and potential problems. The key question - which the chapters in this book emphasise - is what the conditions are, and what policies should be adopted, so that accession may take place in the most favourable circumstances.

The EEC is confronted with a great responsibility and a major task, developing a set of instruments to reduce economic and social structural imbalances (21). This theme was developed in Volume I of this series. Aspects of such a strategy would include what Vaitsos calls 'a common and diversified industrial policy' and regionalisation of the instruments of economic policy, giving greater emphasis to structural policy than to price policy (as Pepelasis suggests). This would entail a series of instruments of aid and transfers of various kinds. An effort of national economic policy 'to create and develop the fundamental nucleus of the productive machinery on a national basis' as requested by Cal (see Chapter 7) or the establishment of a policy of sectoral reconversion which facilitates entry under the best conditions of competition for Spain. The new countries have to make efforts so that accession has some possibility of success.

The implication is that there is a pressing need to integrate the instruments of economic policy within a consideration of regional development programmes: sectoral policies cannot be indifferent to regional effects. In conclusion, a fundamental problem of the second enlargement is that the agreements and policies of the EEC which were established for six members are not adequate for an EEC of twelve with different structural characteristics in a different world situation.

NOTES

1. Enlargement of the Community: Economic and Sectoral Aspects, Bulletin of the European Communities, supplement 3/78, presented to the Council on 20 April 1978. For reasons of economy of language, I shall call the three countries new members, although only one is actually a new member at the time of writing.
2. The reference to Greece was issued 20 January 1976, to Portugal 19 May 1978, to Spain 29 November 1978.
3. See Constantine Vaitsos, 'Conclusions: Economic Effects of the Second Enlargement' in Dudley Seers and Constantine Vaitsos (eds), The Second Enlargement of the EEC: The Integration of Unequal Partners, London, Macmillan, 1982.
4. See Dudley Seers, 'Introduction: The Second Enlargement in Historical Perspective' in Dudley Seers and Constantine Vaitsos, ibid.
5. See Enlargement of the Community ..., op.cit.
6. See A. Wright, 'Libertad de Movimiento de Trabajadores en Europa', in Espana v el Mercado Comun: Politicas v Alternativas, Instituto de Empresa, Instituto Nacional de Industria and The Financial Times, Madrid, 1980.
7. See Chapter 3(a) where Pepelasis discusses the figures, giving 28.8 per cent, even higher than the estimate by the German Development Institute (S. Musto) which is 26.6 per cent.
8. According to figures given by Pepelasis (see Chapter 3(a)), in Greece, only 9.3 per cent

of cultivated land is estates of more than twenty hectares; while in Spain (Opinion on Spain's Application for Membership, November 1978) 0.3 per cent of exploitations cover 27 per cent of cultivated land (estates of more than 1000 hectares) (Chapter 9) and in Portugal (Chapter 6) the situation is similar.

9. See Constantine Vaitsos, 'Transnational Corporate Behaviour and the Enlargement' in Dudley Seers and Constantine Vaitsos (eds), *op. cit*.
10. See Stefan Musto, 'Structural Implications' in Dudley Seers and Constantine Vaitsos (eds), *ibid*.
11. *Opinion on Greek Application for Membership*, January 1976, Official Bulletin, supplement 2/76.
12. *Opinion on Portuguese Application for Membership*, May 1978, Official Bulletin, supplement 5/78.
13. *Opinion on Spain's Application for Membership*, November 1978, Official Bulletin, supplement 9/78.
14. *Ibid*.
15. See reference in Note 9.
16. See reference in Note 10.
17. See reference in Note 3.
18. Juan J. Bueno Lastra, 'Las Empresas Multinacionales v la Economia Espanola', Madrid Universidad Complutense, 1980 (unpublished doctoral thesis).
19. See Chapter 7 and Conclusions in Dudley Seers and Constantine Vaitsos (eds), *op. cit*.
20. See Musto, *op. cit*.
21. *Ibid*.

Part I

Historical Framework

1 Economic Development of the Mediterranean Countries in Historical Perspective

JOSEP FONTANA

The role of the historian in the study of economics may lie in two different directions: on the one hand, to place economic change in the context of the social structure and its evolution, to relate it to politics, culture etc.; on the other, to examine long-term transformations of economics according to a different perspective, not limited to the normally short- or medium-term horizon of the economist. The object of this chapter is to approach certain aspects of the problem of disparities in economic growth, particularly differences between the economies of some of the European Mediterranean countries (Spain, Portugal, Italy and Greece) and those of countries farther north, that might be characterised by earlier and more advanced industrialisation (the United Kingdom - England, Wales and Scotland, Ireland not included; France and Germany).

THE GENESIS OF UNEQUAL DEVELOPMENT

The interest aroused by the genesis of unequal development is not new, but interpretation of it is closely related to the way we explain the very process of modern economic growth. Those who believe that the development of trade and the establishment of a world market were essential, seek in the nature of trade the reasons for maladjustments. Such was recently the case of Immanuel Wallerstein. According to him, the establishment of a world capitalist market dates back to the sixteenth century - to the major discoveries, particularly of America - and implies the polarisation of growth in the 'core-states' of the system as well as a comparative impoverishment of the peripheral and semi-peripheral areas. 'Hence, the ongoing process of a world-economy tends to expand the economic and social gaps among its varying areas in the very process of its development' (1).

There is a major objection to this interpretation. It appears that, until the eighteenth century, only a very small part of the total product of these economies circulated through this world market and, consequently, the enrichment and comparative underdevelopment that were generated were very localised (or must be attributed to the destruction of previous economic progress, as in the case of pre-Columbian American societies). This is supported by the fact that, at the beginning of the nineteenth century, the economic differences between states still seemed to be rather insignificant, which means that three centuries of a world market hardly had any effect on the emergence of the kind of disparities we know. This is supported by all the available evidence as well as by estimations of GNP of countries in the nineteenth century, hazardous though they are.

TABLE 1.1 GNP per capita of today's developed countries (DCs) and less developed countries (LDCs), 1750-1970

(US $, 1960 prices)

Date	DCs	LDCs	DC/LDC x 100
1750	180	202	89
1800	198	200	99
1860	318	183	174
1913	646	196	329
1970	2220	310	716

SOURCE
P. Bairoch, 'Les grandes tendances des disparités économiques nationales depuis la révolution industrielle', in M. W. Flinn (ed.), Proceedings of the Seventh International Economic History Congress, Edinburgh University Press, 1978.

Paul Bairoch asserts that, in the mid-eighteenth century, GNP per capita in European countries was inferior to that of the rest of the world and that differences in their favour were not recorded until after 1830, 'due to the combined effect of the diffusion of the industrial revolution in Europe and North America and the decrease in the standard of living in certain areas of the rest of the world (attributable to the unfavourable effects of economic relations between these two areas)' (2). This statement is illustrated in Table 1.1.

In consequence, it appears that the origin of prevailing economic disparities is to be traced back to the industrialising processes of the nineteenth century. We shall see if this is also valid for differences between the four Mediterranean countries and the industrialised countries of Europe.

THE ISSUE OF THE DECADENCE OF THE MEDITERRANEAN AREA

The topic of the 'decadence of the Mediterranean area' gave rise to an abundant literature where the same platitudes are repeated and explanations given in geo-political terms: the shifting of trade away from the Mediterranean to the Atlantic - forgetting that this does not explain facts such as the ruin of the Hanse (which occurred at the same time as the decline in Mediterranean trade) or the downfall of Portugal (one of the countries best located to take full advantage of the inter-oceanic trade).

Carlo M. Cipolla, who critises this geo-political standpoint as an 'example of simple-mindedness' and shields himself behind the fact that 'the issue is so complex and intricate that in order to treat it adequately, a series of volumes would be, at least, necessary', does not offer any better explanation. Thus, referring to Spain, he affirms that: 'The decadence of Spain in the seventeenth century is not difficult to understand: the main point is that, in substance, Spain never developed itself' (3). This is an irrelevant statement as, if 'development' meant some form of substantial progress towards industrial growth, it is evident that no country in the world, in Europe or elsewhere, had 'developed itself' until the seventeenth century. Moreover, one does not know what the 'decadence of Spain' really means. Even if one ignores the contrasting rhythm of change in certain peninsular areas during the seventeenth century and accepts the identification of Spain with the crown of Castile, the decadence appears highly dubious. If it means that the Spanish state of the Austrians was politically decadent, this is indisputable, but it has nothing to do with the existence or absence of economic development. The existence of 'economic decadence' must be proved by an overall evaluation of the product, particularly in the agricultural sector. The evidence for agricultural production in this period is contradictory and, rather than decadence, it points to a more complex type of change - whereby certain forms decay whilst others rise. Gonzalo Anes formulated the following overall hypothesis: 'The depression of the seventeenth century might thus consist in Spain, as far as agriculture is concerned, in readjustments that took place slowly and automatically between the number of inhabitants and subsistence production, through the emigration of country people from over populated areas and the reorganisation of cultivation that resulted in the worse lands or those farthest away from the main centres of rural population being left uncultivated' (4).

The so-called 'general crisis of the seventeenth century' and its role in the transition to capitalism is irrelevant here. Nevertheless, if we start the comparison between Mediterranean and European industrialised countries on the basis of the only reliable series of data that might be traced back five centuries - those relating to population - we observe that something happened in the seventeenth century in the Mediterranean area that implied a different evolution from that of the rest of Europe (see Table 1.2). Such an analysis shows that, in this period, an economic sluggishness characterised the Mediterranean area, contrasting with the expansion recorded farther north. And, even if the subsequent acceleration of growth rates in the nineteenth and twentieth centuries might induce one to think that the problem has been solved, indexes based on the sixteenth century reveal that this is not the case: even in 1975 the effects of the demographic disparity that appeared in the seventeenth century had not been completely offset.

We have used demographic data for lack of others. According to one widely accepted theory, economic growth is usually related to demographic expansion in a mechanical and linear way. If that were true, we might think that the sluggishness of the seventeenth century reflects an economic decline in the Mediterranean area whilst the rapid rise of the nineteenth and twentieth centuries is representative of a phase of prosperity. Nothing could be simpler. On the one hand, we know that the demographic growth rate at the end of the eighteenth and nineteenth centuries was due, to a large extent, to the increase in birth-rate brought about by the break-down in controls in traditional agrarian society that, through limiting or delaying marriage - but also through contraceptive practices - tried to maintain a certain balance between land and food and population. Nor are optimistic inferences to be drawn from growth rates alone. Even in Spain in 1930, agrarian inland areas were seen as an 'horrendous human slaughter house' where mothers from Extremadura and Aragon lost two children out of five, 'and in certain provinces of Castile and Leon, half of them died' (5). These circumstances were similar to those in the French countryside three centuries previously.

The only conclusion to be drawn from the index relates to the existence of some phenomenon in the Mediterranean area during the seventeenth century that was reflected in population stagnation. But it is necessary to investigate the nature of this phenomenon. In seventeenth-century Spain it appears that the reasons are to be found in the social changes that produced the conditions under which eighteenth-century capitalist and industrial development established itself, whereas in Castile or Valencia these changes were restrained by a process of re-feudalism (6). If these factors influence the population figures, it is probably in relation to the ease with which the shift occurred from subsistence to another kind of agriculture that progressively specialised in market-oriented production which, as is well known, entails a strong increase of production. Thus, the re-feudalism processes might, in turn, act upon the population data, by limiting the increase in food production and the development of capitalism, by hindering the formation of a domestic market.

It is worth taking this explanation into account, as it is endogenous and has a social character only slightly related to the formation of a world capitalist market, and it allows us to point out the reason why industrialisation took place earlier and more easily in certain places. The previous level of economic development, measured according to objective indicators such as GNP per inhabitant, might be similar, as might the availability of resources convertible into capital, but the social conditions under which industrialisation was to take place were completely different (7). It was neither the volume of available resources nor the technological level that was to be applied that delayed industrialisation in the Mediterranean countries. Unfortunately, once the process had started in other European countries, its own dynamics made it more difficult for industrialisation to begin in other countries.

TABLE 1.2 Population of four Mediterranean countries (MCs) and of advanced industrialised countries (ICs), 1500-1975

	Population (millions)		Indices (1500=100)		Annual growth rate (per thousand)	
Year	MC(a)	IC(b)	MC	IC	MC	IC
1500	19	28	100	100	-	-
1600	24	35	126	125	2.3	2.2
1700	24	42	126	150	-	1.8
1800	35	58	184	207	3.7	3.2
1900	61	121	321	432	5.5	7.3
1960	89	161	468	575	6.3	4.7
1975	107	186	563	664	12.3	9.6

SOURCE
C. McEvedy and R. Jones, Atlas of World Population History, London, Allen Lane, 1978.

NOTES
(a) MC: Spain, Portugal, Italy and Greece,
(b) IC: United Kingdom (Ireland not included), France and Germany.

It is not difficult to understand why industrial growth tended, during the first stages, to be oriented towards the outside world. Once the productive structure of the country concerned had changed so that the population employed in agriculture was only a minority (and this occurred prematurely in Great Britain), the extension of growth to the domestic market required an increase in the purchasing power of wage-earners, at the expense, in the short term, of the entrepreneurs' profits. There was a contradiction between the short-term interests of the entrepreneurs (to increase consumption capacity in order to raise production to allow the volume of profits to be maintained, even if rates of profit were to decrease). Under these conditions, it is not surprising that, while foreign markets were accessible, industrialists sought there the solution to their problem - which was to sell ever more without caring about the purchasing power of the domestic market (that is, the standard of living of the workers). This outward growth was to be disguised as a civilising crusade, aimed at extending industrialisation to the whole world, creating mutually profitable interdependencies between the countries that produced primary products and the 'workhouses of the world'(8). But such was not the case. The development of the world economy in the nineteenth and twentieth centuries shows that the articulation of a world market of manufactured products only favoured the industrialised countries whilst maintaining in a backward state those that received their products. The machinery of unequal growth worked also inside Europe, among the economies that had first industrialised and those that did so later.

Table 1.3 shows the reality of this backwardness as regards the Mediterranean countries. As it is difficult to find a satisfactory index - that is, one based on available data - of the shift to industrialisation, the quotient between the value of the industrial product and that of the agricultural product has been used, so that when this value is superior to one - that is, when the share of industry in the total product is superior to the share of agriculture - it might be considered as crossing the threshold of the non-reversing process of industrialisation. The great time lags

TABLE 1.3 Ratio of industrial product (IP) to agricultural product (AP) in selected European countries, 1850-1969

	United Kingdom	Germany	France	Italy	Spain	Portugal	Greece
1850	1.7	0.4	0.6	0.3			
1880	3.6	0.9	0.7	0.3			
1900	6.1	1.3	0.9	0.3	0.4		
1913	5.7	2.0	1.0	0.5	0.5		
1935	7.7	2.8	1.6	0.8	0.9		0.5
1969	12.0	11.2	6.3	2.8	2.6	2.0	0.9

SOURCE
B.R. Mitchell, European Historical Statistics, 1750-1970, London, Macmillan, 1975, pp. 799-816, except for Spain, as a new series calculated by Julio Alcaide was used; this is published in Datos básicos para la historia financiera de España, 1850-1975, Madrid, Instituto de Estudios Fiscales, 1976, I, pp. 1127-50.

show that the difficulty in acceding to the block of industrialised countries cannot be explained merely by a later starting-point.

Certain factors contributed to this delay and their origin is not to be found in the Mediterranean countries. First of all, free trade, that promised joint growth, was deceitful. We can assert this as a general truth. Studying European trade in the nineteenth century and comparing it with the economic growth of different countries, Bairoch concluded: 'For almost all the European countries, the liberal phase was characterised by an unfavourable evolution that increased the distance that separated them from the most advanced countries. On the other hand, the protectionist phase allowed two-thirds of the European countries to reduce this disparity' (9). The experience of Portugal, which agreed to provide Great Britain with agricultural products in exchange for manufactured articles, shows that this course not only led to sluggishness but also hindered the transformation of the social structures of production, perpetuating the forms of the past under new disguises. Neither export agriculture nor emigrants' remittances (when Portuguese went and took the places previously reserved for slaves in Brazilian plantations) nor, finally, the creation of a colonial market in Africa were sufficient to lead Portugal to modern economic growth. In fact, interdependency turned out to be sheer dependency (10).

The figures in Table 1.4 illustrate the problem. From an initial situation, in 1930, of comparative equilibrium for GNP per inhabitant of the two blocks of countries, there was a shift, at the beginning of the twentieth century, to a difference of 1 to 2. And more importantly, this difference remains. Whilst a short-term analysis, based upon post-Second World War data might show a certain convergence, that would re-establish the initial equilibrium, overall data for the twentieth century reflect a simple fact - the fluctuation around an average stable value: 50 per cent GNP per inhabitant of the Mediterranean countries.

To substantiate that these time lags did not reflect any complementarity in the different evolutions, it should be noted that agriculture in one decade at least in the Mediterranean countries also followed an unfavourable trend compared with that of the industrialised countries (see Table 1.5).

TABLE 1.4 Evolution of GNP in Mediterranean (MC) and advanced industrialised countries (IC), 1830-1976

	GNP per capita (in US dollars, 1960 prices)		Indices (1830=100)		GNP per capita of MC expressed as percentage of IC
	MC	IC	MC	IC	
1830	264	277	100	100	95
1860	309	412	117	149	75
1913	398	819	151	296	49
1929	473	928	179	335	51
1950	490	1,142	186	412	43
1960	780	1,723	295	622	45
1976	1,524	2,825	577	1,019	54

SOURCES
P. Bairoch, 'Europe's Gross National Product: 1800-1975', in The Journal of European Economic History, II (1976), pp. 273-340, and 'Les grandes tendances des disparités économiques nationales depuis la révolution industrielle', in Michael Flinn (ed.), Proceedings of the Seventh International Economic History Congress, Edinburgh University Press, 1978, I, pp. 175-86. Data were reprocessed on the basis of the population census of the seven countries.

CONCLUDING REMARKS

It is difficult to escape the fact in 1979, that we face a structural crisis in industrial growth. This should compel us to reconsider much of what we accepted unquestioningly until a few years ago.

The vision of the past elaborated by the historian is often used to justify the rationality of the present. For two hundred years, historians and economists shared a vision of the history of mankind that was basically optimistic whereby they intended to prove that, every time mankind faced a severe crisis, some kind of technological miracle - the invention of agriculture or steam and mechanisation - occurred and allowed a new jump. Most progressive variants would add to the technological miracle various social conditions, but without modifying basically the prevailing view. Thus we saw men emerge from the remotest past, establishing their domination of nature through two great revolutions: the neolithic and the industrial. Now we know that there was never a neolithic revolution, and we should be able, as well, to begin to distinguish capitalism from industrialisation, the latter being, perhaps, a mere cancerous degeneration of capitalism.

TABLE 1.5 Agricultural productivity of Mediterranean (MC) and industrial countries (IC), 1955 and 1965 (IC = 100)

	Per hectare		Per worker	
	1955	1965	1955	1965
Great Britain, France and West Germany	100	100	100	100
Mediterranean countries	63.5	60.6	29.5	26.0

SOURCE
The figures are based on data from Yujiro Hayami and Vernon W. Ruttan, in Agricultural Development: An International Perspective, Baltimore, Johns Hopkins Press, 1971.

NOTE
The comparison is in units of wheat.

Unfortunately, this vision of the past was used to justify the economic forms of the present and the view that progress could be defined as the extension of industrialisation to the whole world, whether under the same social conditions under which it emerged, as Rostow wanted, or under modified social conditions. Even conceptions such as socialism were corrupted when they came into contact with the myth of industrialisation and changed their objectives, giving priority to industrial development and postponing the abolition of forms of exploitation.

While we cannot go back to the past, nor can we be blind to the bitter disillusion that resulted when it became clear that the recipe for economic progress could not be extended to all of mankind. The disillusion is felt not only by those who criticise industrial capitalism, but also by someone less susceptible to such leanings. Otto Schoeppler, Chairman of the Chase Merchant Banking Group, said recently: 'If we expect to solve the world population problem and raise hundreds of millions out of abject poverty, many trillions of dollars will be needed. If the Western world is to remain competitive, more trillions will be needed . . . Can the required capital be raised? I do not know' (11). No one would have expressed such a doubt twenty years ago.

Analysis of the past leads one to think that the machinery of economic growth that permitted the rapid rise of advanced industrial countries cannot be applied as a general rule, as it is based upon inequality and tends to perpetuate it. It does not seem that such growth could be achieved by following the same strategy, either in its 'pure' capitalist form or in 'socialist' state industrialisation. Therefore, it is advisable to look back to the very birth of capitalism, analysing its social articulations, without reducing it to its technical aspects. Above all, we must examine the stage of accelerated industrial growth, in order to be able to organise new strategies of economic progress free from previous flaws and defects. This task is not only incumbent upon the historian. The economist needs to reconsider concepts and words, analyses and measurements. Above all, both must be on their guard against merely repeating combinations of factors that produced results in the past in order to obtain the same results in the present when general conditions have changed.

NOTES

1. Immanuel Wallerstein, The Modern World-system, New York, Academic Press, 1974, p. 350.

2. P. Bairoch, 'Les grandes tendances des disparités économiques nationales depuis la révolution industrielle', in M.W. Flinn (ed.), Proceedings of the Seventh International Economic History Congress, Edinburgh University Press, 1978, p. 178.
3. C.M. Cipolla, Historia económica de la Europa preindustrial, Madrid, Revista de Occidente, 1974, p. 220.
4. Gonzalo Anes, 'Tendencias de la producción agrícola en tierras de la corona de Castilla, siglos XVI a XIX', in Hacienda pública española, No. 55 (1978), pp. 108-9.
5. Severino Aznar, Despoblación y colonización, Barcelona, Labor, 1930, pp. 25-6.
6. I.A.A. Thompson, War and Government in Habsburg Spain, 1560-1620, London, Athlone Press, 1976; James Casey, The Kingdom of Valencia in the Seventeenth Century, Cambridge University Press, 1979.
7. In the Iberian Peninsula, industrialisation began in Catalonia, where existing financial resources were far inferior to those accumulated in Andalucia due to land rents, feudal revenues and profits obtained from trade with South America. The rents of feudal rights that a noble family as the Medinaceli took from Catalonia to Andalucia, where they resided, reached much higher figures than the total investments in new industrial plants in Catalonia during the last decades of the eighteenth century.
8. It is almost incredible that, in 1979, the birth of the cotton industry in England should be commented on in terms such as those used by D.A. Farnie: 'In defiance of all rational expectation it found in India its ideal predestined vent, free from the climatic constraints of European markets, and acquired a reassuring belief in the permanence of its democratic mission to clothe the tropical two-thirds of the world's population.'
9. Paul Bairoch, Commerce extérieur et développement économique de l'Europe au XIXe siècle, Paris/The Hague, Mouton, 1976, p. 294.
10. This analysis and the quotation are extracted from the excellent book of Miriam Halpern Pereira, Livre Cambio e Desenvolvimento

Economico: Portugal na segunda metade do seculo XIX, Lisbon, Cosmos, 1971.

11. Sperry Rand Corporation, Toward New World Trade and Investment Policies, n.d., n.p., p. 33, n. 21.

Part II

Greece

2 Characteristics and Motives for Entry

JEAN SIOTIS

It would be difficult to understand what has been described as the 'Greek obsession' with becoming a member of the Community without taking into account relations between Greece and Western Europe for the past century and a half. It would not be an overstatement to call this a 'love-hate' relationship: love because the great Christian powers were instrumental in ridding at least some Greek territories of the Ottomans; love for cultural reasons and the fact that ancient Greek civilisation was considered as one of the roots of Western civilisation; and love because liberalism and pluralist democracies were spreading in Western Europe and the Greek people recognised in the heritage of the French Revolution and in British parliamentarianism the basic constituents of modern democracy. At the same time, the Greeks felt humiliated, both by the stringent limits placed on their external behaviour as an independent state, and by repeated political, military and economic interventions by the great powers. The country's forward-looking elites resented deeply the constitutional counterpart of this dependence, the successive imposition of two foreign dynasties on the throne of Greece.

Thus Greece's relationship with Western Europe combines contradictory elements. Nevertheless, the 'European model' continues to be a yardstick of progress. The forces which have dominated Greek political life since the Second World War have always made it clear that, in their view, Greece belongs to the West and the only acceptable foreign policy for the country is one linking it to the Western world. The opposite view puts forth the objective of neutralism and non-alignment for Greece.

Strong pro-European trends in Greek political opinion are still prevalent in Greek attitudes towards membership of the EEC. In the 1977 elections, approximately 65 per cent of the electorate voted for parties which held firm pro-Community views. Among the 35 per cent who voted for the Panhellenic Socialist Movement (PASOK) and for the Communist Party, many certainly do not share the anti-Community stands taken by the leadership of these two parties. Unfortunately, opinion polls in Greece are still underdeveloped and one cannot rely on their results. Nonetheless, all of the polls carried out recently and informed, even if impressionistic, assessments indicate that pro-European forces constitute the majority of Greek public opinion.

EUROPE AND DEMOCRACY IN GREECE

The seven and a half years of tyranny in Greece were a 'moment of truth' in the eyes of its people; Greeks became convinced as to their friends abroad, realising that the only support in their struggle against the dictatorship came from Western Europe. Although there were variations and shifts in the policies followed by foreign powers towards the colonels between 1967 and 1974, they can be summarised as follows:

The Democratic administration in Washington accepted, at times begrudgingly, the *fait accompli* and carried on 'business as usual' with the Athens regime, before as well as after the king fled the country in December 1967. The overwhelming majority of Greeks, however, are convinced that this 'acceptance' was a cover for effective support given by the United States to the establishment and maintenance in power of the dictatorship. The US Government was and still is perceived as having been instrumental in bringing about the dictatorship. As a result, even conservative Greek public opinion felt betrayed by their traditional friends.

The Soviet authorities, on the other hand, did not miss an opportunity to make it clear that the internal situation in Greece should in no way affect inter-state relations. The USSR did not simply 'tolerate' the colonels but it often acted as if it expected them to shift to some form of non-alignment possibly following the 'Nasserite' model.

The colonels maintained excellent relations with several Arab and African countries. Libya, Zaïre, the Central African Republic and other African countries were visited officially by Deputy prime minister Patakos and the colonels even elaborated plans for financial assistance to Third World countries. More importantly, officers from Libya and other African countries were trained in Greek military schools.

In the face of such a general external acceptance of the abolition of democracy in Greece, Western Europe was a particularly eloquent exception. The initial reaction of West European political opinion was shock and indignation. Throughout the seven and a half years, this reaction was maintained and the Athens regime was never accepted as a 'respectable' European government. As for political parties - with the rare exception of the extreme right - organised political forces in Western Europe almost unanimously acted against the regime in Athens. The pressure of the media and public opinion made it impossible for any West European democratic political party or government to move in the direction of a rapprochement with the colonels. No government broke off diplomatic relations with Greece; but several downgraded the level of their representation to that of a chargé d'affaires and many more used their diplomatic presence in Athens to help those Greeks fighting the dictatorship.

The nature of European institutions made it possible for them to act against the dictatorship more vigorously than national governments. Already in September 1967 the EEC Commission formulated the basic principles of what came to be known as the 'freeze' of the Treaty of Association with Greece. On many occasions during the military dictatorship, attempts were made by some member governments to normalise relations with the colonels. They all failed because of the firm stands taken by the Commission and by the Parliament.

A year after the collapse of the dictatorship, in June 1975 the democratic Government of Greece officially requested that negotiations be started for Greece's accession to the EEC. The Council replied positively less than a fortnight later and the Commission was asked to present its Opinion which was published in January 1976. However, the Greek Government reacted negatively to the suggestion that a pre-accession transitional period was necessary. Prime Minister Caramanlis, as well as the opposition, also rejected the view that the solution of Greece's problems with NATO and Turkey should in any way be considered as a pre-condition to accession. The negotiations were formally opened on 27 July, but in fact they began towards the end of 1976. The Treaty of Accession was signed in Athens on 28 May 1979.

THE GREEK ECONOMY: A BRIEF OVERVIEW

The performance of the Greek economy over the past seventy odd years has been more than satisfactory. This can be illustrated by the following data:

The average rate of growth in GNP (per annum) between 1962 and 1975 was almost 7 per cent for Greece and close to 4 per cent for the Nine.

During the same period, industrial production in Greece grew at an annual average rate of 9.4 per cent compared to 3.7 for the Nine.

Between 1962 and 1975 the average rate of increase in gross fixed capital formation, at constant prices, was 6.3 per cent for Greece and 3.8 for the Nine.

The share of industrial and manufacturing production in GDP rose from 41 per cent in 1962 to more than 52 in 1975.

Industry and manufactures accounted for a little more than 11 per cent of total exports in 1962, while at the end of the 1970s they accounted for more than 50 per cent.

Total tonnage of the Greek-owned merchant marine fleet rose from 13.3 million in 1962 to over 48 million in 1975. During the same period the increase for the Nine was from 45.6 to 74.3 million tonnes.

The GDP increased between 1961 and 1974 by approximately 500 per cent (at an average annual rate of 7.4 per cent).

The share of agricultural production in GDP decreased between 1961 and 1975 from 25.5 to 17 per cent (1).

As for the active population in the agricultural sector, the 1971 census gave the figure of almost 40 per cent. The Commission, taking into account the rate of decrease recorded over the past decade, calculated the percentage in 1976 at about 34-35 per cent. The Research Department of the Agricultural Bank of Greece, on the other hand, questions these figures. On the basis of sample data collected in 1976-7, the Agricultural Bank places this figure at 25-26 per cent of the total active population. This difference of views relates to the overall state of the Greek economy.

The share of investments in agriculture decreased between 1962 and 1974 from 13.7 to 9.1 per cent of total investments.

In 1970 agricultural exports to the EEC almost balanced imports from the Six ($177 and 180 million respectively); in 1975 Greek exports to the Nine had risen to a little over $300 million but imports from the Community represented $765.6 million.

Industry, Manufacturing and Foreign Investment

The quantitative development of industrial and manufacturing production has been accompanied by a spectacular increase and diversification of industrial/manufacturing exports, and some Greek products are becoming highly competitive on international markets. In addition, some industrial enterprises, such as the cement industry, have introduced highly advanced technologies.

However, in spite of these achievements, large sectors of Greek industry are still characterised by low productivity, the absence of quality control and a totally outdated approach to management and to financial returns from investments. These industrial enterprises survive largely thanks to protectionist barriers and public subsidies, which will be abolished within the next few years. The very concept of management is unknown to many of them, and they have been used to the security offered by trade barriers and the certainty that the state-controlled banks will always 'bail them out' in case of difficulties. A large section of Greek business has also been used to rapid gains which carry few risks. A return on investments of 25-40 per cent is not unusual in Greece, while quality of production is often neglected.

The technologically advanced industries, as well as the smaller manufacturing units which produce essentially for the home market, while respecting certain standards of quality will undoubtedly gain from membership of the Community. On the other hand, it is generally recognised that some enterprises which have grown behind protectionist barriers will face serious difficulties. They will have to limit their gains, step up investments and modernise, accept the introduction of modern management techniques and raise the quality of their products in order to survive. The 'bogey-man' of foreign take-overs is being used by those who oppose accession, but more and more Greeks are asking themselves whether it is preferable to sustain outdated business practices - in the name of 'national' ownership - or to accept willingly the establishment of foreign subsidiaries which will contribute to the modernisation of the economy.

Given the Greek capacity for adaptation - particularly when faced with imminent danger - there are good reasons to be optimistic about the impact of membership on Greek industrial enterprises. Notwithstanding this optimism, it would be fair to state that although large sectors - the most advanced - of Greek industry will gain or, at least, will not be affected negatively by accession, others will face considerable difficulties.

Foreign direct investment - either through equity participation in nationally owned companies or through the establishment of subsidiaries - has undoubtedly contributed to the development of Greek industry. Legislation enacted since 1953 has been particularly attractive to foreign investors but, surprisingly enough, such investments did not exceed 15 per cent of aggregate investments during the decade 1961-70. Moreover, they have tended to concentrate in certain limited sectors, related to the extracting, chemical and iron and steel industries. In spite of quasi-monopolistic privileges, Greece has not attracted an undue volume of foreign investment. The reasons probably lie in the limited size of the national market and in the inflexibility and/or incompetence of the Greek bureaucracy and service sectors.

It is difficult to foresee the effects of membership in the long run but we can reasonably state the following:

(a) The size of the Greek market no longer deters potential investors. In addition, geographic location and traditionally good relations with Middle Eastern countries can increase the comparative advantages of investing in Greek industry.

(b) Such investments could become more diversified than in the past, precisely because of qualitatively new market conditions, and they could contribute much more to the introduction of new technologies and managerial skills.

(c) The monopolistic or quasi-monopolistic positions occupied by some Greek or foreign companies in the past have become illegal under Community law and this represents a substantial gain to the consumer and to the Greek economy in general.

(d) The large number of small enterprises - employing under twenty workers - will necessarily diminish as a result of fusion or take-over. Between 1961 and the late 1970s, their number hardly decreased, from 61 per cent to a little over 50 per cent of the total number of enterprises. To a large extent, the shortcomings of Greek industry and manufacturing mentioned earlier stem from this dispersion of industrial structure, as well as from the outdated family-based ownership of some large enterprises.

(e) Independently of direct foreign investment and of its impact on Greek industry, the competitive framework of the Common Market will force even its most reluctant sectors - as well as the public authorities - to introduce quality controls which are so badly needed in Greece.

The mining and energy resources of Greece represent an important comparative advantage for Greek industry. The proven existence of large base metal resources - Greece is the only country in the Community of Ten to have such resources - will provide raw materials for the development of new industries. Given the dependence of the Community on raw materials imports, this potential should not be neglected in any evaluation of the prospects for Greek industry.

Services

(a) Approximately 90 per cent of Greek banking is publicly controlled and the remainder is under particularly stringent public controls. This is a remnant of the past, the pre-war and the immediate post-war periods. The role of central government authorities in regulating credit goes further than in any other European country. Many of the laws, regulations and practices in force will have to be progressively adapted to conform with the Community banking practices. Some of the major Greek banks are already working in this direction, but the distance to be covered before they become truly competitive within the Community is still large.

(b) The Greek transportation system, which was never particularly good, did not recover fully from the effects of the Second World War and the civil war which followed. The rapid development of the economy as a whole has not been accompanied by a parallel development of transportation infrastructure. The major ports - Piraeus and Salonica in particular - meet international standards, but many others do not. More seriously, the number of motor vehicles which has grown exponentially over the last twenty years has not been followed by a development of the road network likely to meet the needs of a country lacking a satisfactory rail network. As for maritime transport, Greek shipowners have invested heavily in large ocean cargo vessels and tankers, but the network of passenger vessels and ferry boats serving the islands as well as foreign destinations is still totally unsatisfactory. The competitivity of Greek exports depends to a large extent on the lowering of transportation costs for Greek agricultural and other products. The Community has an important role in this development and the European Investment Bank will be called upon to participate in financing projects.

(c) In insurance, the situation is hardly better than in banking. Greek consumers - individuals and business enterprises - are treated as a source of revenue for insurance companies, but very few companies have adapted their practices to the needs of a modern economy. The right of establishment will gradually bring to Greece insurance companies from other Community countries which will inevitably lead to drastic changes in present practices.

Agriculture

In the course of the negotiations for accession, the most controversial sector of the Greek economy was agriculture. But the restrictive approach adopted by the Community negotiators had little to do with Greek agriculture. The real issues were Spanish accession in the future, as well as relations with other Mediterranean countries. Given the volume and possibilities for expansion of Greek agricultural production, any serious apprehensions on the part of other Community farmers are not justified. Moreover, climatic conditions and Greek farmers' capacity for adaptation, as well as the remarkable development of certain categories of production, will, to a large extent, lead to complementarity rather than competition with the Mediterranean products of France and Italy.

In attempting to evaluate the impact of Community membership on Greek agriculture as well as on the Community, we should make the following points:

(a) The present levels and the rate of decrease of the active population in agriculture, as well as the real incomes of Greek farmers, do not justify any fears, expressed during the negotiations, on the part of the Community that Greek products will be 'dumped' on the market following the transitional period. As for agricultural income in particular, labour costs in the more advanced agricultural areas of Greece are higher than in France and Italy, and in the less productive areas they are comparable.

(b) Greek agriculture is characterised by uneven development and serious structural imbalances. Greek participation in a necessarily reformed CAP will bring important benefits to its farmers. The financial support which they will receive from the Community will almost equal the amounts spent by the Greek Government in subsidising agriculture; but what is more important is that the selective nature of Community action in relation to the structure of agriculture could lead to lasting transformations and not only to the supplementing of farmers' incomes. The small size of farms in Greece and the dispersion of land ownership are serious handicaps in any efforts to improve the structure and content of agricultural production. Community financial aids to assist in the regrouping of farms and more generally the nationalisation of land tenure will be valuable in helping Greek agriculture overcome these serious handicaps.

(c) An additional element in relation to Community aids is the support given to exports to third world countries. In the case of Greece these supports could contribute, to a very large extent, to the development of large-scale exports which will, in turn, alleviate the burden on the Community budget of surplus production generated by Greek accession.

(d) Community policy towards agricultural cooperatives strengthens their position in the Greek agricultural system. Although Greece has had a long and rich tradition of cooperative agricultural organisations, difficulties have tended to limit their role to one of support for government policies. Community policies in this field will help the efforts of Greek cooperatives to improve their status and bargaining power.

THE IMPACT ON THIRD COUNTRIES IN THE MEDITERRANEAN REGION

Greek membership of the EEC does not in itself have a significant impact on third countries in the Mediterranean region. Even though Greece's traditional relations with countries in the Middle East, as well as its geographic position, will no doubt prove to be useful in strengthening the Community's positions in the Eastern Mediterranean, the size of its economy is such that its membership has no major effect on the overall picture of Community relations with non-member Mediterranean countries. However, the situation will change considerably following the accession of Spain and Portugal. The importance of the Spanish economy and its politico-cultural influence in Arab countries in the region will add a new dimension to the Community's role in the Mediterranean (2).

The Future of the 'Global Policy' Approach

The difficulties encountered by the Community in its efforts to replace the piecemeal approach which has characterised its relations with the Mediterranean countries are well known; the question is whether the second enlargement will compound these difficulties or contribute to their solution. In my view, a Community of twelve will be in a better position to re-define its role in the Mediterranean for two reasons.

First, the shift of its centre of gravity to the South will strengthen elements in its decision-making bodies which have been pressing for the adoption of policies specifically aimed at reinforcing ties with the countries of the region.

Second, the fact that the other two South European countries will become members of the

Community and participate fully in the integration process will modify qualitatively the basic parameters of Mediterranean policy. Up to now, attempts at the formulation of such a policy have had to take into account the interests of a heterogeneous group of countries whose levels of development and political regimes have ranged from that of Egypt to that of Spain and of Greece and from Kaddafi's dictatorship to the pluralist regimes of Greece, Portugal and Spain. After enlargement the three European countries will no longer be viewed as beneficiaries of the Mediterranean policy, and the Community will find its task of formulating policies for the region as a whole easier.

The Enlarged Community and Crises in the Mediterranean Region

It is not an exaggeration to state that the Mediterranean is potentially the most conflict-ridden area in the world. The East-West and North-South conflictual axes cut across each other in the region and the interests of most European countries and of the Community are inevitably affected by any serious crisis here. The Community of Twelve will find it even more difficult to remain aloof - as it often did in the past - when such crises erupt. This does not mean that the Community of Nine is more immune, but enlargement will, once again, simply introduce into its decision-making processes greater empathy for the region and a more balanced view of Europe's interests as compared with the present central European fixation.

The Middle East. Following a long period of toeing the United States' line in matters related to the Middle East, there has been a gradual shift of European policies during the past five years. The reasons for this are many: Europe's dependence on external energy supplies; the failure of US initiatives to bring about a peace settlement; Israel's intransigence, which has affected even the most pro-Israeli political forces in the Community; the existence of political cooperation machinery enabling the Nine to work out common, or at least non-contradictory, positions; and so on.

Enlargement strengthens the current trends, to the extent that Greece as well as the Iberian countries follow, to varying degrees, policies which place them closer to the Arab side than is the case for most of the Nine. Neither Spain nor Greece maintains formal diplomatic relations with Israel; and although membership in the Community should lead them to re-examine this anomaly, the present situation in the Middle East certainly does not make such a development very likely. On the other hand, no matter how far the Community goes in recognising Palestinian rights, we can hardly imagine that in a Community of Ten or Twelve one or more members will long maintain the diplomatic fiction of unequal treatment of the two sides in the conflict.

The dispute over the Aegean and the occupation of Cyprus. Ever since Greece asked, in June 1975, to accede to the Community, its future partners and the Commission expressed, on various occasions and with a varying intensity, their concern over the possible effects of Greek accession on relations between the Community and Turkey. In the most extreme 'expressions of concern' it was stated that Greek membership could possibly lead to a veto in future decisions affecting these relations. Very early, even before the negotiations were formally opened, the Greek Government stated clearly that it had no disputes of an economic nature with Turkey. Under these circumstances, it was not going to use its future position in the Community's decision-making bodies to impede the strengthening of ties with Turkey (3).

With full membership, Greece is better situated to explain its position, but any future Greek Government is likely to abstain from using its relative advantage to 'drag the Community' into the Greek-Turkish dispute.

The Balkans. Greece's membership has brought the Balkans much closer to the centre of the Community's concerns, from an economic view-point and in a time of potential crisis. Even if security in Southern Europe were in no way troubled, Greek membership means that the whole range of issues affecting the Community's relations with Yugoslavia will have to be faced and dealt with more effectively than has been the case in the past. Yugoslavia is one of the geographic links between

Greece and the Community, and this adds a new parameter to the formulation and conduct of its policies towards that country.

The presence of Greece inevitably strengthens the Community's relations with Yugoslavia and, in turn, these relations will become an element of stability in the Balkans. The US and the USSR both have vital interests in the sub-region; and, in this context, Western Europe, with a distinct policy, could and should contribute to the maintenance of peace and security in the Balkans.

CONCLUSION

We have not attempted to present a rosy picture of the prospects for Greece and for the Community following enlargement. The arguments in favour of or against the accession of Greece have become irrelevant. What is needed now is a clear view of the problems to be faced together during the coming years. Their solution is possible, given the political will of the governments and peoples of the Ten as well as of Community institutions to make the enlargement a success.

NOTES

1. Pepelasis gives this percentage as 16.1, while OECD estimates it as 16.5.
2. For further discussion of the implications of enlargement for the Mediterranean policy of the EEC, see Volume 2 of this series, especially Chapters 9 and 10.
3. The Turkish Minister of Foreign Affairs, Mr Erkmen, at a meeting in Brussels of the Council for the Association of the EEC and Turkey on 5 February 1980 expressed Turkey's wish to 'revitalise the association with the EEC' and its hope of joining the Community as soon as possible. In May 1980 this Committee met again, and the basic features of a 'revitalisation' of the association were put forward: social aspects of agriculture, preparation of the fourteenth financial protocol and economic and technical cooperation.

3 The Agricultural Sector

(a) The Implications of the Accession

ADMANTIOS PEPELASIS

The second enlargement of the EEC will add a new dimension to the Community, making it truly representative of different levels of development and economic and social structures in Western Europe. Greece became a full member of the EEC on 1 January 1981 while negotiations for the accession of Spain and Portugal continue.

Although Greece, Portugal and Spain have been growing at particularly high rates in the post-war period (1), they are at a lower level of development than most members of the EEC, with the exception of certain problematic regions, such as the Mezzogiorno in Italy and parts of Ireland. This lower level of development is expressed mainly in the structural imbalances that characterise the economies of these three countries, and in particular the lagging performance of agriculture vis-à-vis the rest of the economy.

An important common characteristic of the Three is that agriculture continues to be a vital sector as a source of income and employment and, in the case of Greece, a net foreign exchange earner.

Agriculture in Greece, Spain and Portugal accounts for a larger share of output and employment than the EEC average, although the situation is not greatly different to that recorded in certain EEC members, such as Ireland, Italy and, to a lesser extent, France. Furthermore agricultural productivity in each of the Three varies from between two-thirds to around half of that in the EEC as a whole.

The lagging performance of agriculture in Greece, Spain and Portugal is the result of the low level of integration of this sector into the rest of the economy. This is due not so much to the slow rate with which new methods of production have been introduced in relation to change elsewhere (especially in industry), as to the relative inflexibility of agricultural structures.

The question which has been prominent in the debates on enlargement is whether the integration of the Three into a technologically more advanced area of production and exchange is going to help them integrate their own economies into one consistent whole or whether they are simply going to 'export' their problems to other members of the Community.

Greek agriculture is in a new economic environment since Greece's accession to the EEC, defined in terms of greater market competition, as well as narrower limits for national policy-making, which are the obverse of increased market opportunities and a wider framework for policy-making across frontiers. These conditions will be intensified after Spanish and Portuguese entry since their agricultural production is not very different in kind from that of Greece, although much larger in volume, at least in the case of Spain. Will Greek agriculture be able to adjust to the new conditions; does it have the potential to do so, and at what rate?

It will be argued that Greek agriculture does have the potential to meet the challenge. However, the necessary adjustment is not going to happen automatically. Great efforts will be required of Greece, while the EEC will also have to help, given that it is more than a mere customs union among nation states. After all, the long-term aim of the Treaty of Rome is full economic and political union, which can only be achieved if economic and social divergences within the Community are eliminated as far as possible, and, of course, as soon as possible.

GREEK AGRICULTURE TODAY

(a) Growth Record. The share of agriculture in the Greek economy has declined steadily in the post-war period. Its share in GDP fell from over one-quarter (28 per cent) in 1950 to less than one-seventh (13 per cent) in 1979 (at constant 1970 prices). In terms of growth rates, agriculture grew at an annual rate of 3.4 per cent, compared with 6 per cent for the economy as a whole (1950-79).

The share of agriculture in the total labour force also dropped considerably. According to the

1951 population census this stood at 48 per cent of the labour force in 1950, dropping to 41 in 1971 and, by projection, to 30 per cent in 1977/78 (2).

In comparative terms, Greek agriculture in relation to agriculture in the EEC on average is (a) of about the same order of importance as agriculture in Ireland; (b) not very far from the situation in Italy; (c) certainly more important than agriculture in the EEC as a whole.

From the point of view of growth rates, these have been higher for Greek agriculture, although its starting point was lower and the Greek economy as a whole grew at particularly high rates in the post-war period (3).

Finally, the contribution of agriculture to total trade is still significant, although declining, accounting for 34 per cent of exports, and 10 of imports (as at 1977). The significance of the EEC as a trading partner should further be noted. In 1977 the EEC absorbed 46 per cent of Greek agricultural exports, while 26 per cent of Greek agricultural imports came from it.

(b) Productivity. Generally, Greek agriculture has been growing at a respectable rate, while its diminishing share in the economy is explained by the process of structural transformation. However, its level of performance, as measured, for example, by the level of productivity per worker, has been lower than that in the rest of the economy, although the gap has been closing. Thus, in 1971 productivity in agriculture (gross value added per worker) was equal to 43 per cent of that in the rest of the economy, rising to 50 in 1977 (at constant 1970 prices) (4).

Greek agriculture has lagged in productivity compared with EEC countries. For example, in 1977 worker productivity in Greek agriculture was equal to 63 per cent of the EEC average, varying from 73 vis-à-vis Irish agriculture, to 30 vis-à-vis agriculture in the Netherlands.

However, within Greek agriculture there are more and less dynamic units, with some farmers responsive to and able to adjust to changes dictated by market forces. Greek agriculture is characterised by a certain dualism, whereby dynamic units coexist with archaic, or less developed, ones. This is the result partly of structural weaknesses in

Greek agriculture and partly of the failure of policy to tackle agricultural problems realistically and effectively.

The processing, packaging and marketing of agricultural products is becoming more and more important as the level of sophistication in consumer tastes rises and the distance between places of production and sale increases. Greek agriculture faces a number of serious problems in this area, affecting its level of productivity. Many of these are related to both the present structural weaknesses of Greek agriculture, and an inadequate policy response on the part of the Government.

(c) Composition of Output. The structure of agricultural production has changed significantly in Greece in recent years (see Table 3a.1). The general movement has been away from wheat, tobacco, grapes and olives (the traditional mainstays of Greek agriculture) and towards products requiring irrigation and characterised by high income elasticities of demand, as well as towards animal products (some of which - beef and cows' milk - presuppose adequate supplies of animal feeds grown on irrigated land).

This structural shift has been important in Greece's recent record of economic growth and at the same time has accommodated changing patterns of domestic and international demand for agricultural products. However, there are still lags between supply and demand for certain products, mainly in the livestock sector, and in particular the production of beef, which satisfies only part of domestic consumption (5).

Beef is a typical example of a product sector suffering from structural problems and inconsistent policy signals. Generally, pastures are of a poor quality, and the size of herds small, while winter feeding presents problems in the mountainous and hill areas of northern Greece. Furthermore, mainly in an effort to check inflation, in the late 1960s maximum producer prices were set at a level which did not compensate cattle farmers for rising costs. Policy was reversed in the 1970s, especially after 1974, and efforts are being made to deal with the various problems of the sector, as well as to increase the domestic production of feedstuffs,

TABLE 3a.1 Changes in the product mix of Greek agriculture (million drachmas, current prices)

Products	Value of production					
	1959		1970		1978[a]	
	Amount	Percentage	Amount	Percentage	Amount	Percentage
Total	31,941	100.0	60,902	100.0	244,317	100.0
Main crops	20,866	65.3	28,377	46.6	111,952	46
Wheat	4,241	13.3	5,080	8.3	20,175	8
Maize	602	1.9	1,420	2.3	3,655	1
Tobacco	2,048	6.4	3,017	5.0	11,990	5
Cotton	1,224	3.8	2,492	4.1	9,507	4
Sugar beets	-	-	703	1.2	3,324	1
Alfalfa	618	1.9	2,177	3.6	10,724	4
Tomatoes	752	2.4	1,551	2.6	6,494	3
Potatoes	784	2.5	1,282	2.1	4,344	2
Grapes	3,550	11.1	3,319	5.4	13,433	5
Oranges	246	0.8	678	1.1	2,955	1
Peaches	68	0.2	453	0.7	2,602	1
Olives	6,733	21.0	6,205	10.2	22,749	9
Main animal products	7,075	22.1	18,616	30.6	63,547	26
Beef	602	1.9	3,607	5.9	9,932	4
Lamb, goat meat	1,689	5.3	3,481	5.7	14,508	6
Pork	500	1.6	1,567	2.6	8,402	3
Poultry	457	1.4	1,668	2.8	6,459	3
Milk	2,897	9.1	5,899	9.7	19,047	8
Eggs	930	2.9	2,394	3.9	5,199	2
Other products	4,000	12.6	13,000	22.8	68,818	28

SOURCES
Agricultural Bank of Greece, Ministry of Agriculture, and Ministry of Coordination.

NOTE
a Provisional estimates

which are largely imported (6).

One fast-growing sector is fruit and vegetables. Between 1972 and 1978 their share in agricultural production (in value terms) rose from 15 to 25 per cent, while in relation to crop production it rose from 22 to 37 per cent. This increase in fruit and vegetable production, which has been an international phenomenon, has come as a response to an increase in demand due both to rising income levels and to new dietary trends favouring the consumption of 'natural' foods. The soil and climatic conditions of Greece allow a rapid expansion of the cultivation of fruit and vegetables. This expansion has been encouraged by state policy, which has recognised the value of this sector as a foreign exchange earner and a source of income and employment, especially in view of its labour-intensive nature, well suited to the small size of holdings in Greece.

Fears have been expressed that, following accession, Greece may compete against France and Italy over particular products, such as fruit and vegetables. These fears are ungrounded, to the extent that they assume (i) that costs in Greece are markedly lower than those in France and Italy; (ii) that the change in policy following accession is not going to affect cost levels; and (iii)that no efforts are being made to adjust the pattern of Greek production to that of the EEC.

In fact, agricultural wage rates in Greece may be lower than in France or Italy. However, the level of production per worker is also low, bringing the labour cost per unit of production up to a level comparable to cost levels in the rest of the EEC. For example, in 1976, the average agricultural wage rate recorded in Greece was 51 per cent of that of France and 51.3 per cent of that of Italy. Comparing wage costs per unit of output, however, reduces this difference considerably: in 1976 the average cost of labour per unit of production in Greece was 88.4 per cent of that in France and 68 per cent of that in Italy.

Furthermore, production costs are going to rise when the present system of input subsidies, foreign to the CAP, is phased out, to align Greek agricultural policy fully to that of the EEC. Input subsidies accounted in 1977 for approximately 20-25 per cent of total agricultural subsidies, so that their elimination is going to have a significant impact on production costs.

On the whole, Greek agricultural production is largely complementary to that of the rest of the EEC. For example, whereas livestock production accounts for 34 per cent and crop production for 66 per cent of agricultural production in Greece (1978), the corresponding figures for the EEC are approximately 60 and 40 respectively.

(d) Marketing and Processing. Greek agricultural products have been inadequately known by European consumers, with the exception of certain traditional items, such as olive oil, olives, currants, peaches, a number of canned products, such as tomato paste, whole tomatoes, vine leaves, etc. This is largely the result of an inadequate system of marketing.

Efforts in the marketing of agricultural products started only recently, and the results cannot be considered as satisfactory. In particular, standardisation has not been achieved and there is no strict control over private trade practices; legislation covers only fruit and vegetables, and then only in a general way.

Greek agricultural processing industries date from the 1950s. Progress has been made, although there is still room for improvement. Over the period 1970-7, the production of processed goods increased in volume by 30 per cent for foodstuffs and 50 per cent for beverages. In 1977 exports of processed foodstuffs and beverages accounted for 12.5 per cent of total exports of industrial goods.

In relation to Greek industry as a whole, the agricultural processing sector accounted for almost 11 per cent of total assets in 1976, while in 1977 it absorbed 18 per cent of the total gross fixed capital formation. According to the Association of Greek Industrialists, in 1976 sixteen of the 200 largest industrial groupings in Greece were in agriculture and accounted for 10 per cent of the capital resources of the 200.

Most of the processing industries operate at high cost levels, while the quality of their products is not always satisfactory. This is the result of a low level of technology and the small scale of operations, as well as poor coordination between production in the field and absorption by the factories. This state of affairs has been allowed to develop through the failure of policy to guide the sector.

Agricultural Policy

Any student of Greek agriculture cannot fail to observe the influence of policy, which has not always been positive. Development has been conceived traditionally in terms of industrial development, while agriculture has come a poor second. Moreover, the allocation of funds within agriculture has often been based on political influence rather than economic and social rationality. Lastly, agricultural policy suffers from excessive bureaucracy, making for delays, errors, etc. in the application and sometimes the conception of policy.

Over the period 1970-9, public investment in agriculture tailed off from 17 per cent of total public investment to 10 per cent. Thus the low level of productivity in agriculture vis-à-vis the rest of the economy is an indicator of the failure of policy to perceive the true proportions of the problem. There are signs of this situation changing, as Greek society becomes more pluralistic, and a greater variety of interest groups claim a greater say in the country's economic life, while the traditional Right is gradually becoming a more open type of party, more readily influenced by outside changes than in the past. For example, on coming to power in 1974 the Government of Mr Karamanlis satisfied popular feeling by nationalising a number of dominant firms and sectors, such as the Greek subsidiaries of the Commercial Bank of Greece, the oil distilleries at Aspropyrgos, the Olympic Airways Company, and the Athens bus companies. In relation to agriculture, efforts are being made to help the sector operate on a more profit-making basis. Agricultural cooperatives which date from the beginning of the century have been strengthened, so that they can play a greater role in the development of the agricultural sector and of rural society more generally.

At the end of 1979 there were about 7,000 local agricultural cooperatives representing 705,080 members. Classified by main type of activity, over two-thirds (70 per cent in 1979) are credit cooperatives, one-fifth (20 per cent) are production cooperatives and only a very small number are sales cooperatives (3 per cent), although many are active in the export sector, especially for fruit and vegetables. An important task of the cooperatives is the distribution of short-term credit on behalf of the Agricultural Bank of Greece, a service for which they receive a fee.

Another failing of agricultural policy in general is that of long and complicated bureaucratic procedures, often impeding even properly conceived policies. The negative effects of bureaucracy are widely recognised, and it is one of the stated objectives of the Government to rationalise the workings of the State mechanism.

Greece's membership of the EEC puts the question of policy on a new footing. Agriculture cannot continue to be the 'poor relation' of industry. The successful incorporation of Greece into a society of advanced nations demands that a new and more creative view is taken of agriculture and of its role in development.

REGIONAL CONSIDERATIONS

The distribution of income depends on the distribution of the ownership of resources and on the (productive) use made of these. In agriculture the pattern of land ownership is basic to the distribution of income. Given that land concentration is rare - farms of over 20 ha.occupy 13.01 per cent of the cultivated area while 69 per cent of total cultivated land is taken up by farms of less than 10 ha.each (1977), and almost all farms are owner-operated - there are no acute inequalities in Greek agriculture.

Another important aspect of income distribution is the regional characteristics of agriculture - farm size, irrigation and product specialisation - in relation to the share of different regions in agricultural income and in total cultivated area. Greece is divided geographically into nine main areas: Macedonia, Epirus and Thrace (the northern part); Central Greece, Euboea and Thessaly; Peloponnese (in the south); and the islands - Ionian, Aegean and Crete. The largest agricultural area is Macedonia, followed by Peloponnese, Central Greece and Euboea, and Thessaly. This order changes when related to irrigation. Macedonia again comes first with the greatest share in total irrigated land, followed by Thessaly, Central Greece and Euboea and Peloponnese. In both instances, the islands come towards the end of the list, with the exception of Crete, which represents 8 per cent of the total cultivated area, although only about 5 per cent of irrigated land.

On the whole, Macedonia, Thessaly, Central Greece and the Peloponnese are the most favoured agricultural regions, to the extent that there is widespread use of irrigation, as well as a large number of medium to large-size farms (7). This is borne out by the regional distribution of income. Central Greece, Thessaly and Macedonia claim a share which is more than proportionate to their share in cultivated land. This is not the case with Peloponnese, which accounts for 18.6 per cent of cultivated area and only 15.6 per cent of agricultural income (1977). This is partly due to its low share in irrigation. Finally, the islands claim a less than proportionate share in income, in relation to their share in cultivated area. However, one should add that the islands have an important alternative, and often rival, occupation to agriculture - tourism.

The regional distribution of production, and therefore of product specialisation, is particularly relevant to the regional implications of EEC membership for Greek agriculture. That is, the impact of membership will vary from region to region, depending on product specialisation and the effects of accession on particular products.

On the whole, production in each region is fairly widely diversified, depending on climatic and soil conditions. For example, olive oil is produced mainly in high and dry areas, where olives are not of a good enough quality, size, etc. to be processed and sold as such. Similarly, must is produced in dry areas, which favour a high alcoholic content, while table grapes and currants are in well irrigated areas. Across regions there is a similar pattern of diversification, although there is some regional specialisation. Around half of the national output of cereals, tobacco, sugar beet, fodder crops, as well as 68 per cent of apples and 94 per cent of all peaches are produced in Macedonia. Macedonia also produces around one-quarter of the national meat and milk output. Over half of all cotton is produced in Thessaly, while Central Greece produces 61 per cent of all olives and 33 per cent of must, as well as almost one-quarter of meat of all kinds, especially poultry meat, and 38 per cent of all eggs. The Peloponnese is an important fruit and vegetable growing area, accounting for more than half of the national output of some products such as citrus fruits and apricots. The islands, especially Crete, tend to concentrate on fruit and vegetable production. Crete produces 46 per cent of all currants, the remainder being produced in the Peloponnese.

THE IMPLICATIONS OF ENLARGEMENT

The effects of joining a customs union area may be expected to be:

(a) an increase in the volume of trade among member countries, as well as greater specialisation by each in the production of those goods in which it has a comparative advantage in the short run, leading to,

(b) structural improvements in the quantity and/or quality of factor inputs in the long run.

The EEC constitutes a common market where not only trade restrictions but also those on factor movements are abolished. However, the actual effects may be quite different, even opposite, to the above, depending on the circumstances of any particular case. In the case of Greek agriculture, this faces a number of structural problems in its various stages of production, from the tilling of the land to the sale of the final product. At the same time, Greek agriculture has a potential for change, in the form of young farmers willing and able to innovate in order to benefit from changes in market conditions. Thus the question arises: which force will prevail in view of the challenge offered by membership of the EEC? Will the dynamic element prevail over the archaic one? Will the response and the adjustment rate of Greek agriculture be fast enough for it to benefit from the new conditions of production and exchange?

In the first place, the volume of trade between Greece and the EEC may be expected to increase. This is following past trends in trade relations between Greece and the EEC, as well as in intra-community trade. Thus, over the period 1963/5 to

1975/7 Greek exports to the EEC increased four-fold. This was largely the result of the dynamism inherent in Greek agricultural exports over this period, since a similar (proportionate) increase was marked in relation to exports to non-EEC countries. Part of this increase was also due to the Association Agreement formally linking Greece to the EEC after 1962. The effects of the Agreement can be seen more clearly in relation to developments in imports. Between 1963/5 and 1975/7, agricultural imports from the EEC increased more than five-fold, while imports from non-EEC countries increased less than four-fold. The share of the EEC in total agricultural imports increased from 21 per cent in 1963/5 (3-yearly average) to 28 in 1975/7. Over the period 1965-77 the EEC maintained its position as a principal outlet for Greek agricultural exports, absorbing 46 per cent in 1977.

On the other hand, trade among EEC countries has been steadily increasing (from 18,300 m.EUA in 1974 to 34,000 m.EUA in 1979), while in 1979 intra-community trade in farm produce and foodstuffs was equal to 84 per cent of the EEC's agricultural imports from third countries. The tendency for increased trade among member countries, including Greece, may be expected to continue, due to a number of factors, such as the system of community preference, the nearness of markets, convergence in consumer tastes, etc. The extent to which this is going to mean greater specialisation on the part of Greece and the consequences of this for Greek agriculture are more difficult to assess.

Greece is a net exporter of agricultural products; for example, in 1978 its agricultural exports exceeded its (agricultural) imports by 7 per cent. The bulk of its exports is made up of fruit and vegetables (49.1 per cent in 1978) and of its imports of animal products and maize (52 per cent in 1978). Furthermore, this situation has evolved steadily. The extent to which fruit and vegetables will maintain their position as a leading export sector, while Greece remains dependent on foreign, especially EEC, sources of supply for a large part of its consumption of animal products and animal feeds, will depend both on the adaptability of Greek agriculture and on policy measures adopted by the

EEC. The insistence of certain non-Mediterranean countries on producing fruit and vegetables in greenhouses certainly goes against Greece's comparative advantage in these products.

For Greek agriculture to reap the benefits of greater specialisation within the Community it will have to face up to its structural problems and steps will have to be taken to put agriculture on a more rational footing. These can only be political, and will have to be bold in order to be effective.

The CAP has laid more stress on market and price policies than on socio-structural measures. This has been the result of pressures applied by farmers on governments, as well as difficulties inherent in measures causing radical changes. Although the need for greater emphasis on structural policies was stressed by Sicco Mansholt in 1968 (8) the first socio-structural directives were adopted only in 1972 (9), and their application began only recently. Furthermore, the special nature of the Mediterranean regions and their particular problems have only recently begun to be taken into account, and suitable measures taken to deal with them.

The prospects for immediate structural changes in Greek agriculture within the context of the CAP are thus limited. However, what is more important are the trends in the CAP of a wider recognition of the importance of structural policies. Greece will have to add her weight to those pressing for a more comprehensive and effective structural policy within the Community. However, it would be quite wrong to view agricultural development in isolation. Agricultural development is a part of overall economic development: the smoother and steadier the process of the latter, the more successful the efforts to deal with the problems of the former.

The economic and monetary crises of the early 1970s, continuing into the 1980s, have caused a setback in efforts to deepen economic and political integration among EEC members. The second enlargement is a step in the direction of greater unity, if only in terms of area. Nonetheless greater unity across sectors, that is, in depth, needs to be pursued further if the concept of a European Community is to withstand the difficulties of our times.

Efforts to deal with the problems of Greek agriculture have to be placed within the more general context of dealing with the problems of the economy and of promoting overall economic development. Such a policy standpoint does not contradict the spirit or the letter of the CAP. Rather, it is indispensable for the successful adaptation of CAP provisions to the particular nature of Greek agriculture. Finally, a comprehensive approach to agricultural development needs to include adequate social and regional measures to alleviate the impact of structural changes on the agricultural population, as well as to help preserve less favoured farming areas (10). As a recent report on the successes and failures of EEC agricultural policy noted: 'Only a long, intensive and comprehensive development policy is likely to have a lasting impact'.

NOTES

1. The annual rates of growth for Greece, Spain and Portugal over the period 1968-78 were 5.9, 4.9 and 4.8 per cent respectively. The corresponding rate of growth of GDP (market prices) at constant prices for the EEC _on average_ was 3.5 per cent.
2. This figure (30 per cent) is generally believed to be too high, as a recent labour force sample survey carried out by the National Statistical Service has shown, setting the share of agriculture in national employment at 28.8 per cent. ILO statistics put this figure at 27 per cent.
3. 1.6 per cent per annum for Greek agriculture in 1971-9, as compared with -1.5 for the EEC for 1973-8.
4. Between 1971 and 1977, agricultural productivity increased at 10.0 per cent per annum while productivity in the rest of the economy increased at 6.5 per cent per annum. See A. Pepelasis, G. Yannopoulos, A. Mitsos, G. Kalamontosakis, N. Perdikis, _Sussex European Papers 7, The Mediterranean Challenge IV, The Tenth Member, Economic Aspects_, p.12, Table 4.
5. 42 per cent in 1979. Self-sufficiency has been achieved in relation to pig meat, poultry meat

and eggs.

6. Suitable cattle breeding systems are being developed in the mountainous and hill areas, as a result of valuable information obtained in pilot units in Thessaly on simple systems of livestock rearing which can be applied by small farmers.
7. Cf. 'A regional analysis confirms that Greece is fairly homogeneous, the range (of the average area of farms) varies from 2 to 4.4 ha., in Epirus and Thrace, respectively', from the COM (78) 200 Final report by the Commission of the EEC on 'analyses supplementing its views on enlargement' (p. 174).
8. Memorandum on the Reform of Agriculture in the EEC, 18 December 1968, better known as the Mansholt Plan.
9. Directive 72/159/EEC on the modernisation of farms, and Directive 72/160/EEC on encouraging the cessation of farming and reallocation of utilised agricultural area for the purposes of structural improvement.
10. Directive 72/161/EEC on the provision of socio-economic guidance for the acquisition of occupational skills by persons engaged in agriculture. See also Chapter 5 by Christopher Ritson in Volume 2 of this series.

(b) The Impact of the Common Agricultural Policy

SOPHIA EFSTRATOGLOU-TODOULOU

The Treaty of Accession of Greece to the EEC provides for full membership from 1981 and for a five-year transitional period to enable Greek agriculture (except for peaches and processed tomatoes for which a seven-year period was provided) to adjust and become fully integrated into the agricultural sector of the EEC.

This chapter explores some of the likely effects of the CAP (price and structures policy) on the performance of Greek agriculture, after briefly considering some basic structural problems facing Greek agriculture and its main characteristics in comparison with Community agriculture.

THE STRUCTURE OF GREEK AGRICULTURE

Agriculture remains a vital sector of the Greek economy. Its contribution to the formation of GDP is high (15.9 per cent in 1979, current prices) compared to that of the EEC (4.2 per cent), while it employs about 28 per cent (1) of the total labour force. The relative percentage for the EEC is 8.

The importance of the sector is more evident when its participation in GDP and labour force is considered on a regional level. In most regions (2) the share of agricultural product in regional GDP varies between 30 and 42 per cent (see Table 3b.1). Only in the Central and West Macedonian region and the Eastern Continental and Islands, where Salonica and Athens are located and where industrialisation has advanced significantly, is the share of agriculture as low as 17 and 6 per cent respectively. The percentage of people engaged in agriculture on a regional level varies from 44 to 58 for most regions.

During the last twenty years, significant changes have taken place in Greek agriculture. This period has been characterised by a rapid increase

TABLE 3b.1 Regional agricultural product and labour force as a percentage of regional gross product and employment, 1977

	Agricultural product	Labour force
Eastern Continental Greece and Islands	5.6	8.9
Central and Western Macedonia	16.6	32.7
Peloponnese and Western Continental	37.8	56.2
Thessaly	33.3	51.3
Eastern Macedonia	38.0	58.1
Crete	39.6	56.4
Epirus	29.8	57.0
Thrace	41.6	63.3
Islands of Eastern Aegean Sea	20.9	43.7
Country average	16.8	33.4

in farm labour productivity (6 per cent per annum in real terms) compared to most EEC countries. This was mainly the result of capital investment in mechanisation, irrigation, etc. and of the expansion of modern technology, which allowed a rapid exodus of farm population. These structural effects are reflected in the changes in factor ratios utilised in agriculture. Between 1961 and 1977 the machinery/labour ratio increased four times, fertilizer/labour five times, while the land/labour ratio almost doubled.

Despite its rapid long-run growth, Greek agriculture faces several structural problems (3) which constrain self-sufficient growth (at previous high levels) unless significant improvements in structures and institutions take place.

(a) Cultivated land accounts for 3.5 million ha. About 41 per cent is mountainous or semi-mountainous where low-yielding cereals, olive trees, vines and sheep breeding predominate. Soil and climatic conditions contribute to the low elasticity of the production response in these areas.

(b) Intensive farming is limited to 950,000 ha., which is the total irrigated land and which represents only 27 per cent of total cultivated area. Given the water resources available, the long-run capacity in irrigation is estimated at 1.6 million ha.(45 per cent of cultivated land). This constrains the expansion of intensive farming in the sector given the dry soil and climatic conditions.

(c) The small size and fragmentation of farm holdings is a major structural problem in the sector. The situation seems to have evolved slowly with a slight increase in average farm size from 3.2 ha. in 1961 to 3.6 ha. (4) in 1977. In the same period the number of farms fell by 16 per cent while the farm labour force decreased by 40 per cent. These figures indicate the reluctance of people who leave farming to reallocate their land, since land holding is considered a profitable asset.

(d) The relatively aged farm population and the inadequate level of professional skills of Greek farmers compared to Community farmers contribute to the low efficiency of the sector.

(e) Labour productivity in the sector amounts to about half of that in Community agriculture, while per capita income of those engaged in farming remains at about 50 per cent of that of the Greek economy overall. Farm income disparities on a regional level, due to differences in resource endowments, technology and human capital employed (in the regions), accentuate the low-income problem. At a level of disaggregation of nine regions, agricultural product per labour unit varied from 64 to 145 with the country average of 100. If this value added may be taken as a rough indication of farm income, then income disparity between rich and poor regions is approximately 2.3:1. If farm income on a district level is considered (Greece is divided into fifty-one district-nomos), income differences are as high as 6:1.

Similar estimates for EEC countries (5) indicate that Germany has the smallest inequality index (1.7:1) while for Italy and France the index is equal to 4.3:1 and 4.6:1 respectively. However, these indexes are not directly comparable since they are derived from a different number and size of regions: the larger the regions, the smaller the index since local differences are cancelled out in the aggregate.

GREEK AGRICULTURAL POLICY AND THE CAP

The basic objectives of Greek agricultural policy in recent years have been to: raise and stabilise farm incomes; increase productivity; and promote exports of agricultural products.

Farm incomes were supported mainly by providing: (a) Minimum price guarantees for the main agricultural products combined with intervention schemes (cereals, tobacco, cotton, olive oil, raisins, etc.). Minimum prices were also implemented along with production quotas for rice, tobacco, sugar-beets and with production contracts between farmers and processors (processed tomatoes). There were minimum prices for fruits and vegetables but only for those quantities sold to exporters or processors provided they paid producers at least at the minimum prices. There were no minimum prices or intervention mechanisms for livestock products, with the exception of milk (price guarantee). A maximum producer price (beef) and a wholesale price (pig meat, poultry) were fixed along with price controls at the wholesale and

retail level for consumer protection.
(b) Direct subsidies, for example, to small farmers producing wheat and barley in mountainous areas, and to tobacco producers, etc.
(c) Import restrictions (licences) controlling product supply and regulating markets.

To increase productivity:
- subsidies on means of products such as fertilizer, pesticides, quality seeds, machinery, etc. were granted to farmers for expanding modern technology use;
- programmes, through public investment funds, were carried out for improving infrastructure (irrigation, marketing facilities, land consolidation, etc.);
- low-interest loans were granted to farmers by the Agricultural Bank, contributing significantly to capital formation in the sector.

To promote exports, agricultural products were subsidised so as to reduce the gap between higher Greek farm prices and low world prices.

Although Greek agricultural policy objectives do not differ from those of the CAP, as outlined in article 39 of the Treaty of Rome, there are some basic differences in mechanisms applied to achieve the objectives.

The basic adjustments in mechanisms which will affect Greek agriculture are:
(a) the removal of input subsidies (fertilizer, pesticides, etc.) which are not compatible with EEC regulations and which will increase the cost of production;
(b) the abolition of import restrictions which will open up the sector to competition from EEC farm products. At the same time the adoption of the Community's more flexible scheme of protection (entry prices-levies) against third countries leaves room for third country exports to Greece whenever market forces allow this;
(c) the adoption of a minimum price guarantee for livestock products (beef, sheep meat, dairy products) and the introduction of withdrawal mechanisms for some fruits and vegetables will improve farmers' bargaining power;
(d) adjustment of generalised investment aids on farm machinery, animal breeding, marketing and processing facilities, etc. to selective investment aid schemes to zones and/or farms that fulfil

certain requirements.

THE IMPACT OF THE CAP ON GREEK AGRICULTURE

Greek accession to the EEC will add 7 per cent to the total utilised area of the Community, 13 per cent to the labour force and only 4 per cent to the value of agricultural production. These figures indicate the relatively small size of total Greek agriculture and the marginal effects it could have on EEC agriculture. However, integration into the Community of such a small sector with a lower level of development and less-favoured structures will have significant effects on the sector.

Common Market organisation effects on production

The pattern of production in Greece is typically Mediterranean. Final production consists of about 70 per cent of crop and 30 per cent of animal products. For several crops, production exceeds domestic demand and depends, to a large extent, on export markets (durum wheat, tobacco, raisins, citrus, certain fresh and processed fruits and vegetables and recently hard wheat due to some high yielding varieties). In other crops such as soft wheat, sugarbeets, potatoes, poultry, pig meat and eggs, the country is about self-sufficient (see Table 3b.2). However, there are permanent large deficits in feed-grains (6) and beef and rather small deficits in milk products.

On the whole, Greek agricultural production is complementary to rather than competitive with that of the EEC. In those products in which Greek production amounts to a significant percentage of that of the Community (Table 3b.2) the Community has deficits (tobacco, cotton, raisins, citrus, sheep meat, olive oil). For products for which the Community faces permanent or occasional surpluses (milk products, beef) Greece has deficits. On the other hand, wine production and certain fruits and vegetables (peaches, grapes, canned fruits, etc.) could be considered competitive, but the relatively small production of wine and the possibilities for seasonal adjustment of the supply of Greek fruits and vegetables (by taking full advantage of climatic conditions) make the competition problem less acute.

Adjustment of prices to those of the EEC is going

TABLE 3b.2 Degree of self-sufficiency in Greece and EEC for basic agricultural products, 1978

	Degree of self-sufficiency		Greek production as a percentage of EEC production
	Greece	EEC (the Nine)	
Crop products			
Soft wheat	107	102	6.1
Hard wheat	196	57	22.4
Maize	34	58	3.3
Rice	117	53	15.8
Sugar	104	125	2.7
Wine	130	94	3.6
Olive oil	130	83	47.3
Tobacco	217	24	75.4
Potatoes	107	101	2.3
Fresh vegetables	102	92	12.8
Citrus fruits	161	41	27.5
Fresh fruits	118	73	7.4
- apples	102	93	4.6
- pears	100	95	6.1
- peaches	128	101(a)	26.0
Livestock products			
Beef	44	95	1.8
Sheep meat	91	65	23.2
Pig meat	90	100	1.4
Poultry meat	100	103	3.4
Milk	90	-	1.6
- whole milk-powder	-	310	
- concentrated milk	-	107	

SOURCES
Yearbook of Agricultural Statistics, Eurostat 1980;
The Agricultural Situation in the Community, Report, 1979, Centre of Planning and Economic Research, Division of Agriculture.

NOTE
(a) Data for 1977

to affect the pattern of production in Greek agriculture. Table 3b.3 shows that for certain products (durum wheat, olive oil, red wine, and some fruits and vegetables) Greek prices are lower than those of the Community. For other products (beef, pig meat, milk, apples, soft wheat) prices are almost the same, while for maize, barley, sugarbeets, pears, etc. Greek prices are higher than Community prices.

If product supply elasticities were available one could draw some conclusions about the effects of prices on production. However, such estimates would be based on other prices being constant (7), while readjustment involves a great number of factor changes.

The pattern of farm production is expected to be affected by changes in the following which are involved in the integration process:
(a) removal of input subsidies not compatible with EEC regulations, which will increase the cost of production;
(b) price changes in other factors of production (wages, machinery, etc.);
(c) structural aids (non-price) to areas with poor structures;
(d) improvements in market efficiency due to CAP implementation; and
(e) increases in irrigated land, which will allow intensive farming, to the extent allowed by Community-financed development programmes.

The combined effect of these factors on the relative competitiveness of Greek farm products is very difficult to project without a highly sophisticated econometric model. On the other hand, qualitative effects of the price policy, such as the expansion of protection schemes to livestock products, the new organisational system in the fruit and vegetable markets, the encouragement of group farming activities in the marketing and processing of agricultural products, and the strengthening of farmers' bargaining power are expected to have favourable effects on production.

Trade effects

Greek agricultural exports account for 36 per cent of total exports and consist mainly of crop products. Traditional export products such as tobacco, raisins, olive oil, cotton and wine account for

TABLE 3b.3 Comparative support prices in Greece and the EEC (the Nine), 1980-1

	Price	(ECU/ton) Greece	EEC (the Nine)	(percentages) Greece to EEC
Common wheat	Reference price	172.37	175.20	98.4
Durum wheat	Intervention price	242.88	260.33	93.3
Barley	"	165.23	155.88	106.0
Maize	"	165.23	155.88	106.0
Rice	"	242.95	233.71	104.0
Sugarbeets	Minimum price	38.83	33.10	117.3
Wine (0°/HL) I	Guide price	2.51	2.51	100.0
II	"	2.41	2.68	90.0
III	"	2.41	2.68	90.0
Olive oil	Intervention price	1693.80	1801.22	94.8
Oranges	Basic price	19.38	28.59	67.8
Lemons	"	26.32	29.02	90.7
Pears	"	29.83	21.46	139.0
Apples	"	25.92	25.92	100.0
Peaches	"	22.82	34.42	66.3
Table grapes	"	27.06	23.74	114.0
Beef	Intervention price	1446.80	1446.80	100.0
Pig meat	Basic price	1587.21	1587.21	100.0
Cows' milk	Indicative price	222.60	222.60	100.0

42 per cent of agricultural exports (1977-78), while fresh and processed fruits and vegetables account for the rest, but at a continuously increasing rate. About 50 per cent of the agricultural exports flow to the Community, which provides about 30 per cent of Greek agricultural imports.

The removal of import restrictions in EEC markets (quotas, levies) raises expectations for an increase in exports of certain Greek agricultural products (olive oil, rice, durum wheat, citrus, peaches, out of season vegetables, etc.). The effects in the transitional period will be rather limited, given that compensatory levies may be imposed to reduce price differences.

However, how fast exports will move will depend to a large extent on the improvement of marketing conditions and of farm productivity to allow the supply of farm products close to institutional prices (the low-price benefit for Greek products will be outweighed by the fixing of common prices and the application of MCA).

Removal of import barriers and adoption of the generalised preference system from the Greek side will expose the sector to competition from the EEC and third countries. Products facing competition are olive oil from low-price vegetable oil imports, tobacco from low-quality product imports, some fruits and vegetables (seasonally) (8), and animal products. Free movement of Community farm products, while maintaining some forms of protection against imports from third countries (levies, quotas), will affect traditional Greek trade flows in favour of the EEC. Imports for certain products such as beef, milk products, cereals, etc. from third countries will be replaced by imports from the Community.

Structural policy effects

Community policy on agricultural structures is an indispensable component of the CAP. It is largely by means of it that the Community can take account of the special characteristics of farming imposed by the social structure of the sector and the structural and natural disparities between the different agricultural regions (9).

Before considering the possible effects of that policy on Greek agriculture, it is appropriate to refer to its impact on member countries. Although there have been some effects on the Community's agricultural structures, it is generally accepted that its impact has been rather limited. Its implementation has been confronted with difficulties such as inadequate infrastructure, lack of vocational training in farmers and limited financial resources (10). For 1981 only 3.5 per cent of budget appropriations for the CAP will go under the structural policy.

Structural policy has proved unable to resolve the problem of structural disparities or to palliate the effect of the price policy (11). The main criticisms of the policy are:

(a) 'It favoured the better farmer through the granting of a selective system of investment aids, provided in the context of farm modernisation directive'(12).

(b) 'Research has shown that payments do not merely flow into the regions and farm holdings of low income, but rather into those of medium or high income'(13) in the framework of the Dir. 268/75 for the less-favoured areas.

(c) 'The types of agriculture, which have responded best are those which at the outset were already better organised, farmed by those who had reasonable professional skills and who owned efficient farms' (14).

Greek agriculture faces several structural problems and has a poorer structure than EEC countries. Structural policy in its present form is likely to have rather limited effects on Greek agriculture for the following reasons:

(a) Considering its small farm size, it would be difficult for a great number of Greek farmers to achieve a 'comparable income' and to fully employ one or two labour units in order to have access to the benefits of Dir. 159/72 for farm modernisation. It seems that only few, relatively large farms, with intensive types of farming (horticulture, animal breeding) could benefit in the context of that Directive.

(b) Directive 268/75 benefits farms in less-favoured areas with total utilised land of more than 3 ha. Application of that Directive to Greek agriculture leaves out a great number of farms in less-favoured areas, since in those areas 60 per cent of the farms are smaller than 3 ha. Unless community pastures in those areas are taken into consideration for calculating total utilised land, it does not seem possible for small farmers to benefit from Community aids.

(c) In the past Greek farmers have been granted investment subsidies and low-interest loans, which has had a significant effect on productivity in the sector. Adoption of the selective investment aid schemes for specific zones and/or farms that fulfil certain requirements could deprive a lot of farmers of the possibility of benefitting from low-cost investment aid and could have a negative effect on capital formation.

(d) Opening the sector to competitive conditions is expected to affect low-efficiency farms in areas of poor structures. These are expected to be the first to leave the sector unless regional development programmes provide for better utilisation of agricultural resources and support non-agricultural activities.

However, new tendencies in Community structural policy are encouraging for Greek agriculture. Regionalisation of policy (e.g. Mediterranean package), development of specific programmes for areas or sectors (Dir. 355/78 for improving marketing and processing conditions) as well as of integrated programmes for agricultural areas with diversified economic and social conditions, will have favourable effects. Agricultural areas, poor in structures, suffer from lack of resources, inadequate infrastructure and aged farm population. In many of those areas, agricultural development is possible only if accompanied by regional development programmes aimed at encouraging non-agricultural activities and at fully utilising available agricultural resources such as forests, pastures, waters, etc.

Considering that structural disparities in EEC agriculture have widened with Greek accession, structural policy requires more flexibility in development plans, to allow access to a greater number of Greek farmers.

Regional effects

Farming conditions differ significantly among regions, with differences reflected in disparities in labour productivity (value added in agriculture per labour unit) and in the level of resources employed in farming (see Table 3b.4). The labour

TABLE 3b.4 Average labour productivity (Y/L) compared to factors of production per labour unit, average farm size and land productivity (Y/Land)

(index values with country average = 100)

	Y/L	Land/L	C/L	Irrig/L	M/L	F/L	LS/L	Average farm size	Y/Land
Eastern Continental Greece & Islands	145	124	120	102	104	93	142	109	121
Central & Western Macedonia	110	140	159	146	192	142	119	119	77
Peloponnese & Western Continental Greece	100	77	72	78	48	84	77	93	134
Thessaly	91	108	121	152	137	119	90	117	81
Eastern Macedonia	100	106	146	141	153	120	116	99	94
Crete	109	83	73	52	61	97	68	84	138
Epirus	69	56	37	63	25	37	100	59	130
Thrace	64	112	94	76	137	126	123	136	53
Islands of Eastern Aegean Sea	74	90	44	35	28	44	103	69	84
Country	100	100	100	100	100	100	100	100	100

NOTES
Y/L = gross value-added in agriculture per labour unit.
Land/L = cultivated land per labour unit.
C/L = value of capital in agriculture per labour unit.
Irrig/L = irrigated land per labour unit.
M/L = machinery horsepower per labour unit.
F/L = metric tons of fertilizer per labour unit.
LS/L = livestock units (homogeneous) per labour unit.
Y/Land = gross value-added in agriculture per ha. of cultivated land.

productivity index varies from 64 (Thrace) to 145 (Eastern Continental and Islands), while the land/labour index varies from 56 to 140, irrigated land/labour from 35 to 152 and machinery/labour unit from 28 to 192.

From Table 3b.4 it can be observed that regions with labour productivity above the average (Eastern Continental and Islands region, Central and Western Macedonia, Eastern Macedonia) have a relative abundance of natural resources (land, irrigation), utilise more capital and their farms are organised on a larger scale. At the opposite end, low labour productivity regions (Epirus, Islands of Eastern Aegean Sea) are characterised by relative scarcity of natural resources and of capital and by small-scale farming. Crete and Peloponnese as well as Thrace and Thessaly are exceptions for the following reasons:

- although land, irrigation and capital use in Crete and Peloponnese is below the average level, labour productivity is above it because of the high value of their produce (out of season vegetables, citrus fruits, olive oil), which is reflected in the high index of gross value added per ha. of cultivated land (138 and 134 for Crete and Peloponnese respectively as shown in Table 3b.4).
- Thrace and Thessaly present the opposite picture. Although favoured with resource endowments, modern technology (machinery, fertilizer) and large-scale farming, their labour productivity is below the average due to the low value of products produced in the regions, reflected in the low index of land productivity (53 and 81 for Thrace and Thessaly respectively).

Although the pattern of production in the country is typically Mediterranean, there is some differentiation of production among regions (see Table 3b.5). This can be attributed to differences in resource endowments as well as to climatic conditions.

Southern regions (15) produce a high percentage of Mediterranean products: 90 per cent of olive oil, 88 of wine, 85 of citrus production and 60 of vegetables. Northern regions produce 77 per cent of cereals, 90 of cotton, 67 of tobacco. As far as livestock production is concerned, 78 per cent of beef and 60 of milk production come from Northern regions while 67 of poultry and 52 of sheep and

TABLE 3b.5 Percentage distribution of production of basic farm products on a regional level, 1977

	(Country total = 100)									
	1	2	3	4	5	6	7	8	9	Country
Cereals	11	34	7	17	13	(a)	1	16	1	100
Tobacco	6	40	23	11	15	-	-	5	-	100
Cotton	10	31	1	52	4	-	1	1	-	100
Vegetables	18	17	31	5	8	8	5	5	3	100
Citrus fruits	4	-	61	-	-	8	26	-	1	100
Fresh fruits	2	74	7	9	2	2	2	1	1	100
Wine	29	4	33	7	1	18	2	-	6	100
Olive oil	9	-	41	1	-	33	8	-	8	100
Beef	8	34	8	10	14	3	4	17	2	100
Sheep meat	17	11	25	14	7	7	11	5	3	100
Pig meat	18	16	24	15	4	7	7	6	3	100
Poultry	46	9	14	5	4	6	13	1	2	100
Milk	14	25	18	15	6	5	8	6	3	100

SOURCE
Agricultural Statistics of Greece, Year 1977, National Statistical Service of Greece.

NOTES
1 Eastern Continental Greece and Islands
2 Central and Western Macedonia
3 Peloponnese and Western Continental Greece
4 Thessaly
5 Eastern Macedonia
6 Crete
7 Epirus
8 Thrace
9 Islands of Eastern Aegean Sea

(a) Less than 1 per cent production in the region

pork are from Southern regions. Nevertheless, Northern and Southern regions share approximately the gross agricultural product (46 and 54 per cent respectively). Despite the above pattern of production, there is product diversification within regions and even within districts.

Price differences in Table 3b.3 indicate that for most products in Northern regions, prices have reached the EEC level, while for products produced mainly in the South there are still margins for increases. Thus one could expect, *ceteris paribus*, a positive effect on farm incomes in Southern regions and a likely upward shift in the supply of those products in these areas, but in other areas also to the degree that soil and climate allow. For the reasons stated above, it was not possible to draw conclusions on likely changes in the regional pattern of production (16).

Redistributive effects of common price policies

CAP implementation involves transfers of income to farmers. What are the redistributive effects of those transfers going to be on regional farm incomes? EAGGF expenditures on Greek agriculture in a full membership year were estimated, based on the existing pattern of production in Greek agriculture and the present system of Community aids (17).

Guarantee expenditures for farm products were allocated to the nine regions proportionally to the quantities produced. Transferring resources resulted in a marginal reduction of the farm income disparity ratio from 2.3:1 to 2.2:1 (see Table 3b.6), although there was a widening in the income gap in absolute terms (13 per cent increase in the absolute difference). The non-deterioration in relative income levels could be attributed to product diversification within regions, absorbing aids from almost all products under Common Market organisation. Thrace remained the lowest income region and Eastern Continental and Islands the highest (see Table 3b.6). The relative income position for most regions remained the same, with the exception of Crete which seemed to benefit most and which moved to the second position after the allocation of EAGGF transfers.

Guarantee expenditures were also distributed

TABLE 3b.6 Percentage allocation of Guarantee receipts among regions, and regional farm income index before and after allocation

		Country average = 100		
	Guarantee receipts (percentages)	Farm income	Farm income(a)	Increase in farm income (percentages)
Eastern Continental Greece & Islands	9.9	145	135	14
Central & Western Macedonia	19.7	110	113	25
Peloponnese & Western Continental Greece	28.6	100	103	25
Thessaly	9.7	91	89	18
Eastern Macedonia	5.7	100	97	17
Crete	14.6	109	120	34
Epirus	5.1	69	68	20
Thrace	3.3	64	61	15
Islands of Eastern Aegean Sea	3.4	74	76	25
Whole country of which:	100	100	100	22
- less-favoured areas	38	52	55	26
- favoured areas	62	161	157	18

NOTE
(a) Farm income after the allocation of Guarantee receipts in the regions

between less-favoured and favoured areas. Less-favoured areas, according to the criteria of Dir. 268/75, cover 51 per cent of total agricultural land and produce 37 per cent of the gross value of agricultural output; two-thirds of that value comes from products heavily protected from EEC price policy (livestock products, olive oil, cereals). Allocation of budgetary receipts between less-favoured and favoured areas resulted in 38 per cent of the receipts going to the less-favoured. With the average country index being 100, Guarantee expenditures per farm in favoured areas were 142 compared to 67 in less-favoured. Thus areas with higher farm income absorbed a larger percentage of community aids. Despite that, allocation of these resources resulted in reducing, although only marginally, the farm income inequality ratio from 3.1:1 to 2.9:1 (see Table 3b.6).

CONCLUSIONS

This chapter has presented some of the possible effects that the CAP (price and structural policy) could have on the development of Greek agriculture, given its structural problems and regional inequalities.

In summary, the main points are:

- Greek agriculture is complementary to rather than competitive with EEC agriculture, since its export capacity lies in products in which the EEC has a deficit.
- Removal of import restrictions in EEC markets raises prospects for an increase in exports of certain products. However, export prospects depend mainly on improvements in Greek marketing strategies and in farm productivity. On the other hand, abolition of import barriers will expose certain Greek farm products to EEC competition.
- As far as price policy effects are concerned, although there are still margins for increases in certain products, it is not possible to estimate quantitative effects on the pattern of production due to the great number of factors involved in the readjustment process which will affect relative competitiveness.
- Common Market organisation is going to have qualitative effects such as expansion of protection schemes, encouragement of group farming activities, strengthening of farmers' bargaining power that

will affect farmers favourably. On the other hand, opening the sector to competitive conditions will affect low-efficiency farms in less-favoured areas, which are expected to be the first to suffer unless supported with more effective structural measures.
- Allocation of budgetary receipts from the EAGGF (Guarantee Section) in the regions, given the existing regional pattern of production and under the present system of Community aids, did not increase farm income inequalities (in relative terms). Distribution of the same receipts between less-favoured and favoured areas resulted in reducing the farm income inequality ratio from 3.1:1 to 2.9:1. In both cases though, the gap in farm incomes increased in absolute terms.
- Community structural policy in its present form is going to have rather limited effects in improving regional structures, unless more flexible schemes are adopted that will allow access to development plans to a greater number of farmers.
- Recent tendencies in the regionalisation of structural policy, such as the development of special programmes, and of integrated programmes, could have favourable effects on structures.

NOTES

1. That is, farmers employed more than 140 days a year in agriculture.
2. The country is divided into development regions, which served as the base for the development of the Regional Plan 1981-85.
3. For a detailed exposition of structural problems in Greek agriculture see S. Efstratoglou, 'Developments in the Greek agriculture and its prospects in the EEC', Mimeo, KEPE, 1979.
4. This is not comparable to average size for the Community which is 17.5 ha., since Community estimates are based on total utilised area, Greek estimates on cultivated land. If pastures and grazing land are included, total utilised land per Greek farm amounts to about 9 ha.
5. Agricultural Situation in EEC, Report 1978 (p. 123). EEC, Brussels.
6. Maize production for 1981 was expected to almost cover domestic needs and to reach 1,600 thousand tons compared to 560 thousand

tons in 1977. This is due to the development of a high-yielding variety that made the crop quite competitive.

7. S.M.C. Rollo, 'The second enlargement of the EEC - Some economic implications with reference to agriculture', J.A.E., Vol. XXX, Sept. 1979, p.336.
8. During the first months after accession, despite Greece's self-sufficiency, there were imports of potatoes and onions from Holland and pears from Italy that benefitted from relatively high market prices because of a seasonal low supply.
9. Doc. COM(80) 800 final, September 1980 (p.24).
10. Doc. COM(77) 650 final and COM(79) 438 final.
11. Price policy has often been criticised for working to the benefit of the larger producers, who already have the most favourable structures.
12. J.J. Scully, 'Agricultural regionalised measures under the CAP', paper presented at the Congress of the European Association of Agricultural Economists, Belgrade, September 1981.
13. W. Peters and U. Langendord, 'Direct income transfers for the agricultural sector in less-favoured areas', paper presented at the Congress of the European Association of Agricultural Economists, Belgrade, September 1981.
14. European Parliament, Doc. 1-824/79.
15. The Southern regions comprise Peloponnese, Crete, Islands of Aegean Sea and Eastern Continental and Islands; the Northern regions are Thessaly, Epirus, Eastern Macedonia, Central and Western Macedonia and Thrace.
16. For a detailed treatment of the subject, see S. Efstratoglou-Todoulou, 'Common Agricultural Policy and regional development in Greek agriculture', paper presented at the Congress of the European Association of Agricultural Economists, Belgrade, September 1981.
17. Estimates were produced by the Ministry of Coordination.

4 The Industrial Sector

ACHILLES G. J. MITSOS

The number of studies on the effects on Greek industry of accession to the EEC is extremely small compared to those on agriculture, and they lack depth and clarity (1). The complexity of the issues could provide an explanation, but in no way justifies the myth of a huge market of 250 million people being opened up to Greek manufactures - or the myth that multinational monopolies will swallow infant Greek industry.

In reality, the large market was, to a large degree, open to Greek products before accession; the multinationals had no reason to await Greece's entry to the EEC; and Greek industry was not at the infant stage before accession.

EEC membership is exerting both direct and indirect impacts on Greek industry. Among the former are the lifting of restrictions on the free movement of goods, services and capital; Greece's obligation to accept Community legislation concerning state aids, indirect taxation, etc.; and new sources of finance for Greek economic development. On the other hand, indirect and much less quantifiable are the effects of the closer ties between Greece and EEC member states on the structure of industry, workers' position, employment, etc. Some of these changes may very well turn out to have radical effects, others marginal, mainly because the Association Agreement of 1961 has already paved the way. Furthermore, some of these changes have already occurred, while for others a transitional period of up to five years has been established 'to solve any problems of adjustment which may arise on either side'(2).

THE NEW ENVIRONMENT

Tariff Protection

The gradual abolition of tariffs protecting domestic

production was the only part of the 1961 Agreement of Association between Greece and the EEC that was fulfilled (3) and, prior to accession, Greek tariff rates for EEC products were either totally non-existent or reduced by 60 per cent compared to those existing in 1962 (depending on whether or not they were manufactured in Greece) (4). The main exception concerned iron and steel products which were not covered by the Association Agreement.

Contrary to the common belief that 'whatever evil the reduction of protection could cause is already done'(5), it has been argued by Buck (6) that 'trade liberalization has just started for the most important products'.

Until accession, 1.5 per cent of total Greek imports faced a tariff rate of 20 per cent or higher (7), but it should be remembered that high tariffs were imposed on 'high demand elasticity' products, which means that a 20 per cent price increase for the imported good could exert a decisive impact (8), and the sectors enjoying high tariff protection employed a major portion of the Greek labour force (especially clothing, footwear and some chemical industries).

With regard to tariff protection from non-EEC countries, gradual alignment to the Common Tariff of the EEC had been established by the Association Agreement. What is new with accession is Greece's obligation to accept and apply the Community's preferential agreements and the Generalised Preferences Scheme. The five-year transitional period may help in minimising problems. It is important to note that the main problem for Greek products was raised by the agreements between EEC and third countries and not by their acceptance by Greece. It is wrong, therefore, to connect (as Hummen does (9))both of these problems with Greece's accession.

Non-tariff Protection

The Greek system of non-tariff protection is extremely complex and this is an area where accession may play a major role. The main non-tariff barriers prior to accession have been (10):

(i) Quantitative restrictions. A special import licence was required for 'luxury' goods and for goods for which sufficient domestic production existed. This licence was given only if total imports did not exceed a pre-determined level. Quantitative restrictions between Greece and the Community have been abolished on accession, with the exception of a number of products for which quotas are continued (but which will be progressively increased) during the transitional period.

(ii) Discriminatory taxation. In many cases the indirect tax levied on an imported good was only in theory equivalent to that imposed on domestic production.

(iii) Advance deposit requirements. Each commodity was included in one of the many 'commodity lists' determining the percentage of import duties payable in advance, the time and manner of settlement of the value of imported commodities, and the length of the period for which advance deposits had to be made. This system is being phased out over three years after accession.

In addition to these non-tariff measures, such devices as invoice control by the Chambers of Commerce, the whole system of government procurement and other less obvious measures, prove that the protection enjoyed by Greek industry was mainly non-tariff and its abolition could generate serious problems.

Accession has not opened a huge market for Greek industrial products simply because this market has existed, in theory at least, since 1 July 1968. Furthermore, there is no reason to believe that EEC restrictions on certain Greek textile exports will not continue during the transitional period: the 'safeguard mechanism' of Article 135 of the Act of Accession provides full rationale for such restrictions.

State Aids and Regional Development

The complex system of state aids (11) is not being abolished altogether but will probably have to be changed. The system of 'incentives for profits' is being replaced by 'incentives for investment' (direct grants, etc.). This means a shift from incentives aiming at economic development in general towards those directly linked to the development of underdeveloped areas. This shift will be reinforced by the regional policy of the Community. To illustrate the importance of the Regional Fund for Greece, it is sufficient to note that the 105 million EUA (the Commission's original estimate for annual allocation of this Fund for Greece (12)), account for approximately 10 per cent of total public investment in Greece (without counting additional expenditure that the government will make in order to absorb this amount).

The degree to which regional inequalities exist can be seen by simply pointing out that 35 per cent of the total number of manufacturing units are in the Greater Athens area, employing 46 per cent of total labour force in manufacturing industries. Moreover, the S-shaped development axis based on the four largest Greek cities (Patras, Athens, Volos and Thessaloniki) accounts for approximately 50 per cent of total manufacturing establishments and more than 60 per cent of the total labour force.

Indirect Taxation

The obligation to adopt Value Added Tax within a three-year transitional period could have some impact on Greek industry, mainly because of the negative characteristics of the structure of existing indirect taxation (13):

(i) The system has been extremely complicated. The introduction of the single tax, VAT, replaces at least 46 existing taxes.

(ii) The system has been mostly regressive (14). The VAT, on the other hand, with the possibility of 2 or 3 rates, may leave some limits of progressivity. This comparison becomes more important if we take into account that indirect taxation in Greece covers 45 per cent of total tax receipts, compared to 28 per cent for the Nine (15).

(iii) The tax on imports has only in theory been equal to that on domestic production; this *de facto* discrimination against imports almost automatically disappears with the introduction of VAT.

(iv) Exports have only partially been exempted from indirect taxation. Thus VAT may encourage them.

(v) Investment has also been only partially exempted from indirect taxation, an exemption that will be generalised by the introduction of VAT.

(vi) The number of firms obliged to keep books, etc. has been much smaller than under the VAT system. Thus the tax burden is being spread more widely, but this could pose serious problems for many small enterprises which represent a very important proportion of the total (16).

New Sources of Finance

The main new sources of finance are the European Investment Bank and the Community Funds. On implications of membership in the EIB the only available estimate is in a study by the German Development Institute. According to this, if Greece had been an EEC member in 1975, the total of EIB loans would have been approximately 160-200 million EUA (17).

With regard to Community funds and based on the hypothesis that enlargement occurred in 1979, it was estimated that total expenditures going to Greece would have been 806 million EUA (EAGGF Guarantee section 489 million, EAGGF Guidance section 95 million, Social Fund 50 million, and Regional Fund 105 million).

The financial instrument (the 'Ortoli facility') could play an important role in promoting further industrialisation in Greece, mainly because it will not be based strictly on 'banking' criteria. The sectors which encounter the greatest financing difficulties (medium-sized firms and projects with deferred returns) are not favoured by the EIB; the 'Ortoli instrument' could fill this gap.

Foreign Investment

The importance of lifting foreign exchange restrictions following accession must be seen in the context of the system which operated before it, viz:

(a) Foreign investment in Greece could be freely undertaken, except in the sectors of mining, banking and insurance, where prior approval was required.

(b) In principle, the repatriation of capital, profits and capital gains was restricted. In the case of investment undertaken with the consent of the authorities, investors were usually allowed to export 10 per cent for capital depreciation and 12 per cent for profits. Investment projects lacking such consent did not qualify for the export of interest and profits. The export of capital gains was entirely prohibited.

(c) A wide range of incentives and privileges existed for the purposes of attracting foreign capital.

Throughout the period 1961-77, the total inflow of

capital according to the provisions of Law 2687 of 1953 ('for the attraction of foreign capital') was $613 million, and at the beginning of 1977 the stock of foreign capital imported with the approval of the Greek government totalled $1,310 million (18). From the foreign exchange point of view, these figures are not very important. During the period 1973-7, the total inflow of capital under Law 2687 covered only 3.2 per cent of the current account deficit.

However, recent studies have drawn attention to the qualitative importance of these investments, because:

(a) in manufacturing as a whole, foreign firms controlled nearly 30 per cent of total capital held by 'sociétés anonymes' and 'limited liability companies' in 1972 (19);
(b) foreign firms have a larger share in the technologically advanced and therefore more dynamic branches of manufacturing (20);
(c) after 1970 there was a shift towards European investment (and away from American) and, subsequently, towards minority participation (instead of participation granting full control); furthermore, European investments seem to be directed to different sectors (mainly metal industries, machinery, clothing, food and some chemical industries (21)).

There is no clear indication that the Association Agreement played any major role in these developments.

The entire system of incentives and privileges now has to be replaced. Export restrictions on profits and capital gains have to be eliminated, together with the special privileges granted to foreign firms (22).

None the less, it is likely that accession will not, in the end, effect a radical change, for several reasons. In the past, all foreign firms wishing to come to Greece were free to do so. In most cases, exports of profits were systematically less than the officially authorised amounts; multinational firms were able to export profits by other means (23); and in the EEC countries despite the prohibition of any control over imports and exports of capital, it is known that such control was exercised to some extent.

LESSONS FROM THE PAST

The only goal of the Association Agreement of 1961 between Greece and the EEC that was attained was the Customs Union. The evolution of international trade, therefore, is probably the only area where one can test whether this Association has helped Greek economic development, and to what degree.

Greek Exports

In the period 1961-78 total Greek exports (at current prices) increased from $223 million to $3335 million, which corresponds to an annual average growth rate of 17 per cent (9.7 per cent at constant prices - see Table 4.1). In the same period the annual average growth rate of Greek exports to the EEC was even higher (at current prices 20 per cent to the Six and 19 per cent to the Nine). Consequently, the EEC share in total Greek exports increased considerably, absorbing approximately half the total by the end of the period (see Table 4.1).

TABLE 4.1 Greek exports (total and to EEC), 1961-78

Year	Total exports ($ m.)	Exports to EEC-6 ($ m.)	Exports to EEC-9 ($ m.)	Share of EEC-6 in total exports (%)	Share of EEC-9 in total exports (%)
1961	223	68	87	30	39
1970	643	295	336	46	52
1978	3,335	1,527	1,695	46	51

SOURCE
OECD, Trade by Commodities, Series A.

This important growth of Greek exports does not suffice to characterise the Association Agreement as positive (24). However, the importance of the Community market for Greek exports should not be ignored, especially if we want to assess the cost of a certain deterioration in Greece-EEC relations.

The penetration of Greek exports into the Community market was considerably more rapid than that of all non-EEC countries that may be considered as competitors of Greece. (In the period 1961-78, EEC imports from Greece increased by more than 2000 per cent, while those of 'competitor' countries increased from 260 to 1600 per cent; see Table 4.2.) However, this may not prove the positive effects of the Association but may simply reflect the improvements in the overall international competitive position of the Greek economy.

To distinguish the impact of the Association Agreement from this overall improvement, the relative change in the degree of penetration of the Community is compared to that of the world as a whole (25). The results are impressive and show that the growth of Greek exports to the EEC (compared to those of Spain, Portugal and Turkey) is not fully explained by the improvement in the overall international competitive position. There is one element that clearly distinguishes the Greek case - and this may very well be the Association Agreement.

The most drastic changes in the period since 1961 have not occurred in overall figures but in the structure of exports. The contribution of industrial exports to total Greek exports was 16 per cent in 1961 and over 69 per cent in 1974/75 (26). Exports of Greek industrial products (SITC 5-8) increased from $24 million in 1961, to $252 million in 1971, and $1675 million in 1977. (The corresponding annual rate of growth at constant prices is 22 per cent.) A disproportionate part of these industrial exports was made by a few large units. In 1976 exports of the four biggest firms covered 10 per cent of total industrial exports; those of the ten biggest 27 per cent, and those of the fifty biggest almost half the total (27).

The growing importance of the Community market for Greek industrial products may be seen from the fact that the EEC absorbed 16 per cent in 1961 and 50 per cent in 1976 (28). Total Greek industrial exports account for only a very small proportion of the Community market (around 0.5 per cent). However, this does not hold for specific products where Greek exports have been concentrated. Greece accounts for over 30 per cent of total EEC imports from third countries in eight out of twenty-four products (representing over 50 per cent of total EEC imports from Greece), and in six other products the relative portion is between 10 and 30 per cent (see Table 4.3). In nine of these products, Greece

TABLE 4.2 EEC external trade with Greece and competitive countries, 1961 and 1978 ($ m)(1)

	Imports of EEC-6			Exports of EEC-6		
	1961	1978	1978/61	1961	1978	1978/61
Greece	93.4	1,979.3	21.19	281.6	3,517.6	12.49
Portugal	79.9	922.6	11.55	261.8	1,858.1	7.10
Spain	374.6	5,694.5	15.20	363.0	5,347.0	14.73
Yugoslavia	159.6	1,984.2	12.43	159.6	4,326.0	27.11
Turkey	152.9	917.0	6.00	201.2	1,763.8	8.77
Morocco	270.7	981.3	3.62	251.5	1,542.8	6.13
Algeria	663.3	2,793.9	3.73	917.0	4,331.3	4.72
Tunisia	120.6	709.0	5.88	137.1	1,375.8	10.03
Egypt	83.3	1,061.5	12.74	159.8	1,885.5	11.80
Israel	65.5	1,139.8	17.40	173.3	1,589.4	9.17

SOURCE
Eurostat, *Monthly External Trade Bulletin*.

NOTE
(1) The 1978 figures are given in EUA and they are converted to US dollars on the basis of the following parity: $1000 = 784.72 EUA.

held the first place among non-EEC member states prior to accession.

It has often been argued that, although the growth of industrial products in general may be rapid, that of exports 'of high technology' has been minimal (29). To test this hypothesis, various indices measuring export performance by industrial sector were correlated with the different structural characteristics of these sectors (30). Among the export performance indices, some are static and others dynamic (31). The results for thirty-four Greek industrial sectors were correlated with fifteen structural characteristics of each sector measuring factor intensity (32), technology intensity (33), size of units and economies of scale (34), stage of production, product differentiation, 'age' of products, and nominal tariff protection.

The main conclusions were as follows:

(a) The correlation between the 'static' and 'dynamic' indices of export performance was unimportant or often negative. This proves that the sectors that recently experienced more rapid growth are not the same as the traditional ones where the country used to have, and still has, 'comparative advantage'.

(b) In twelve of thirty-four sectors, the export/import ratio was greater than one, while in twenty-eight of the thirty-four this ratio increased - which shows a positive trend.

(c) The same positive trend was shown by the fact that in twenty sectors the Greek share of total OECD imports increased.

(d) 'Comparative advantage' was apparent in the highly protected (35), traditional consumer-goods sectors.

(e) The correlation among all 'dynamic' indices and the skill ratio and the other 'technology intensity' indices is positive. In other words, the greatest recent progress was in the modern, technology-intensive sectors (36).

Greek Imports

Total Greek imports at current prices increased from $714 million in 1961 to $7556 million in 1979, which corresponds to an annual average growth rate of 14 per cent (7.5 per cent at constant prices - see Table 4.4). However, the rate of growth of imports, at current prices, was considerably higher

TABLE 4.3 Greece's position in the Community market for major Greek industrial products, 1977

NIMEXE	Product	EEC imports from Greece (1,000 EUA)	Greece's share of EEC imports from third countries (%)
2710	Petroleum products	75	2
430330	Fur clothing	104	42
6004	Underwear	75	14
5505	Cotton fibres	126	27
760111,15	Aluminium (raw)	64	9
2519	Magnesite	37	43
240138	Tobacco	31	42
2006	Preserved peaches, apricots	39	35
6005	Jerseys, pullovers	41	9
200230	Tomato paste	38	31
730257	Ferro-nickel	24	14
3814	Chemicals	16	89
580218,19	Carpets	17	52
430215	Furs	29	73
282011	Aluminium oxide	27	14
890161	Ships and boats	6	1
640251,57	Leather shoes	18	6
200260	Olive oils	13	23
260173	Bauxite	9	4
410162	Horse leather	2	19
260160	Zinc	7	2
260150	Lead	7	7
5501	Cotton	3	-
410111	Ship leather	2	6

SOURCE
Eurostat Analytical Tables, NIMEXE.

in the years after the inflationary pressures of 1973 (the average rate of growth during the period 1961-72 was 11.4 per cent; during 1973-7 it was 23.6 per cent); while, on the contrary, the rate of growth of total imports at constant prices decreased in recent years.

With regard to imports from EEC countries, contrary to what is often argued, their total share did not increase (see Table 4.2), although the picture is more complicated when the EEC share in certain products rather than in total is examined (see Table 4.5).

The importance of the EEC in the domestic market can be seen from the fact that in twenty-two of these products, Greek imports from the EEC cover more than 50 per cent of total Greek imports, and in sixteen products they account for over 70 per cent (see Table 4.6). The question of how important the gradual decrease in tariff protection has been for the EEC share in Greek imports remains unsettled. Figures published by Hummen (37) show that the correlation between the 'tariff advantage' enjoyed by Community products in Greece and the share of the EEC in the Greek market is minimal (38), which at least does not prove that the tariff reduction has improved the EEC's relative position.

Using the same methods for imports as for exports, it is evident that:

(a) contrary to what happened with exports, Greek imports from the EEC did not increase as much as EEC imports from other 'competitor countries' (see Table 4.2);

(b) the results of comparing the penetration of Greece by the EEC (in relation to that by the world as a whole) are less convincing than in the case of exports - for certain sectors (mainly food and chemicals), the Association Agreement was positive for the EEC, while for others (beverages, tobacco, machinery, etc.) the results were the opposite.

Greek industry is now functioning in a new environment after accession. The lifting of tariff and non-tariff restrictions on the free movement of goods, the new regime in the fields of competition, taxation and the movement of capital, and the new sources of finance are some aspects of this new environment. Past trends and present performance are useful analytical tools only if one remembers that

TABLE 4.4 Greek imports (total and from EEC), 1961-78

Year	Total imports ($ m.)	Imports from EEC-6 ($ m.)	Imports from EEC-9 ($ m.)	Share of EEC-6 in total imports (%)	Share of EEC-9 in total imports (%)
1961	714	272	355	38	50
1970	1,958	792	976	40	50
1978	7,556	2,939	3,308	38	44

SOURCE
OECD, Trade by Commodities, Series A.

TABLE 4.5 Greek imports (total and from EEC) per product group, 1961 and 1977 ($ m.)

SITC	Product group	1961 Total	1961 EEC-6	1961 (%)	1977 Total	1977 EEC-6	1977 (%)
0	Food and live animals	88	12	13	588	139	24
1	Beverages and tobacco	-	-	-	16	5	33
2	Crude materials	65	9	14	545	92	17
3	Mineral fuels	52	5	9	1,160	85	7
4	Oils and fats	7	1	7	14	10	72
5	Chemicals	60	38	62	609	416	68
6	Manufactured goods	133	75	56	986	513	52
7	Machinery - transport equipment	290	123	42	3,484	1,376	40
8	Miscellaneous manufactures	19	10	56	224	125	56
9	Other	-	-	-	7	6	78
5-8	Total industrial	502	246	49	5,304	2,429	46
0-9	Total	714	272	38	7,633	2,766	36

SOURCE
OECD, Trade by Commodities, Series B.

Table 4.6 Greece's major imports by origin, 1976

Greek statis- tical number	Product	Imports (m. drs)	EEC (%)	Eastern Europe (%)	Other Europe (%)	Other indus- trial (%)	Othe (%)
2010101	Veal meat, fresh	1,134	1	4	94	-	1
2010109	Bovine meat, frozen	2,606	31	2	2	14	51
2010112	Sheep meat, frozen	619	-	-	-	68	32
4020105	Evaporated milk	1,101	100	-	-	-	-
9010100	Coffee	1,453	-	-	-	-	100
0050200	Maize	3,442	-	-	-	97	3
3070000	Feedstuff for animals	692	64	-	2	29	5
5100000	Calcium phosphate	616	-	-	-	-	100
7010100	Coal	889	-	22	-	78	-
7090000	Petroleum, crude	38,173	-	-	-	-	100
7100201	Jet fuel	1,216	100	-	-	-	-
7100301	Diesel oil	1,303	30	66	-	-	4
7100302	Fuel oil	1,751	16	40	-	-	44
0030231	Medicines	852	53	-	42	5	-
8110203	Baits etc.	770	58	6	9	17	10
8191900	Chemicals	739	89	-	4	7	-
9020363	Polyethylene	1,697	93	-	1	5	1
3020500	Fur pieces	1,455	81	-	1	18	-
4030302	Wood, rough	996	2	1	-	1	96
4050101	Wood, sawn	1,530	-	39	53	8	-
7010106	Paper pulp	703	22	-	25	53	-
8010100	Newsprint paper	551	7	1	90	2	-
1010100	Synthetic fibres	561	94	-	5	1	-
3010102	Sheep wool	1,458	5	-	-	88	7
3050101	Carded wool	868	50	-	2	5	43
5010202	Cotton	820	-	1	-	16	83
5090202	Cotton fabrics	543	29	13	16	32	10
6010102	Textile fibres	787	89	1	3	1	6

Continued

TABLE 4.6 Continued

Greek statis- tical number	Product	Imports (m.drs)	EEC (%)	Eastern Europe (%)	Other Europe (%)	Other indus- trial (%)	Other (%)
3080101-7308	Iron & steel products	1,632	27	3	-	70	-
3120202	Iron bands	537	22	9	6	63	-
3130213	Tin	981	92	-	-	7	1
401001	Copper	1,260	28	-	-	7	65
4060102	Jet engines	719	11	-	-	89	-
4060402	Engine parts	801	75	2	5	18	-
4330000	Paper industry machinery	642	92	3	4	1	-
4360000	Textile machinery	1,454	66	3	25	6	-
4370100	Textile machinery	724	47	3	49	1	-
4370200	Textile machinery	538	83	3	12	2	-
4590507	Other machinery	908	80	3	12	5	-
5130201	Telecomms equip.	767	77	21	2	-	-
5150104	Radio receivers	555	9	-	1	78	12
7010200	Agricultural tractors	2,068	73	16	11	-	-
702+ 249	Motorcars	6,875	75	7	7	11	-
702++ 249	Trucks and lorries	4,623	64	-	4	32	-
7060207	Parts of motorcars	1,114	88	1	4	7	-
9010100-9050000	Ships and boats	42,174	22	2	27	46	3
	TOTAL	137,697	27	3	12	24	34

SOURCE
National Statistical Service of Greece.

accession is not a simple continuation of association, and that there is no reason to believe that the external conditions experienced in the sixties and early seventies which were favourable to growth will hold in the decades to come.

APPENDIX

Indices Y and Z

These indices (with some variation and not per product but for the sum of products) were utilised in McQueen, 'Some Measures of the Economic Effects of Common Market Trade Preferences for the Mediterranean Countries' in A. Schlaim and G. N. Yannopoulos (eds), The EEC and the Mediterranean Countries, Cambridge University Press, 1976.

$$Y = \frac{A}{B}, \quad Z = \frac{C}{D}$$

$$\text{if } A = \frac{\Delta Xe}{\Delta X'e}, \; B = \frac{\Delta Xw}{\Delta X'w}, \; C = \frac{\Delta Me}{\Delta Mw}, \; D = \frac{\Delta M'e}{\Delta M'w},$$

where X : Greek exports per product,
X' : exports of 'competitive country' per product,
M : Greek imports per product,
M' : imports of 'competitive country' per product,
e : to/from EEC,
w : to/from non-EEC countries.

If A is greater than one, Greek exports of the particular product to the EEC have increased more than the respective exports of the 'competitive country'.

If B is greater than one, Greek exports of the particular product to non-EEC countries have increased more than the respective exports of the 'competitive country'.

If C is greater than one, Greek imports of the particular product from the EEC have increased more than Greek imports of the same product from the rest of the world. In other words, the EEC has increased her share in Greek imports.

If D is greater than one, the EEC has increased her share in the 'competitive country's' imports.

If Y is greater than one, the growth of the particular product's Greek exports to the EEC was

TABLE 4.A1 Indicator of trade for Greece, Turkey, Spain and Portugal with EEC and other countries, by SITC group, 1976 (1961 = 100)

	Greece				Turkey			
SITC	ΔX_e	ΔX_ω	ΔM_e	ΔM_ω	ΔX_e	ΔX_ω	ΔM_e	ΔM_ω
0	1,497	852	1,041	436	543	349	5,150	46
1	227	262	2,300	4,000	297	289	500	5,500
2	440	371	884	605	321	907	1,082	655
3	287,000	456,000	1,440	2,475	43,500	3,750	1,994	2,173
4	73,500	305	198	58	1,200	733	11,250	31,700
5	3,274	924	911	685	5,550	1,800	1,538	1,501
6	20,832	5,224	490	636	7,779	1,542	743	899
7	91,500	3,461	806	901	10,500	20,400	1,152	860
8	205,300	4,685	853	852	409,000	29,500	707	592
9	3,500	500	17,000	900	100	100	100	100
Total	1,691	898	762	892	627	528	1,097	926

	Spain				Portugal			
SITC	ΔX_e	ΔX_ω	ΔM_e	ΔM_ω	ΔX_e	ΔX_ω	ΔM_e	ΔM_ω
0	595	467	996	942	169	333	807	1,064
1	1,720	750	2,250	794	613	369	233	292
2	379	504	1,973	1,042	782	430	877	419
3	6,058	428	1,367	2,955	571	467	652	1,227
4	111	460	566	124	111	216	217	333
5	1,583	1,506	1,454	1,736	955	299	814	913
6	2,149	1,784	1,761	2,529	824	395	340	730
7	13,057	7,200	1,715	1,238	17,000	1,510	538	548
8	7,228	2,228	3,727	3,348	58,000	1,898	1,071	
9	5,500	1,125	3,000	4,000	15,000	3,000	28	64
Total	1,241	1,224	1,678	1,549	763	502	543	729

SOURCE
OECD, Trade by Commodities, Series B.

NOTES

$\Delta X_e = \dfrac{\text{Exports to EEC-6, 1976 (x100)}}{\text{Exports to EEC-6, 1961}}$

$\Delta X_\omega = \dfrac{\text{Exports to non-EEC countries, 1976 (x100)}}{\text{Exports to non-EEC countries, 1961}}$

$\Delta M_e = \dfrac{\text{Imports from EEC-6, 1976 (x100)}}{\text{Imports from EEC-6, 1961}}$

$\Delta M_\omega = \dfrac{\text{Imports from non-EEC countries, 1976 (x100)}}{\text{Imports from non-EEC countries, 1961}}$

TABLE 4.A2 Indicators of trade for Greece and competitive countries, by SITC, 1976 in relation to 1961

		0	1	2	3	4	5	6	7	8	9	Total
A	c	2.82	0.33	1.12	55.64	644.74	2.18	10.63	6.81	21.92	0.17	1.69
	t	2.76	0.77	1.37	6.60	61.25	0.59	2.67	8.71	0.50	35.00	2.70
	s	2.52	0.13	1.16	47.38	662.16	2.07	9.69	7.01	28.40	0.64	1.36
	p	8.86	0.37	0.56	502.63	662.16	3.43	25.28	5.38	3.54	0.23	2.22
B	c	2.09	0.65	0.56	690.91	0.70	0.90	5.27	0.67	2.13	2.31	1.05
	t	2.47	0.91	0.41	121.60	0.42	0.51	3.39	0.17	0.16	5.00	1.70
	s	1.85	0.35	0.74	1,065.42	0.66	0.61	2.93	0.48	2.10	0.44	0.73
	p	0.59	0.71	0.86	976.45	1.41	3.09	13.23	2.29	2.47	0.17	1.79
Y	c	1.35	0.51	2.00	0.08	921.06	2.42	2.02	10.64	10.29	0.07	1.61
	t	1.12	0.85	3.34	0.05	145.83	1.16	0.79	51.24	3.13	7.00	1.59
	s	1.36	0.37	1.57	0.04	1,003.27	3.39	3.31	14.60	13.52	1.45	1.86
	p	3.42	0.52	0.65	0.51	469.62	1.11	1.91	2.35	1.43	1.35	1,24
C		2.39	0.58	1.46	0.58	3.41	1.33	0.77	0.89	1.00	18.89	0.85
D	c	1.37	1.49	1.99	0.45	3.39	0.91	0.62	2.19	0.98	0.45	0.95
	t	111.96	0.09	1.65	0.92	0.35	1.02	0.83	1.34	1.19	1.00	1.18
	s	1.06	2.83	1.89	0.46	4.56	0.84	0.70	1.39	1.11	0.75	1.08
	p	0.76	0.80	2.09	0.53	0.65	0.89	0.47	0.98	0.88	0.44	0.74
Z	c	1.74	0.39	0.73	1.29	1.01	1.46	1.24	0.41	1.02	41.98	0.89
	t	0.02	6.44	0.88	0.63	9.74	1.30	0.93	0.66	0.84	18.89	0.72
	s	2.25	0.20	0.77	1.26	0.75	1.58	1.10	0.64	0.90	25.19	0.79
	p	3.14	0.73	0.70	1.09	5.25	1.49	1.64	0.91	1.14	42.93	1.15

greater than could be expected on the basis of Greece's overall improvement in her international competitiveness as shown by index B.

Finally, if Z is greater than one, the EEC has penetrated the Greek market more than the market of the 'competitive country'.

Tables 4.A1 and 4.A2 present the full results of this exercise for Greece compared to Spain, Portugal and Turkey.

NOTES

1. The most profound analysis of the future of Greek industry was prepared at the German Development Institute (see W. Hummen, Greek Industry in the European Community - Prospects and Problems, Berlin, German Development Institute, 1977). Work being carried out at the Greek Institute for Economic and Industrial Research (IOBE) is as yet unfinished. For a review of Greek literature on the subject, see my survey in Synchrona Themata (Contemporary Issues), Summer 1979, pp. 31-57.
2. The expression was used by the Commission's Vice President, L. Natali, in his report on Greece's Treaty of Accession, Agence Europe, Document No. 1054, 29 May 1979.
3. The other two objectives - the financing of Greece's economic development by Community sources and, most importantly, the harmonisation of agricultural policies - were not realised, mainly because during the military dictatorship (1967-74) relations between Greece and the EEC were frozen.
4. For products which were not manufactured in Greece, the gradual abolition of tariffs ended in 1974, while for the others a twenty-two year transitional period was established.
5. See, for example, X. Zolotas, Greece in the European Community, Bank of Greece, 1976.
6. K. H. Buck in M. Nikolinakos (ed.), EEC, Greece and the Mediterranean (in Greek), Athens, Nea Synora, 1978, p. 270. See also Hummen, op. cit., who includes among the main reasons for the expected deterioration of Greece's trade balance (a) the fact (?) that the tariffs which remain to be reduced are much higher for individual sectors than previous tariff reductions, and

(b) the price sensitivity of the highly protected sectors.

7. In 1976 the value of total Greek imports was $221.8 million and the value of imports for which the tariff rate was 20 per cent or higher was only $2.7 million.
8. Hummen, op. cit., p. 30.
9. Ibid.
10. See also my 'The New Role for the Greek Government after Accession to the E.C.' in The Mediterranean Challenge: IV, Sussex European Papers, No. 7, University of Sussex, 1980.
11. For a brief description of Greek state aids see, for example, the study of the National Bank of Greece as reported in G. Yannopoulos, 'The Effects of Full Membership on the Manufacturing Industries' in L. Tsoukalis (ed.), Greece and the European Community, Farnborough, Saxon House, 1979.
12. EEC Commission, Economic and Sectoral Aspects (of Enlargement), COM (78) 200 final, 27 April 1978.
13. On VAT in general, see K. Georgakopoulos, The Value Added Tax in Greece, KEPE, Athens, 1976.
14. See the study by S. Karayiorgas in Politis, January-February 1976, pp. 10-19.
15. OECD, Revenue Statistics of OECD Member Countries, Paris, 1977.
16. In 1974 52 per cent of the total labour force employed in manufacturing was working in firms employing less than twenty persons, and 31 per cent in firms employing less than two persons! Similarly, 26 per cent of total value added was produced in firms employing less than twenty and 12 per cent in firms employing less than five. National Statistical Service of Greece, Statistical Yearbook of Greece, Athens, 1977.
17. German Development Institute, 'Etude sur l'adhésion à la Communauté Européene de la Grèce, de l'Espagne et du Portugal', Européenne Berlin, 1977, p. 40 (unpublished).
18. Data from the Bank of Greece.
19. A. Yannitsis, 'Foreign Capital in Greece', Oikonomikos Tachydromos, 24 April 1975 (in Greek), and S. Babanassis, Greece on the

Periphery of the Developed Countries, Athens, Themelio, 1976 (in Greek).

20. ELEMEP, 'Technological Dependence and the Prospects of Greek Industry in the EEC', Synchrona Themata, Vol. 1, May 1978, pp. 8-17 (in Greek).
21. A. E. Yannitsis, 'Economic Integration of Greece to the European Communities and Foreign Direct Investment' in M. Nikolinakos (ed.), EEC, Greece and the Mediterranean, Athens, 1978, pp. 139-41 (in Greek).
22. Strictly speaking, these remarks refer only to investment from the EEC countries. In practice, however, it would be very difficult to distinguish between EEC and non-EEC investment (for instance, in the case of a US firm investing in Greece through its West German affiliate).
23. See P. Roumeliotis, Study of the Negative Effect of Overstating the Cost of Imports on the Greek Balance of Payments and the International Experience, Athens, n.p., 1976 (in Greek).
24. The 'classical' methodological error has been used by almost every study to 'prove' either the positive effects of the Association Agreement or that positive effects were 'tariff induced' and, thus, exhausted; see, for example, Hummen, op. cit., p. 34.
25. See Appendix to this chapter and M. McQueen, 'Some Measures of the Economic Effects of Common Market Trade Preferences for the Mediterranean Countries' in A. Schlaim and G. N. Yannopoulos (eds), The EEC and the Mediterranean Countries, Cambridge University Press, 1976, pp. 13-32.
26. Federation of Greek Industrialists, Bulletin, vol. 342-3.
27. This estimate was based on figures published in Federation of Greek Industrialists, Bulletin, vol. 365, and National Statistical Service of Greece, Statistical Bulletin of Foreign Trade, January-December 1976. Hummen's assertion, according to data he does not publish, that 'almost 50 per cent of exports are undertaken by only 8 companies' (Hummen, op. cit., p. 251), is at least unfounded.

28. See G. Rigas, 'Greek External Trade in the Last Fifteen Years', Our Entry to the EEC, Athens, Themelio, 1978, pp. 293-309 (in Greek).
29. See, for example, PASOK, Greece and the Common Market, second edition, 1976, p. 33.
30. See my 'Export Performance of Greek Industry', Bank of Greece, June 1978, unpublished.
31. The eleven export performance indices included: export/import ratio; net exports as percentage of domestic production; Greek share of total OECD imports; Greek share of total EEC imports; export growth; Balassa's revealed comparative advantage (see B. Balassa, 'Trade Liberalization and Revealed Comparative Advantage', The Manchester School, 1965); Goodman-Ceyhun index (see B. Goodman and F. Ceyhun, 'U.S. Export Performance in Manufacturing Industries: An Empirical Investigation', Weltwirtschaftliches Archiv, 1976/3, pp. 525-55); change in export/import ratio; and change in Greek share of OECD imports.
32. Number of employees per value added; total horsepower of installed machinery - as an approximation for the capital stock per employee Vanek's natural resources index (see J. Vanek, The Natural Resource Content of US Foreign Trade 1870-1955, Cambridge, Mass., MIT Press, 1963); and dummy variable for raw materials intensity.
33. Skill ratio; average wage; and unskilled workers in relation to value added.
34. Average size of units; average employment of the biggest units; proportion of total value added accounted for by 'small' units; elasticity of value added with respect to the number of employees per establishment.
35. This does not confirm the common view that tariff protection discourages export growth. There are two possible explanations: (a) both export performance and protection are related to the traditional character of Greek industry; (b) export performance is a direct function of the various incentives, aids, etc., given which, in turn, depend on the political and economic power of the sector, as much as tariff protection does. Cf. A. Mitsos, 'The Rationale of Tariff Protection of Greek Industry', University of Pittsburgh, PhD Dissertation, 1975.

36. These results agree with a study by the Society for the Study of Greek Problems (ELEMEP) which shows that most progress (in production terms) has occurred in the modern sectors and that Greece is not only producing consumer goods and raw materials.
37. *Op. cit*., p. 73.
38. Correlation coefficient: 0.222.

Part III
Portugal

5 Characteristics and Motives for Entry

JOÃO CRAVINHO

Portugal is the poorest country in continental Western Europe. Why should her governments try so earnestly to enter into what is supposed to be a rich countries' club? Integration will only have a chance of success if Portugal is allowed to benefit from substantial transfers of resources during an extended period. Also, the transfer of resources will only work if a purposeful set of programmes is launched to bring coherence, depth and articulation to an open development process increasingly able to satisfy the pressing needs of the Portuguese population. Have the Portuguese correctly assessed their requirements? And has the EEC considered them in a seemingly compatible manner? If the answer is dubious, motives and characteristics will hardly match, with all the inherent consequences.

Most motives for entry developed during the 1960s and early 1970s. An appraisal of changes that occurred in that period is crucial for understanding Portugal's posture relative to the negotiations.

PORTUGAL AND EUROPEAN INTEGRATION IN THE 1950s AND 1960s

A central concern with European affairs as a European nation is fairly recent in Portugal. Up to the 1950s the African colonies were widely regarded as a sufficient outlet for any ambition Portugal might nurse for the future. Putting aside difficulties stemming from the extreme divergence in levels of development in the Community and in Portugal, in the 1950s the regime could not accept the EEC philosophy and EEC members could not extend full membership to Portugal under an anti-democratic regime.

Paradoxically, from the political point of view, Portuguese participation in EFTA was very clearly a choice for non-commitment to European affairs. At first sight EFTA made a very significant impact on Portuguese exports in the 1960s. While in 1958 it only represented 18 per cent of Portuguese export markets, in 1971/2 it accounted for 35. EEC shares in the same years were, respectively, 23 and 20 per cent. The importance of colonial markets declined from close to 25 per cent to less than 19. While they were of first importance at the beginning of the decade, by the end they occupied third place after EFTA and EEC. EFTA had an important impact on Portuguese exports, while not causing significant disturbance in the domestic market (1). Though only textiles and apparel made significant breakthroughs, those successes very effectively drove home the importance of European markets for the future development of Portuguese industry.

In little more than ten years the ruling élite veered from stubborn ignorance of European integration to acceptance of full EEC membership as a desirable medium-to long-term objective. This remarkable turnabout is the result of a complex network of interrelated political, social and economic events, at home and abroad.

In the second half of the 1960s, as far as long-term prospects were concerned, the dominant questions among the ruling élite were related to the following problem areas: first, the growth model that had been put into effect immediately after the war was exhausted and had long outlived its useful role, but it did not seem that a clear alternative was being prepared; second, the colonial option had to be re-examined, but this was not an easy task because it touched the very core of the regime's ideological basis; third, a serious crisis in leadership was surely on the way, in part because of lack of appropriate reaction to the above problems, but in fact because Salazar and the gerontocracy surrounding him were, no doubt, approaching their expected biological term of service.

The colonial problem had taken on alarming proportions and the military solution had failed. It only fuelled opposition to the regime, at home and abroad. Social unrest could be detected in many areas. Emigration had changed the traditional passive picture in the rural areas, which gradually came closer to Europe, in a certain sense, than urban centres.

The economy had grown in complexity. Important structural changes had occurred which, on the one hand, emphasised the need for long-overdue, deep reforms of the basic corporative framework of the system. On the other hand, they signified a wider role for export markets in the future, and, thus, the need to dispose of domestic political uncertainties relative to European integration.

Naturally, the increasing contradictions of the regime's African and European policies were among their most damaging blind alleys. Only a total change in leadership could eventually supersede the impasse. And European political systems started to be looked at seriously as possible sources of inspiration for gradual change.

THE CAETANO PERIOD AND THE 1972 AGREEMENT WITH THE EEC

In September 1968 the nearly 40-year-old Salazar era came to an abrupt end and the 4½ years of the Caetano period started.

The tasks the regime could not avoid facing can be summarised as follows: (i) to define and implement a political solution for the colonial question; (ii) to accommodate demands from several quarters in Portuguese society for political liberalisation; (iii) to provide an operative framework for new economic policies designed to accelerate the industrialisation process and modernise agriculture; (iv) to accept rapid increases in the workers' standard of living as a necessary ingredient for keeping power. All these tasks were directly as well as indirectly interlinked; economic and political tasks were deeply interrelated, as one would expect.

Nevertheless, 1972 was dominated by the Agreements with the Communities, due to the combination of two types of events. The first had to do with the clear definition of the future growth model. A rather elaborate blueprint for a new model existed in the 1965-7 and 1968-73 plans (2). The solution was obvious enough: in 1969 and part of 1970, the Caetano Government set itself the task of making these ideas compatible with the interests of big business groups, using an approach similar to that of the Japanese regarding problems of a highly dualistic semi-industrialised economy.

Emphasis was on, first of all, concentration of

financial resources through banking, insurance and stock exchange manipulation, including the concentration of emigrants' remittances. Next came the search for huge sources of cash flow in the form of real estate operations and European-scale capital-intensive projects (refineries, petrochemicals, steel, fibres), supported by massive public subsidies for infrastructure, low-interest finance, etc. The third element was a vigorous small business revitalisation programme, supposed to act, somewhat contradictorily, as a flexible element in the socio-political system and/or a preparatory device for indirect satellitisation through the big groups' banking and trading activities.

The fourth, and most interesting element for the present discussion, was the design of a strategy of appropriate agreements with foreign big business, especially in domains where the Portuguese could take advantage of political control of access to huge (at the international level) Angolan and Mozambican natural resources, combined with a generous public subsidisation of necessary infrastructure.

Regarding small and medium-sized business reaction to closer ties with the EEC, it was expected that many members would fare well on their own, while others would become satellites, and many others would just collapse. But that was regarded as the normal price of modernisation of the Portuguese economy, provided the social and political consequences could be accommodated without excessive risks.

In due time everything would fall into place (actually it did, but in a different way). Thus, the internal push towards Europe distinctly outpaced other logical, complementary movements. This helps to explain why political and business circles at the centre of the decision-making process were looking forward to a decisive move towards Europe, while the regime as a whole was manifestly marching back to its traditional colonial and political blind alleys.

Another important contribution was in the first enlargement of the EEC from six to nine, which triggered off the negotiation for the 1972 Agreements. At that stage Portugal had to face the consequences of the EFTA crisis prompted by the entry of UK and Denmark into the EEC. In 1971/2 the UK was, by far, Portugal's first client, representing 52 per cent of Portugal's EFTA markets. Adding Denmark, the two accounted for 21.4 per cent of total Portuguese trade, or 61 per cent of EFTA. The simple arithmetic of market shares shows that on the eve of the first enlargement, the EEC would jump from 20.1 to 41.5 per cent of total external Portuguese markets, while EFTA would decline from 35.3 to a meagre 13.9 per cent. Thus Portugal had to entirely revise her trade policies in order to avoid a dramatic disruption of her export markets.

The Portuguese leadership did not need to wait for the end of the first enlargement negotiations (mid-1971) to conclude that an agreement with the EEC had to be reached immediately at practically any price. In July 1972 the Agreements with the Steel and Coal Community and with the EEC proper were signed. The first did not pose difficult problems. The EEC Agreement was negotiated under Article 113 (Commercial Agreements), and covered industrial products, some processed food products, as well as some agricultural and fisheries products. Industrial products represented 80 per cent of Portuguese exports to the enlarged EEC, and Portuguese industrial goods, subject to important exceptions, could benefit from a progressive five-stage agreement to be completed on 1 July 1977.

The exceptions were the 'sensitive' products, some paper, cork manufactures, textiles and apparel items. 'Sensitive' textiles and apparel exports under this agreement represented 7 per cent of total exports to the Six and 22 per cent of total exports to the UK. 'Sensitive' products accounted for nearly one-quarter of total exports to the enlarged EEC. This illustrates the significance of the problem. The concessions for agricultural and fisheries products were also relatively limited. These and the sensitive goods were among the few items that Portugal could export in significant quantities in the near future. Thus, the Agreement conveyed the usual message that the rich and strong must be defended from the poor and weak. Portugal got a rough deal on the export side.

On the import side, Portugal agreed to dismantle the tariff under the general regime in five stages up to mid-1977. This concerned 40 per cent of imports from the enlarged EEC. As concessions she obtained: (i) a second, slower, pace of liberalisation up to 1980, as in the EFTA Annex G, for goods amounting to 40 per cent of EEC imports; (ii) a third time limit up to 1985 and a few limited special arrangements (vehicle assembly, ball bearings, machine tools); (iii) the new industry clause which allowed the rise of tariffs to a maximum of 20 per cent *ad valorem*, to protect new industries (subject to a global limit of 10 per cent of the total value of imports from the Nine in 1970). This clause could be invoked up to December 1979 and the related duties had to be eliminated by the end of 1984. On the one hand, the first concession implied a tough effort for Portuguese industry, given the much greater aggressiveness of EEC exporters relative to those of EFTA. On the other hand, the new industry clause would be entirely exhausted by the few big projects which the main economic groups had under preparation. Thus the Agreement offered little cause for optimism regarding imports.

The politically very important evolutionary clause was included in both Agreements. It stated that Portugal and the Communities were willing to enlarge their relationship to areas not covered by the commercial agreements. Such extensions would take the form of supplementary agreements as required by the evolution of future relations between the parties. No limits were defined. So a flexible indirect entry route was opened.

In line with this, Chapter 4 of the 1974-9 Plan on development policy objectives and directives confidently affirmed that: (i) the new phase would profoundly deviate from the growth path of the two preceding decades; (ii) the point of no return relative to European integration had *already* been passed; (iii) future evolution could only be directed to a 'congruence with developed countries'.

The arguments supporting these far-reaching revelations were based on the national significance of emigration and EEC markets, as well as on the novelty of the new development model, described as a crash modernisation programme to be conducted by private business with the full infrastructural and supplementary backing of the State.

However, the constraints jointly imposed by EEC competition and the concentration of resources mainly for the benefit of the big units, combined with the low standards of management in most family concerns, would necessarily mean a high mortality rate for traditional firms. Moreover, even without EEC competition, concentrated growth would also accelerate trends in the economy against job creation. Thus unemployment would be a residual variable to be accommodated by massive emigration according to the death rate of traditional firms. That, in turn, would swell resources controlled by the core units through increased availability and collection of emigrants' savings.

From the point of view of equitable development, the 1972 Agreement and the growth model of the 1974-9 Plan were unlikely to be achieved. It is a sign of the irreversible nature of Portugal's integration into Europe that the Revolution expressed full acceptance of the 1972 Agreement while it destroyed the economic system that made such an Agreement a cornerstone of future prospects.

POST-REVOLUTIONARY DEVELOPMENTS UNDER PROVISIONAL GOVERNMENTS

Simultaneous internal and external events precipitated a request for immediate entry to the Community. Have those circumstances sharpened motives for entry? And have they been conducive to a balanced appraisal of the nature and significance of negotiation problems and issues, as well as to a search for effective solutions? Or have they encouraged a superficial approach? It seems that the answer to the first question is positive, while for the second and third, it can only be reserved since negotiations are not at an advanced stage. However, there is a real need to assess the situation and to offer effective solutions to the difficulties enlargement will necessarily bring.

As early as May 1974, the publication of the Constitutional Law provided an opportunity for stressing the importance of ties with the Communities (4). Also, in the first meeting after the Revolution of the joint managing committee of the

1972 Agreement, held in June 1974, Portugal officially expressed the desire to enlarge the field of cooperation by applying the evolutionary clause. Broadening of the 1972 Agreement continued to be a high priority.

Meanwhile, it was evident that democratisation would be rather superficial and subject to some of the setbacks that plagued the Caetano period if the economic system continued to be based on the concentrated network referred to previously. Cosmetic changes would only hurt democracy. Consequently, important nationalisations occurred after April 1975. In addition another pillar of the old regime, decadent colonialism, had been shattered. But all was not well in Portugal. In late spring of 1975, ultra-leftists made clear their intentions to take over, an attempt that led to confrontation which at times came close to civil war.

In this context, in July, the EEC Council of Ministers approved in principle immediate and important financial help to Portugal, but under the proviso that pluralistic democracy be upheld. Given the difficulties the country was facing, this political aim became the principal motive for EEC behaviour towards Portugal.

In October 1975 the first emergency loan was approved (180 million EUA) and it was decided to negotiate a long-term financial arrangement, as well as other extensions of cooperation requested by Portugal under Article 35 of the 1972 Agreement (evolutionary clause), and the revision of the EEC trade concessions. In September 1976 the Additional Protocol gave better terms for Portuguese exports of 'sensitive' products and some non-industrial goods, and greater cooperation with respect to the welfare of migrants, industrial technology and finance. It also allowed Portugal to postpone to 1985 the elimination of duties which should have been abolished by 1980. Finally it permitted the rise of duties, to 20 per cent, for products included in Annex II, beyond the limit imposed by the new industry clause. Some of these new concessions practically meant that the EEC recognised that Portugal had been given a rough deal in 1972. A Financial Protocol, encompassing 200 million EUA, of which 150 could receive a 3 per cent subsidy, was also signed.

The first Constitutional Government (Socialist)

announced in its programme (July 1976) that it would request negotiations for entry in the short term, a formality it accomplished in March 1977 after intense diplomatic contacts in Brussels and other capitals.

NEW POLITICAL MOTIVES FOR ENTRY

In principle, there were other options, namely: (i) the evolutionary clause approach leading eventually to association and medium-to long-term entry; (ii) an immediate association deliberately aiming at later entry. However, political developments had strengthened considerably the motives from both Portuguese and EEC sides for immediate entry.

From the EEC side, there was an urgent political and economic need to define and execute a global, coherent South European policy, within the limits of a larger Mediterranean policy, because of the simultaneous demise of dictatorial regimes in Portugal, Spain and Greece and the difficulties facing their democratisation processes. In the particular case of Portugal, the problem was seen mainly from the political point of view; the Community was defending the best interests of West European political and economic systems but it was also responding to the political demands of the Portuguese parties with influence in Brussels and other EEC capitals.

The CDS and PPD/PSD are wholeheartedly in favour of entry. Apart from the usual arguments (importance of economic, financial and emigration ties), they have political reasons to look forward to entry, believing that accession will move the internal balance of power to the right.

Socialist Party leadership, on the other hand, believes that entry is the best way of ensuring two of their political aims and of giving expression to an old reflex: first, to consolidate democracy and due democratic processes of change (political, economic or social) in Portugal, defending them against dictatorial threats of any kind; second, to provide the framework for a new, grand, political and economic project able to fill the void left by sudden and dramatic decolonisation; and third, to give substance to an old political reflex rooted in the struggles of the sixties and seventies according to which democratic Europe and its prospects formed a contrast with totalitarian Portugal and African colonial wars.

The Portuguese Communist Party has always been against integration. After the Revolution, it accepted the need for the Agreement but maintained total opposition to EEC entry.

Finally, the possible entry of Spain and Greece is a factor to be reckoned with. One idea is that if Portugal enters much later than Spain and Greece it will have more difficulties in getting a proper share of Community markets and benefits.

Be that as it may, post-revolutionary developments at home and abroad intensified reasons for entry, especially by adding to the old economic reasons new, though divergent, political arguments. But has this pushed aside consideration of the problems of integration?

THE NEGOTIATIONS AND AFTER: UNRESOLVED PROBLEMS

At 1979 exchange rates per capita GDP for 1975 in West Germany was four times that of Portugal. That of Ireland was approximately 1.5 times that of Portugal. In real terms it is 2.5 times in the former and 1.7 in the latter. The contrast with Spain and Greece, whose GDPs per capita are close to the Irish level, is clearly unfavourable to Portugal (5). At this level, regional polarisation and dependence theory are well established.

The legacy of the deposed regime and IMF restrictive policies. The Commission's Opinions on Portuguese Application rightly stress the heavy price the Portuguese have paid for half a century of dictatorial government. Welfare levels, available social capital, in broad terms, and production structure are so far from West European standards that it will take a prolonged, highly sustained effort to come to terms with the most damaging implications of these gaps. The essential nature of the problem is structural, and there is no shortcut to promoting equitable development.

After the Revolution, a sudden increase in population of the order of 7 per cent (refugees from the ex-colonies) placed greater social demands on the economy, adding to existing problems. This was true for agriculture, industry and services.

The situation has been aggravated by the restrictive policies imposed by the IMF. The strength of these policies has been such that the authorities in charge of their application publicly concluded that there had been a substantial over-shooting of the targets agreed with the IMF. A price has been paid in terms of growth and over-all development. Real wages fell steadily after mid-1976 and functional income distribution is not so different from in 1973. Unemployment remains above 10 per cent. Investment has also been restricted. The capacity of the IMF to understand the political and developmental implications of its policies is more and more in question. There is a clear contradiction between the structural nature of Portuguese problems and the shock treatment imposed by the IMF.

Trade balance issues. In Portugal some people believe that accession will bring about a significant export boom which will reverse the typically heavy negative trade balance into a surplus. For several reasons, this is an over-optimistic expectation. On the export side, the Portuguese record is far from outstanding. In the late 1960s and early 1970s Portugal lost ground in comparison with the Newly Industrialising Countries and with Greece and Spain. Comparison of Portuguese, Greek and Spanish performances in EEC markets in 1964-71 and in 1971-6 supports similar conclusions for both periods.

Data in Table 5.1 on commodity composition, market structure and competitive effects of Portuguese exports show these to have been clearly inferior in comparison with Spanish or Greek exports. Recent export policies might aggravate very significantly the commodity composition effect in the medium term, at least.

On the import side, two factors are important. The first is that EEC exporters now pose a much greater threat than EFTA exporters did in the sixties and early seventies.

Data in Table 5.2 show that the EEC increased its share in all import categories, for instance, in list A from 56 to 72 per cent of total list A imports. In general terms, these increased EEC shares have mainly been the result of imports from the Six and not so much from the UK, Ireland or Denmark.

TABLE 5.1 Sources of the growth of export of manufactures to the EEC from Spain, Greece and Portugal, 1971-6

(percentages)

Sources of growth	Portugal	Spain	Greece
Overall growth of EEC markets	+214	+ 64	+ 35
Changes in commodity composition	- 14	- 3	- 2
Changes in market structure	- 49	- 2	-
Competitiveness	- 51	+ 41	+ 66
Total	+100	+100	+100

SOURCE
GEBEI, according to methodology in H. Tyszinski, 'World Trade in Manufactured Commodities 1899-1950', The Manchester School, September 1951.

NOTE
- = zero/negligible

Another important aspect is that the increase has been much more pronounced for list A than for list B goods. A possible interpretation can be offered in terms of what we might call an integration awareness effect. That is, perceived economic distance probably diminshes at an accelerated rate once a certain threshold in the integration process is passed. Awareness of the inclusion of new territory in the integrated space feeds an impulse in the most aggressive exporters to occupy this new territory over and above the share implied by the simple price advantages derived from the tariff cut. If this interpretation holds, the integration awareness effect will be translated more and more into a trade creation affect. Also, it will be translated into the job destruction associated with domestic output being displaced by imports. The integration awareness effect also works on the export side. But the asymmetries between centre and periphery regarding information, executive resources, commercial ability and monopoly drive may shift the balance more in favour of imports to Portugal than exports from Portugal, to the disadvantage of the latter's balance of trade.

TABLE 5.2 Shares of imports from EEC and EFTA according to agreed schedules, 1973 and 1977

(percentages)

	EEC (9)		Mini-EFTA	
	1973	1977	1973	1977
List A	56	72	15	10
List B	62	64	27	27
Annex G - new industries	72	74	15	13
Annex G - others	57	69	16	13

SOURCE
GEBEI

NOTES
List A: goods subject to July 1977 schedule;
List B: goods subject to January 1980 schedule;
Annex G - new industries: goods covered by Annex G in 1973 and protected in 1977 according to the new industries clause;
Annex G - others: remainder of Annex G.

The second aspect that has not received sufficient attention is the threat created by imports from Spain and third countries. In the first case Portuguese producers will have to face competition from a country that can establish easy commercial links and knows Portuguese needs very well. On the basis of the Linder hypothesis (6), implying that countries export better what they produce for their home markets, Spain may achieve considerable gains in those markets that are most interesting for upgrading the output mix of many Portuguese firms. In the second case, Portugal will also have to admit imports from third countries. In a few cases, these may damage Portuguese producers in industries like textiles, apparel, etc.

Another significant dimension of the trade

balance problem relates to possible export curbs on a sizeable list of sensitive products. Of course, it is not in the best Portuguese interest to ignore present adjustment difficulties in EEC members. But the truth is that, for a while, the range of products which can contribute in a decisive manner to improving the trade balance is relatively concentrated in areas where adjustment problems already exist or may exist. If export curbs are deemed to be necessary, then some kind of appropriate compensation should be negotiated.

It also seems wise to admit that if development in Portugal is to proceed at a pace and direction in agreement with sustained harmonisation efforts within the EEC, then balance-of-payments problems will persist in the 1980s. That is, foreign savings will have to supplement resources generated at home in order to allow for a sustained transformation of existing structures.

The transfer of resources. In previous negotiations trade policy issues, such as concessions on agriculture exports, slower dismantling of tariff structures or protection to new industries, determined the balance of negotiations. Thus, they received concentrated attention. Now, to some extent, they have been overtaken by a more fundamental problem of a global nature, that of the transfer of resources.

The key aspect to consider is that, while within national boundaries there are very active transfer mechanisms, supported by appropriate fiscal and budgetary policies, under existing Community arrangements, mechanisms to transfer resources within the Community are rather weak and, moreover, highly uneven in their equity effects across countries, regions and people. This has been clearly shown in a variety of studies. In the great majority of these, including the MacDougall report, no account has been taken of enlargement problems (7). If these are considered, the nature and significance of the transfer issues assume dimensions which have received little attention. Certainly for Portugal no effective proposals in this area have been made.

There are three issues that deserve attention. One is the size of net transfers according to the various existing or possible mechanisms, determining the total available. A second one is the aims, the operating characteristics and the immediate destiny of specific mechanisms. A third one is the proper use of resources whenever the mechanism implies a choice among institutions, people and objectives which might benefit from its existence.

The Commission estimates that if present mechanisms were applied in 1978 to an enlarged EEC, net transfers to Portugal would amount to something like 2.5 per cent of her GDP. Assuming, for the sake of the argument, that this is correct, the first type of issue is addressed primarily to the question: will this level of transfers meet development finance needs? The answer seems to be no, bearing in mind the marked deficiencies of the Portuguese economy at present. What then is the role of Community solidarity in closing such a gap?

No less significant than the level of transfers is the structure, and the specificity according to source, beneficiary and effect. With the same level of transfers there might be widely divergent results if the composition of the different mechanisms is changed. The third type of issue can also be framed in terms of source, beneficiary, and effect framework. But here it is clear that an important discriminatory element exists, so that the question: who decides what? cannot be avoided.

From a narrow point of view, this calls attention to existing problems regarding the state of development administration in Portugal, whether we look into planning, execution or control aspects. However, this is only a reflection of deeper problems related to the use and abuse of state power as a producer of social cohesion and integration in some areas and, at the same time, of disintegration in others. Though this battle is to be fought mainly in the domestic arena, it would be naive to believe that EEC negotiations will not shift the internal balance in one way or another. Also, we have to consider that although some of those shifts will occur by accident, others will be promoted by design, external and internal.

These questions have hardly been tackled in a systematic manner; yet it seems they form an essential part of negotiations purposefully addressed to the creation of conditions conducive to more equal development within the Community, among and within countries.

Integration and disintegration at different levels: future development and equity. In the Caetano period the integration strategy seemed to be centred on the extension and deepening of the areas controlled by the leading economic groups, coupled with the possible rise of independent, dynamic, small and medium-sized firms. At the same time, foreign import penetration of the domestic market and national export gains in foreign markets would be combined with previous patterns, the result being the simultaneous development of integration and disintegration effects at the regional, national and international levels, according to an overall concentrated growth model.

According to the Caetano Plan, there would be a new wave of import substitution in capital-intensive sectors (basic chemicals, plastics, fibres, steel, etc.) by means of backward integration of second and third stage light manufactures. This would extend the area under the control of big business, but at the same time it would provide some kind of depth to the industrial structure on a national integration basis. Simultaneously, temporary excessive capacity would be allocated to exports. Specialisation based on the upgrading of the big and medium-sized firms' product mix was also supposed to occur.

To a certain extent market forces would shape the course of events; more so in some areas than in others. But there is no doubt that purposeful use of state power was supposed to be the main vehicle for projected changes. This model provided a framework for integration.

With regard to future development patterns, political forces behind accession diverge on fundamental issues.

It should be noted that the leading economic groups dismantled by the Revolution had a high potential for reorganising large areas of the economy on the basis of national integration, but at the social cost of an overriding lack of concern with equity issues.

Now, the question is: how can depth, coherence and articulation be given to whole sectors in order to combine national and international integration with concern for the needs of the population?

Different social and political forces may have different answers. It seems that the nationalised sector, in cooperation with private firms, has a worthy, though far from exclusive, role to play. However, in the absence of any overall framework, its contributions have been rather limited. Since the nationalised sector is formed by the core of the old economic groups, this behaviour creates a void that must be filled in the future. The notion that it will be filled by private big groups, reborn out of the ashes, does not seem to be a practical proposition for at least a number of years. Thus the present state of affairs works against national integration and in favour of a mix of international integration and national disintegration.

This matter requires urgent attention in relation to equitable development patterns. At the present stage of European integration, it may be true that in the next few years the chances of more equitable development in Portugal will be determined to a greater extent by domestic factors, including the combination of political and economic aims behind the negotiating process.

CONCLUSION

In two decades Portugal has moved almost from secular isolationism from West European affairs to deep, irreversible insertion in an integrated Europe. The way she approached Europe has left behind a host of unresolved problems. The negotiations are vital to providing conditions to solve these problems in a context of equitable development within Portugal. However, there is reason to believe that a recurrent error in past dealings with European integration issues is discernible again. This error is rooted in a relative failure to connect political aims and economic realities. In the past, political aims tended to ignore or underestimate changes exerted by increased integration. Now they may tend to take too much for granted their beneficial consequences. Motives for enlargement, economic aspects and the aims of integration should be analysed carefully. If not, the chances of equitable integration, at both national and international levels, will be lessened.

NOTES

1. See, for instance, EFTA, Les Effets de l'AELE et de la CEE sur les Echanges 1959-1967, EFTA Secretariat, 1972.
2. See Plano Intercalar de Fomento (1965-67) and III Plano de Fomento (1968-73).
3. According to OECD, Trade by Commodities, the UK accounted for 23.1 per cent of Portuguese exports in the period 1971-3.
4. See A. Cordeiro, Portugal e as Comunidades Europeias, Editorial O Seculo, 1977; and J. Candido de Azevedo, Portugal Europa Face ao Mercado Comum, Livraria Bertrand, 1968.
5. Bulletin of the European Communities, 'Opinions on Portuguese Application for Membership', Supplement 5/78, Table 1.
6. See S.B. Linder, An Essay on Trade and Transformation, Stockholm, Almqvist & Wiksell, 1961.
7. On the other hand, see various chapters in D. Seers and C. Vaitsos (eds), Integration and Unequal Development: The Experience of the EEC, London, Macmillan, 1980.

6 The Agricultural Sector

ARMANDO TRIGO DE ABREU

THE CRISIS IN AGRICULTURE

Persistent crisis has characterised Portuguese agriculture throughout this century. Explanations for and consequences of this crisis have varied widely but the essential fact that agriculture has not responded or contributed adequately to the process of Portuguese economic and social development is uncontested.

Among tentative explanations one must list unfavourable climatic conditions, which have been the favourite scapegoat for poor agricultural performance, a long-term maladjustment of crops to soil and climatic conditions - the historical problem to which Salazar referred in relation to cereal production in Portugal (1) - lack of entrepreneurship, low levels of production due to traditional systems, etc.

Whatever the real causes of that crisis, the fact remains that long stagnation of agricultural production transformed Portuguese agriculture from a dynamic sector into a static pool of resources - mainly labour - whence the development of industrial sectors in Portugal or abroad has drawn without any deep restructuring effects on agriculture.

Economically, stagnation of agricultural output is probably the best indicator of the seriousness of the crisis. Taking the last two decades, annual rates of growth of gross agricultural product varied from 0.7 per cent in 1953/5-1974/6 to 0.5 between 1963/5-1974/6. The same stagnation applies to composition of agricultural product. For the 1960s and 1970s, rates of growth for livestock, crops and forest products corresponded, respectively, to 1.6, 0.4 and 1.2 per cent and 1.8, 0.6 and 0.4 per cent (2). The only sizeable exceptions, in this regard, were fruits which grew at an annual rate of 6 per cent and wood products with a similar rate of growth.

Between 1963/5 and 1973/5 yields per hectare were variable but stagnation was the dominant characteristic. For example, wheat production rose from 0.82 tons per hectare in 1963/5 to 1.18; maize went up from 1.08 to 1.30 tons/ha.; rice decreased from 4.38 to 3.25 tons/ha.; and potatoes went down from 9.98 to 9.50 tons/ha. (3).

Areas for major crops showed a steady decline over the last two decades, probably as out-migration and the physical and economic limits of mechanisation tended to restrict agriculture to the more profitable and easily mechanised areas. Between 1963/5 and 1973/5 almost all major crops showed a sizeable decline in their areas of cultivation: wheat lost 47 per cent of cultivated area in 1963/5; rye - 37; maize - 24; pulses - 31; and rice - 8 per cent. There were some exceptions such as potatoes (+5 per cent) (4).

The stagnation of output was accompanied by a decline in fixed capital formation. Some estimates point out that capital formation in agriculture does not cover the rate of depreciation.

Social crisis in agriculture is another aspect of the general pattern of stagnation. Consequences of that crisis are well known and we shall point out its central features later, but the basic feature is the incapacity of the agricultural sector to provide full employment and an acceptable standard of living for its active population. Data on rural employment are scarce and generally unreliable even if some social groups (day labourers in the south) retained a sharp memory of seasonal unemployment which led them to a particular form of participation in recent agrarian reform (5).

Labour productivity in agriculture lagged well behind non-agricultural labour productivity over the last twenty years. The relative position has deteriorated and net annual gains in agricultural labour productivity may be estimated at 0.5 per cent for 1954-61 and 0.8 per cent for 1962-73. It must be stressed that these results are mainly due to massive rural-urban and out-migration that reduced the active population in agriculture from 1.41 million in 1950 to 1.29 million in 1960, 0.98 million in 1970 and approximately 0.84 million in

1975. The share of active agricultural population in total active population decreased from about 47 per cent (1950) to 41 (1960) and dropped dramatically to 30 in 1970 and 27 per cent in 1975 (6).

Effects of this massive transfer of resources into other sectors and economies have been felt at all levels of rural social structure. Looking at the period 1960-70 in more detail, it is worth noting that wage-labour farms were greatly affected - their numbers dropped from 70,000 in 1960 to 16,000 in 1970 - meaning that, in the absence of large-scale and intensive land concentration, wage labour abandoned the rural sector, changing wage-labour farms into family-labour farms. This is confirmed by a large increase in the number of family-labour farm managers (about +20 per cent). Also family farms were deeply affected: family helps - non-wage labour - increased the migration flows and their numbers dropped dramatically (175,000 in 1960 against 99,000 in 1970, that is -55 per cent). Finally, wage labourers, either from the imperfect family-farm system or from the typical large capitalist farming of southern Portugal, declined from 770,000 in 1960 to 450,000 in 1970 (-42 per cent) (7).

There is a third level of the general crisis which is less commonly commented upon, relating to conservation and the efficient use of energy. If, in the beginning of the period, strong pressure on land meant over-exploitation of resources, with severe degradation of the eco-system (erosion, flooding, deforestation), out-migration and rural-urban transfers eased that pressure, as the figures for cultivated areas for some crops show. However, the adaption of the agricultural system to a less labour-surplus economy seems to have led to some extent to less efficient energy use. In fact, studies show that modernisation and innovation, along the lines of new input utilisation in mechanisation and husbandry, tend to result in reduced energy efficiency. Ratios of energy outputs/energy inputs seem to decrease with the dominant pattern of modernisation (8).

RECENT DEVELOPMENTS

The general consequences of this crisis are evident in the agricultural sector itself and cut across the Portuguese economy and society. Social inefficiency, for example, shown in persistently low labour productivity, was a determining factor in the waves of out-migration that swept Portuguese society, especially from the sixties onward (9).

The economic consequences of the long stagnation of Portuguese agriculture are felt at two different levels. On the one hand, the stable composition of the agricultural product tends to show that, in relation to a period of profound change in population (urbanisation, out-migration), agricultural supply does not match the actual composition of demand, as this was affected by changes in dietary habits over the last twenty years. On the other hand, the level of production falls far short of actual demand, even for branches where no marked change in consumer preferences has occurred.

Both these phenomena are responsible for a total inversion of the agricultural trade balance which, from a small surplus in the sixties, proceeded to show an increasing deficit. The rate of increase of the deficit is staggering. From 1965 to 1975 it increased more than tenfold. In 1974 agricultural imports (27 billion escudos) represented 58 per cent of gross agricultural product, 9 per cent of GDP and the agricultural trade balance deficit (12 billion escudos) was 26 per cent of gross agricultural product and about 4 per cent of GDP (10).

The structure of imports underwent some important changes in the 1970s. Apart from traditional imports like wheat (162,000 tons in 1963, 160,000 in 1973 and 680,000 in 1979) and sugar (125; 247; 303), new imports took a major share in the total balance. This is the case for cereals for animal consumption as well as mixed feed. The new importance of this import sector is directly linked with expanding demand for meat and dairy products on the one hand, and with profound changes in systems of animal production, where natural resources were progresively displaced in the food chain by mixed feed of high protein content on the other. Table 6.1 shows the importance of this switch in techniques. The proportion of these imports to total agricultural imports shows the significance and suddenness of the change: in 1963 they represented about 3 per cent of total agricultural imports and ten years later 20 per cent.

TABLE 6.1 Portuguese imports of selected agricultural products 1963, 1973 and 1979

(1000 tons)

	1963	1973	1979
Maize	71	794	1990
Sorghum	0	234	300
Meal	28	157	234

SOURCES
World Bank, Portugal: Agricultural Sector Survey, Washington, 1978, Table 3.1; and Perspectivas da situação do Abastecimento de pais em bens agricolas e alimentares para 1979, Lisbon, Ministerio do Comercio e Turismo, D. G. Coordenacao Comercial, 1979.

A DEVELOPMENT STRATEGY

One development strategy for Portuguese agriculture that enjoys some consensus has indicated a number of production aims, in order to overcome the situation described above. These aims are (11): (i) to increase agricultural production in order to (a) satisfy internal demand for essential products, (b) respond to the need to improve the diet of the Portuguese people,(c) contribute, directly and indirectly, to the trade balance; (ii) to increase productivity by means of (a) improving production technologies,(b) rationalising the use of factors of production,(c) making better use of soils.

This strategy may be discussed at three different levels: first, requirements for its implementation; second, the institutional framework needed;

and third, its compatibility with the development path implied by the evolution of EEC agricultural policies.

Regarding the first level, which is the same as asking what resources and endowments Portuguese agriculture has for this new take-off, a number of questions may be raised. The deterioration of the agricultural situation and the lack of certain resources points to the need for a massive transfer of resources from all over the economy, as it seems that neither the capacity to invest nor the ability to do so is to be taken for granted given past performance of the sector. One may think that the capacity for these transfers is strictly limited in the Portuguese economy, as general economic conditions indicate a low-growth strategy, and industrial investment is badly needed for modernisation of traditional sectors. To stabilise industrial employment and transfers from consumers to agricultural producers would have a dramatic impact on urban living conditions.

Consumption requirements do not seem to have changed perceptibly as new habits continue to be adopted, increasing the strain on sectors where adaptation has been more difficult or where the consequences of adaptation have been felt at the trade balance level (meat and milk production). Given the present state of agriculture, to satisfy consumer preferences will aggravate the trade deficit.

One may ask if accumulation in the agricultural sector is possible given the employment pressure discussed above, or, in other words, if a massive outflow of agricultural population would:(1) be possible under prevailing economic and social conditions; and (2) lead to an increase in production and a higher degree of flexibility in adjusting production to consumers' requirements.

Regarding the first question, where a positive answer would mean that much higher returns to labour would be possible, there is the broad employment situation to be considered. If a suitable target for labour transfers in the next ten years were to attain the proportion of agricultural population to total population current in Central Europe, that is, to decrease that share from the actual 25 per cent to something closer to 10, in absolute terms this would mean reducing the labour force in agriculture from around 0.8 to 0.3 million, or finding 500,000 new jobs outside agriculture. What this would mean to agriculture itself is hard to estimate, as the major exodus of the sixties affected only 310,000 people throughout that decade, with the social and economic consequences described above. Even if agriculture could dispense with almost two-thirds of its labour force in a short period, the question remains - where and how to find alternative employment for half a million people.

Typical outlets for surplus agricultural labour have been industrial growth, the urban informal sector or out-migration. As far as industrial job creation is concerned, one may gather from the evidence on Portuguese industry, that for the next few years the main thrust on the employment front will be the restructuring of industry itself as the labour-intensive traditional sector will have to adapt to new competition.

On the other hand, the Portuguese urban informal sector has absorbed in the last few years, in the aftermath of decolonisation, a sizeable proportion of the displaced labour force, and doubts may be expressed about its ability to expand productively even further. Finally, with regard to out-migration, mainly to Europe, the continuing economic crisis will transform the issue into a main point of discussion regarding entry to the EEC.

But even if job creation, internally or externally, were possible at this level, a question remains about the consequences for agricultural performance of the labour out-flow. Going by past experience, the impact of such out-migration on production structure and performance would not be very encouraging. In fact, out-migration contributed in the last two decades to a process of agricultural stagnation characterised by: (1) a general reduction in cropland; (2) a changeover from a grazing system to a mainly mixed feed system; (3) increased misuse of natural resources; (4) increased strain on the trade balance due to (1) and (2). In the light of this, the answer to the question of the influence of out-migration on modernisation of Portuguese agriculture seems to be that declining population pressure on land due to out-migration has not played a significant role in the modernisation and adaptation of Portuguese agriculture.

PARTIAL REFORMS IN AGRICULTURE

Certain changes have occurred in Portuguese agriculture which may contribute to its modernisation and adaptation to new demands. These are both institutional and functional, and brief reference must be made to them in order to assess their impact and compatibility with European demands on Portuguese agriculture. On the institutional side, three points deserve a mention: agrarian reform, tenancy modification and part-time farming.

The central aim of the redistribution of land was to replace an historically *rentier* class by active entrepreneurship based upon self-managed or cooperative units, in order to move from extensive and excessive cultivation to intensive and balanced agriculture. The course of events, however, emphasised extension of the existing crop system rather than the reversal and intensification of the traditional pattern of cultivation. Scattered experiences, though, point to a new ability to move away from old systems, under conditions of excessive labour charges and capital scarcity.

As far as tenancy is concerned, the changes introduced after 1974 tended to redress the situation of tenants and landowners, asserting the predominance of profits over rents. However, implementation of those changes seemed to lag well behind the intention of the legislator as well as the need to enhance entrepreneurship. Also, lack of supporting facilities (e.g. credit schemes) reduced the impact of changes.

Industrialisation in traditionally agricultural areas brought part-time farming, where workers divided their occupation between the farm they came from and the new industrial jobs that were created mainly in the sixties. Research on the type of change in agriculture induced by this change in status is very scarce but some results tend to show that, in the small farms which characterise the industrial/rural interface, changes in the cropping system are very few, with only the general pattern of replacement of forage crops by the use of mixed feed in cattle production.

Two main trends in functional modernisation have appeared in recent decades. On the one hand, in the early sixties mechanisation progressed quite rapidly, mainly in the wheat plains of the south. On the other hand, as we have already underlined, mixed feed took an important place in the food chain, restricting and eliminating the use of natural grazing lands and imposing new strains on the balance of trade. Use of fertilizers and new chemical inputs also progressed, even if consumption continues to lag well behind European levels.

On the whole, institutional or functional modernisation failed to introduce profound changes in agriculture, if we except the top size class of farms in southern Portugal where ownership and managers were replaced to some extent by the implementation of agrarian reform laws. Farm structure is still distorted by very small units. Of the 0.8 million farms, 300,000 have less than one hectare, another 300,000 fall between one and four, and in 1968 the top layer above 1000 hectares included only 500 farms (12).

AGRICULTURE AND INTEGRATION

The central question is how Portuguese agriculture will adapt to European integration and to the implied changes in market conditions.

The results of this process are certainly minor, in economic terms, for the Nine as Portuguese agriculture is but a small part of an enlarged community: gross agricultural product for Portuguese agriculture represents 3 per cent of the aggregate for the Nine; agricultural area amounts to 5 per cent and even for agricultural population the share is about 10 per cent of total farm population in the EEC.

On the other hand, functional links between the two economies are already well developed. Imports from the EEC amount to 12 per cent of total Portuguese agricultural imports, and the share of the EEC in Portuguese agricultural exports is about 42 per cent (13).

But those economic consequences, as well as the social and political implications for Portugal, are of some concern. Moreover, integration will be a fair test of the ability of the Community to integrate economies and societies which, in their structure and functions, present sharp differences from the core of the Community. The composition of the EEC suggests a dominant pattern of working agreements among already assimilated partners. Thus the question arises of the possibility of maintaining these agreements when the partners show a high degree of heterogeneity.

An additional problem concerns the optimal result of these agreements, as they might aim at reducing disparities - economic, social, cultural - or at maintaining a working relationship between different partners.

Some elements of these problems may be illustrated in a comparative study of Portuguese and EEC agriculture, taking as a starting point the importance of particular products in terms of consumption and prices (see Table 6.2).

A number of conclusions may be drawn from Table 6.2:

(1) The relative importance of agricultural production in Portugal and in the Nine shows that the impact of integration on total production is very low. The only products of some importance on a Community scale are tomatoes for processing, wine, olive oil, lamb and rice.

(2) Surpluses, that is, capacity for exports, are to be found in wine, nuts, tomatoes for processing, and there is near self-sufficiency in barley, lamb, eggs, fresh fruits and citrus fruits.

(3) On the other hand, EEC export capacity exists for wheat (Portugal is an importer), milk (the same applies) and near self-sufficiency for meat, pork, eggs, potatoes, wine and sugar.(14)

(4) The ability to export in either direction under free trade conditions depends also on prices. Information on relative prices in Portugal and the Nine is given in Table 6.2, but before examining it, one must say that before 1974 prices were very similar; after 1974 exchange rates moved rapidly against the escudo and were higher than the rate of growth of farm-gate prices in Portugal, implying a growing gap between Portuguese prices and EEC institutional prices.

TABLE 6.2 A comparison of Portuguese and Community agriculture, mid-1970s

	Production in Portugal/ production in the Nine (1974-6)		Self-sufficiency Portugal (1975-6)	Self-sufficiency The Nine	Farm-gate price Portugal/ farm-gate price the Nine (1977-8)
	(percentages)				(ratio)
Wheat	1.6 -	1.7	75	106	0.76
Barley	-	-	102	101	1.09
Oats	1.3	1.6	n.a.	n.a.	n.a.
Maize	3.2	3.5	26	49	0.90
Rice	11.3	15.7	54	76	0.69
Meat	1.2	1.6	69	99	1.02
Pork	0.8	1.0	88	99	1.08
Lamb	8.3	9.0	100	64	n.a.
Eggs	1.2	1.2	100	100	n.a.
Milk	0.7	0.7	88	101	1.05
Potatoes	2.7	3.0	91	98	n.a.
Apples	2.0	2.2	n.a.	n.a.	n.a.
Pears	2.6	2.6	100(a)	79(a)	n.a.
Peaches	4.1	5.1	n.a.	n.a.	n.a.
Citrus fruits	5.2	5.7	40(b)	98(b)	n.a.
Olive oil	8.2	11.4	65(d)	22(d)	0.73
Wine	5.5	8.1	140	98	0.92
Tomatoes for processing	24.4	40.9	n.a.	n.a.	n.a.
Sugar	-	-	-	98	n.a.
Tobacco	-	6.0	-	n.a.	n.a.
Nuts			143(c)	57(c)	n.a.

SOURCE
A. Cortez Lobão, 'Agricultura Portuguesa e Integracao Europeia', Economia, forthcoming.

NOTES
(a) Fresh fruits, excluding citrus
(b) 1973/4
(c) 1973-5
(d) Olive and vegetable oils
n.a. = not available.

(5) Portuguese farmers receive higher prices than their European competitors for barley, meat, pork and milk, where export or near-export capacity exists in the EEC, as self-sufficiency indexes for these products are respectively 101, 99, 99, 101. Except for barley, where self-sufficiency also exists, Portugal is a net importer of meat and milk.

CONCLUSIONS

Thus the impact of enlargement on areas of the Portuguese economy may be estimated roughly: the more important points to consider are the impact on producers, on consumers and on the trade balance. A product by product analysis of impact on internal supply, internal demand, agricultural imports, balance of payments, changes in official agricultural policy and transfers for consumers and producers has been made, on a qualitative basis. From this study a number of conclusions may be drawn (15).

(1) For producers integration would mean higher prices for most products included in Table 6.2, as internal prices are generally lower than EEC institutional prices; pork, meat and milk would be the exceptions to this rule as their prices are already higher in Portugal than in the Community.

(2) Consumers would also bear the burden of enlargement, as in the absence of any basic restructuring of marketing channels the rise of farm-gate prices would be passed on to them.

The application of Community rules regarding consumer subsidies would mean an increase in the cost of living as a number of products (e.g. milk) are now heavily subsidised.

(3) The rise in farm-gate prices does not imply any major consequences for internal supply, as past history shows that supply elasticity in relation to prices is usually low.

(4) On the contrary, higher prices for consumers would probably imply a reduction in demand for some products, namely meat and milk.

(5) The limited reaction of internal supply to a rise in prices and an eventual reduction of internal demand would contribute to a fall

in agricultural imports, either directly on the demand side or indirectly on the supply side on account of the stability of the use of imported inputs. However, in this respect, any gain would probably be counteracted by the change in import flows and prices of some inputs, namely maize and mixed feed. In fact, the lower prices of these inputs in the international market would mean that compensatory payments should be made to Brussels.

Thus a grim picture for consumers seems to emerge. However, there are also areas of concern regarding producers, mainly for those who specialise in branches with lower prices in the Community than in Portugal and where there are actual or potential Community surpluses. This is the case, typically, for meat and milk.

A study of the implications of changed production conditions for these products in Portugal under the integration agreements would have to be made in terms of regions and social groups. In the absence of such a specialised study, a few indicators show the magnitude of the problem.

In regional terms, animal production is very important in north-eastern Portugal. Four districts out of the eighteen existing districts in Portugal account for 36 per cent of the total value of meat production. Also, meat (including lamb and pork) and milk (in Aveiro, Braga, Porto and Viana do Castelo) represent a significant proportion of agricultural production in these districts (see Table 6.3). In global terms, meat/milk production represents from 26 to 42 per cent of the produce of these districts.

The distribution of land in this area reflects a minifundium structure, with a high density of agricultural population. For example, in Braga, farms with less than one hectare accounted for 49 per cent of the number of holdings and 7 per cent of total farm land. If farms between one and four hectares are included, the corresponding figures are 83 and 38 per cent (16).

But a more precise picture of the social impact of changes in the market for animal products may be drawn on the basis of the size of the milking herd in Portugal (see Table 6.4). It should be noted that the 59.2 per cent of milk producers with one cow are responsible for about 30 per cent of the total supply of milk.

TABLE 6.3 Production of livestock products in districts of northern Portugal, 1973

	Meat	Milk
	(percentages of gross agricultural output)	
Aveiro	18	18
Braga	19	16
Porto	15	11
Viana	20	22

SOURCE
M.H. Caramona , M.M. Conceição and F. Tavares, Repartiçao do Producto Agricola en 1973, Lisbon, INE, 1975.

TABLE 6.4 Importance of Portuguese milk production relative to herd size (a)

Herd size	Percentage of milk producers
1	59.2
2-5	36.5
6-10	2.8
11-20	1.0
21-50	0.4
+50	0.1

SOURCE
E.Castro-Caldas, A Agricultura Portuguesa no limiar da Reforma Agraria, Fundação Gulbenkian, Oeiras, 1978.
NOTE
(a) Date not supplied in source, but probably 1975.

Small producers concentrated in a homogeneous small area provide the ingredients for a social crisis. It remains to be seen what the enlargement must provide to avert any such crisis.

One should, however, qualify the above scenario. The first point concerns the state of Portuguese agriculture - the persistent crisis and lack of ability to adjust - and the very course of its development. The picture presented above corresponds to an abrupt confrontation of Portuguese and European agriculture. However, a transition phase probably gives more room for more gradual modification. The problem lies on two levels: (1) is there a definite and successful course of development for Portuguese agriculture? and (2) is that course of development compatible with smooth integration in the near future?

Elements mentioned above indicate that most of the problems now arising in relation to the enlargement are themselves problems of Portuguese agriculture itself. For example, low productivity and high costs of production that imply a burden for consumers or heavy subsidies are internal structural problems, related to either land tenure and management or linked with low use of modern inputs. The high levels of compensatory transfers on large imports of maize and mixed feed are linked with a distortion of factor use in agriculture that leads farmers to replace abundant natural resources by costly imported inputs. That is, evidence indicates that the needs and shortcomings of internal development correspond to a certain extent with problems posed by European enlargement.

These few examples illustrate not so much the existence of a particular course of development as some problems whose resolution will enhance the possibilities of preventing later difficulties over integration.

But the integrative process is also a problem of adjustment, at least of the instruments that were used at other stages of Community development. These instruments, unified in the CAP, aim at promoting increased agricultural productivity, an increase on farmers' income, stabilisation of markets and reasonable prices for consumers, by means of guaranteed prices for a certain number of products, trade barriers against the outside world and subsidised disposal of surpluses. The operation of the system tends to show a bias, since the price system is not as comprehensive as the range of crops, and plays only a minor role in directing structural change and places an increased burden on consumers.

It is likely that some change in the instruments will result from the combined pressure of the agricultural demands of the three Mediterranean countries, particularly concerning the extension of the guaranteed price system to Mediterranean crops. This would mean that from a system which protects some crops and therefore only some peasants, one could move to a system where the farmer, irrespectively of what region he is in, is the focus of the integration process.

There are, however, certain instruments which are much more dependent on the dominant paradigm of agricultural progress in EEC; in this sense, a critique of the working of a number of funds, instruments and proposals may well miss the central question which is the relevance of a dominant theory of rural development to the central problems of Mediterranean agriculture.

One document that has played a dominant role in shaping EEC concepts and instruments regarding rural change is the Mansholt Plan. It was written during a phase of expansion, adopted the broad framework of population pressure in relation to technical change, and to simplify, promised <u>much for the few</u>. Is this a suitable paradigm for solving the problem of Mediterranean agriculture in the near future? It may be argued that 'much for the few' worked systematically at the expense of consumers, and also that the political equilibrium that sustained that policy was only possible due to the low weight of agricultural population in the EEC. The fact that farmers were few was a precondition for them to have the 'much'.

Moreover, this policy is not only an instrument of distribution among several social groups but it also contributes to the shaping of the groups themselves. In other words, the CAP is an adjustment instrument for the distribution of the labour force, enhancing the traditional out-flow of agricultural population. This adjustment, however, is strictly linked with the dynamics of the economy as a whole. In the case of Portuguese agriculture, as stressed above, the problem is twofold, in the sense that adjustment pre-supposes industrial or services growth and population transfers do not necessarily mean progress in agriculture. In a period of general economic crisis, transfer of active population implies a high social cost, and even measures aimed at the older strata of population lose their appeal as compensations for retirement are bound to be eroded by severe inflation.

The accent on the increase in labour productivity which is a central tenet of the CAP is hardly coherent with an employment situation where the marginal labour productivity outside agriculture is very low. An adequate strategy for Portuguese rural development would tend to emphasise the rise in land productivity. In this sense the new slogan for agrarian policy could not be _much for the few_, but _equitable income for all_.

Under prevailing conditions in the Portuguese labour market, the philosophy of modernisation along the lines of the Mansholt Plan lacks relevance, even if transfers from the EEC were to make possible an improvement in the economic situation in order to re-establish 'normal' intersectoral labour flows.

The Portuguese experience illustrates the need for a new political equilibrium between consumers and a large agricultural population to replace the previous situation (more criticised than praised), which formed the basis of EEC agricultural integration. But this new political equilibrium requires a redistribution between social groups and regions. Will this new reality be examined in Brussels?

NOTES

1. A.O. Salazar, _A questão cerealífera: O trigo_, Coimbra, 1917.
2. World Bank, _Portugal: Agricultural Sector Survey_, Washington, 1978, pp.118 ff.
3. _Ibid_., Annex I, Table 2.0.
4. _Ibid_., Annex I, Table 2.0
5. A.T. Abreu, 'Agrarian Reform and Development Issues in Portugal 1974-78', _Derap Working Papers_ A-124, Bergen, 1978.
6. World Bank, _op.cit_., p. 124.

7. Data from 1960 and 1970 population censuses.
8. C. Borges Pires, Estudo Energético de Duas Explorações Agrícolas no Baixo Alentejo (forthcoming).
9. On migration to the EEC, see Statistical Annexe, Table 4.
10. World Bank, op. cit., Tables 1.0 and 3.0.
11. Diagnóstico de Situação e Estratégias de Desenvolvimento do Sector, Gabinete de Planeamento, M.A.P., Lisbon, 1977.
12. INE, Inquérito às Explorações Agrícolas do Continente, Lisbon, 1968.
13. Data for 1979 were, respectively, 13.57 and 49.43 per cent.
14. On agriculture and the CAP, see Volume II in this series.
15. A.C. Lobão, 'Agricultura Portuguesa e Integração Europeia', Economia (forthcoming). This work is quoted freely in following paragraphs.
16. Data from the General Survey, 1968.

7 The Industrial Sector

VASCO CAL

There are three main problems in analysing the likely impact of integration on Portuguese industry: lack of comprehensive data on Portugal's economic situation; the passive or active resistance on the part of the main project advisers; and the different facets of integration itself.

Some consider that enforced modernisation of Portuguese industry through the impact of joining would fulfil the conditions demanded by multinationals for investing in Portugal.

The negotiations between Portugal and the EEC have been characterised by discussion of time limits until the Community's rights are fully established. As in the case of Greece, Portugal and Spain will benefit mainly from such schedules in order to 'accept the contractual rules of the Community and all the political, economic and social objectives contained therein, as well as the decisions and resolutions of all kinds made from the day the treaties come into force', as expressed by the Social and Economic Committee (SEC 766/79). Furthermore, during negotiations, they must follow various common and well defined precepts so that the coherence of the Community is not endangered (as referred to in the 'global reflections on the problems of enlargement' issued by the Commission).

The dynamics of enlargement and its effect on the Community's institutions are not dissociated from recent efforts to reinforce the supranational thesis (Tindmans' Report), presented as the only way to avoid present or future partition and dilution of the Community. The elections to the European Parliament and changes in decision-making processes in Brussels have come about at a time when it is becoming clearer that 'the liberalisation of industrial exchanges between member countries, the free movement of capital and workers and the support given to the agricultural sector through the common agricultural policy (CAP), simply allow the multinational companies to enjoy total freedom in determining the economic structure of Europe to further their own immediate interests'(1).

The controversies and changes in orientation and priorities of member countries have an effect on Portugal's interests. The inclusion of Portugal within the economic space of Western Europe - which was a reality - encouraged on the whole the adoption of traditional forms of international division of labour, in spite of exceptional conditions which the country could have benefited from, especially in regard to developing industries.

If adequate corrective policies are not adopted, Portuguese entry into the EEC will reinforce previous forms of the division of labour at the industrial level, and will contribute decisively to maintaining and strengthening the development gap between her and other European countries, thus rendering more acute the ever-increasing regional disparities.

INDUSTRIAL STRUCTURE

International specialisation is found more at the product level than at the sector level which is quite aggregated. Various studies, however, point out the correlation between the growth of GDP and a larger share of modern sectors in total manufacturing industry. In Spain, for example, the rate of structural transformation (1960-70) was larger than that experienced by more developed European countries.

In Portugal, estimates for 1978 indicate that the industrial sector accounted for 43 per cent of GDP (manufacturing industry 31 per cent), these figures being larger than those for the majority of the Community countries as well as for Spain and Greece (2). The annual average growth rate of manufacturing industry was 9.7 per cent between 1963 and 1973.

The rate of structural transformation (obtained by computing the difference between its weight at the start and at the end of the given period for each sector and by taking the average of the absolute values of those differences) was 1.12 for Portugal, while for Spain it was 2.69, for Greece

3.34 and for Turkey 3.57.

One should not draw the simple conclusion that there was total industrial stagnation, since within each sector significant changes took place (as in the textile industry) or no progress was made (as in the steel industry).

It should be noted that in the same period the end product of the industrial sector (of which the export of manufactured goods play an important role) grew at a lower rate than the gross value added (GVA) and the import of manufactured goods. This means that there was an infiltration by the industrial sector into the other productive sectors as well as a probable change in the ratio GVA/industrial sector production (3).

PRODUCTIVITY

Portugal has the lowest average productivity rates among the Twelve in practically all sectors (not excluding firms of international standing). Marginal and badly structured units are to be found in every country but, in the case of Portugal, it is alarming that these employ at least one-fifth of the whole industrial workforce. This is a significant indicator when one is assessing the impact of the present opening-up process (see Table 7.1).

According to estimates for 1972 (4) Portuguese productivity levels in twenty-three sectors of manufacturing industry were generally lower than those of the developed countries of the EEC and EFTA and those of South European countries. Only half the sectors showed net productivity levels above those for Yugoslavia and only in four and three sectors were the rates higher than those for Greece and Spain respectively (drink, tobacco and non-electric machines).

As far as productivity rates are concerned, Portugal reaches 3,700 SDRs followed by Spain where the SDR value amounted to 7,500.

In spite of the rapid growth registered in Portugal since 1962, the gap in development mentioned earlier is confirmed by the discrepancy which exists at the sectoral level between Portugal and the four largest EEC countries. It should be noted that, with the exception of cotton textiles, the present weight of Portuguese private enterprise is not significant in any of the other sectors mentioned, since these are either nationalised or under the direct or technological control of multinationals.

TABLE 7.1 Number of firms, volume of employment and output according to production per head in Portugal, 1973

Value added per worker (thousands escudos)	Number of firms	Employment	Value added
40	46.7	19.0	5.6
41 - 80	34.5	39.5	24.3
81 - 150	13.6	27.8	30.7
151 - 300	3.8	9.8	21.0
301	1.4	3.9	18.4
Total		100.0	100.0

SOURCE
Grupo Estudos Básicos de Economia Industrial.

EMPLOYMENT AND WAGES
Considering manufacturing industry as a whole, employment is largely concentrated in the traditional sectors, with low productivity and problems over external competition. The annual rate of growth (0.4 per cent between 1965 and 1970, 0.5 per cent between 1960 and 1970) was completely inadequate to compensate for the release of active farm workers and led to a premature loss in relation to the services sector.

In the last few years the employment structure in various sectors of manufacturing industry has not changed considerably. The ratio between wage earners and total working population was kept high at about 75 per cent, similar to that of the EEC countries, but higher than that of Spain and Greece.

Emigration was stimulated by the policy of the fascist regime that this was a way to 'compensate' for non-creation of jobs (between 1960 and 1976 there were an estimated 1.6 million emigrants) and as a means to keep the balance of payments in equilibrium (remittances from emigrants accounted for 10 per cent of GDP in 1973, or about 60 per cent of total exports of goods and services).

The employment structure (5), together with the negative effects of the recent return of ex-colonial nationals and the stagnation of emigration, explain the increase in the unemployment rate (as well as underemployment in agriculture), which has increased dramatically since 1975.

Past experience confirms that the development of traditional export industries does not contribute to the creation of a great number of jobs. The likelihood is that it will not do so in the future since the present company structure demands the adoption of centralising measures to ensure a better impact by Portuguese exports in international markets. The support given to the reconversion of sectors could, at most, play an important role in maintaining the existing level of employment rather than creating new posts.

The largest share of wage earners in national income - 49.8 per cent - was registered in 1975, whereas the Community average went up to 58.1 and in Spain to 54.5 per cent (6).

On the other hand, the Budget has failed to adopt redistributive measures (except among workers themselves) since our own estimates reveal that only 25 per cent of the total tax return is from unearned income - this shows the importance and urgency of fair fiscal reforms.

As regards working hours in manufacturing industry, there has been steady progress towards standardisation among the Twelve (7). As far as wages are concerned, the levels per sector in the Community are all 160 to 489 per cent above the corresponding Portuguese levels. In Portugal the increase in wages in 1974 and 1975 was followed by the IMF policy, and devaluation of the escudo, which had the immediate effect of lowering the price of the labour force (and consequently increasing exports of the more traditional export goods and the price of imports).

Since Portuguese exports must compete with those

from countries with an even lower wage level (the NICS), and because they are dependent upon products with a low income elasticity (8), the devaluation of the escudo tends to be self-perpetuating, so that competitiveness can be safeguarded at all costs. With these additional difficulties, both the development of the export structure and the modernisation of the production structure would be prevented.

MULTINATIONALS

The internationalisation of economic life and the growing role of the multinationals have had, and still have, profound effects in Portugal. Meanwhile, due to the measures taken and the characteristics of the Portuguese economy (natural resource endowment, cheap and semiskilled labour, geographical situation and membership of EFTA), the establishment of multinationals in industry can be classified as follows:

(a) A first phase which, through export/import firms selling direct or through national enterprises, or producing by licence in national enterprises, aimed to penetrate the Portuguese market in mining, simple consumption goods and conversion of farm produce.

(b) Between 1960 and 1973 (during the colonial war), through direct investments, acquisition or participation in national enterprises or financing through the national capital market made available by multinationals who had built a number of plants in the country (first in Lisbon - Setubal), the aim was to gain control of the market, taking advantage of the weakness of national enterprises in the pharmaceutical, chemical, refining, automobile assembly, domestic electrical appliances, radios, television sectors and others.

(c) After 1968, the larger concerns encouraged the transfer of their factories to the south of Europe, taking advantage of low wage levels and the absence of autonomous trade unions, in the sectors of clothing, footwear, electronics, electrical goods, light machinery (printing and textile machines), toys, precision engineering and optics (especially in the Oporto - Braga region).

(d) More recently, the amount of foreign investment has become stagnant at about $60 million per annum, aiming to maintain the value of existing investments and to penetrate the intermediate product sector, especially chemicals and allied end-products (glues, synthetic fertilisers, paper).

The Portuguese data show, sector by sector, the much bigger average size of companies with foreign participation (minor or major holdings), their important weight in employment and their higher average productivity. Among the 100 largest manufacturing enterprises (classified according to their sales volume) in 1971, forty-two had foreign capital participation. As far as the employment level is concerned, foreign capital plays a significant role in the mining industry (even though there are only five companies), as well as in the electrical materials, chemical, rubber and transport goods, tobacco (only one firm) and metal products sectors. It is important to note the share in gross production of the mining industry and in the electrical products, rubber, transport equipment, metallurgical, other manufacturing, non-electrical machines and chemical sectors.

Direct investment represented 44 per cent of total gross domestic fixed capital formation in the mining industry and only 6 per cent in manufacturing (9).

In terms of the effects on the balance of payments, available data are inconclusive. Considering that foreign concerns work in the more export oriented fields, they have naturally made a decisive contribution to increasing and 'modernising' exports. However, the resultant increase in imports cannot be quantified due to reluctance of foreign firms to obtain supplies on the internal market, to inadequate internal market capacity in terms of machinery and equipment, or to the 'draw back' system for imported raw materials.

EXTERNAL TECHNOLOGICAL DEPENDENCE

The dependence of Portuguese industry is not confined to commercial exchanges or foreign investment. Dependence on technology, 'know-how', and capital goods assumes particular importance when defining the correct strategy for industrial independence in the framework of the present international market.

Portugal's suppliers of technology and equipment are similar: about two-thirds come from the EEC, namely France, West Germany and the United Kingdom; about 10 per cent come from the United States, followed by Switzerland, and 7 per cent from Spain. Of imported technology 75 per cent goes to manufacturing industry (to the chemical and electromechanical sectors). (See Table 7.2).

The chemical industry imports technology mainly from the United Kingdom and West Germany, and the metallurgical and electro-mechanical industries import it from France, with West Germany as the second main supplier. France is the main supplier of technology for the textile industry, followed by Switzerland. Italy's technology is almost exclusively directed to the non-metallic minerals sector at par with Spain, following the main supplier, France.

The greatest technological dependence (10) is in the metallurgical, chemical and metallo-mechanical industries, followed by pulp, paper and cardboard, rubber and non-metallic minerals industries. The less dependent sectors are timber, furniture and cork, food, drink and tobacco, clothing and footwear.

In global terms, the analysis also shows that in the manufacturing industry technological imports related to investment are of most importance, followed by those necessary to maintain normal production. The burden imposed by the use of patent licences and the acquisition of know-how, as well as the lack of marketing, viability, establishment and engineering studies (and considering the weaknesses in effective transfers of technology) are characteristics inherent in the import of technology which reflect the lack of dynamism and the heavy and old-fashioned structure which characterises Portuguese industry.

It has been calculated that in 1972 the royalties paid to foreign firms by Portuguese firms, even though they represented only part of expenditure, were approximately equal to the amount of foreign investment made in the same year.

Regarding the supply of equipment, manufacturing industry as a whole imported 37 per cent of its total equipment, but the printing, textiles and clothing, cement, tobacco, paper and allied

(percentages)

Sectors	Origin							
	France	West Germany	Britain	Sweden	Switzerland	United States	Spain	Total
Food, drink, tobacco	1.7	0.8	1.4	0.8	0.2	0.8	0.5	10.2
Textiles, clothing, footwear	2.5	0.2	1.2	1.0	2.0	1.0	0.2	10.2
Timber, furniture, cork	0.2	0.6	0.2	0	0.2	0.3	0	1.5
Pulp, paper, cardboard	0.6	0.4	0.6	1.5	0.5	1.0	1.2	7.2
Rubber industry	0	1.0	0.2	0	0	0	0	1.2
Chemical industry	3.3	4.6	5.2	0.4	2.1	3.1	1.2	26.1
Non-metallic minerals	1.8	0.6	0.4	0	0.2	0.6	1.2	6.6
Metallurgical	3.3	1.7	1.4	0	0.8	0.4	0	9.5
Electro-mechanical	4.6	3.9	3.3	1.5	1.9	1.2	2.3	24.1
Other manufacturing	0.6	0.6	0.8	0	0.2	0	0.6	3.4
Manufacturing industry	18.6	14.4	14.7	5.2	8.1	8.4	7.6	100

SOURCE
Data obtained from 'Transfer of Technology and Technological Dependence in Portugal', Study by Gabinete de Estudos e Planeamento of the Ministry for Industry and Technology, Lisbon.

NOTE
(a) Technological dependence is measured here according to number of contracts signed.

products and metal production sectors all imported more than 50 per cent of their equipment.

Manufacturing industry is only able to supply 70 per cent of the total needs of the internal market. The following sectors stand out: chemicals (51 per cent), petroleum and coal (65), metallurgical (54), metal products (26), non-electrical machines (9), electrical material (40), transport material (51) and other manufacturing (55). (Figures relate to 1973.) In 1975 the sectors that stood out were non-electrical machines (18 per cent), electrical material (46), metal products (37). However, there were exceptional circumstances in that year.

THE WEIGHT OF THE PUBLIC SECTOR IN THE PORTUGUESE ECONOMY

The State's coercive intervention accelerated and guided the centralisation and concentration of capital (11), and by 1973 the Portuguese economy was controlled by seven large monopolist groups: CUF, Espirito Santo, Champalimaud, Português do Atlântico, Borges & Irmão, Nacional Ultramarino and Fonsecas & Burnay. The names themselves indicate that in some cases the financing capital was formed by linking industrial sectors (CUF and Champalimaud) to the banks; in other cases, banks took over industrial capital. 'Industrial conditioning' meant that any new investment had to receive prior approval from the Ministry for Economic Affairs, whose decision depended upon whether it considered the productive capacity sufficient for current demand. This system strengthened existing monopolies, and protected the low level of productivity and inefficiency which prevailed in many industrial sectors.

The corporative organisation, market and prices controlled by the monopolist system, the regressive fiscal policy, the subsidies, the tax exemptions and the State's direct financial aid to monopolist groups, the use of social security funds for financing the large companies, State expenditure on non-viable sectors, are examples of the forms used for the creation of an 'endless succession of new market imperfections which together with the effects of the "industrial conditioning" caused an acute rigidity in the productive process' (12).

In this context, colonial exploitation had

contradictory effects: on the one hand, the excessive colonial profits and the creation in Portugal of surplus value originated in the colonies established a source of additional accumulation; on the other hand, the investments in and characteristics of the colonial markets slowed down the rate of accumulation in Portugal and rendered less pressing, for the monopolies, the need to stimulate development and technological advance in the Portuguese economy.

As a rule, the structures of the monopolist groups were of vertical integration with autonomous operational and cumulative mechanisms which gave a certain coherence to their activities and to their joint decision-making processes. The groups shared the market in an essentially peaceful manner, with total control over basic industrial industry and the main centres of capital accumulation (13). The close relationship between their activities and the logic of the existing political regime made inevitable the process of profound transformations in the direction of economic democratisation, together with the socio-political democratisation started by the April 1974 Revolution. The nationalisations, whose aim was control of the basic sectors of the economy, hit the firms and sectors owned by the monopolist groups, which have disappeared from the country's present economic scene.

Today the public and nationalised sector is, due to the qualitative and quantitative weight of its enterprises, decisive for the evolution of the Portuguese economy. By virtue of its own strength, it must be considered when it comes to defining any strategy for growth, any industrial policy, any integration.

The public sector has a very high share of gross fixed capital formation (14), which, if considered in terms of manufacturing alone,reaches 56 per cent of the total, which in turn shows its capital-intensive nature. Within the total manufacturing industry, the public sector shares 15 per cent of gross value added, 20 of gross production, 15 of wages, 9.7 of employment, 23 of raw material consumption and 38 of energy consumption.

The nationalised sector comprises 100 per cent of four basic sectors - the petroleum-based products and coal; cement; iron and steel; and electricity

(15). Other industries such as production, transport and distribution of electricity, steel, fertilizers, petroleum refining, petrochemical, cement, tobacco, beer, banking, insurance, airways and railways are public and nationalised. In cellulose, shipbuilding, heavy engineering, urban and suburban passenger transport, shipping, oil distribution and cereals the nationalised sector is also dominant. In a small economy such as the Portuguese, the size and qualitative weight of the nationalised sector stands out, independently of the indicators used.

As regards investment projects, the nationalised sector is important not only because replacement investments are in general much higher than those in the private sector, but also because the two most important investment projects are also included in the present sphere of activities of the nationalised sector, namely the project for the total processing of pyrites and iron ore and those for the chemical industry at Sines.

The stimulating and catalytic effect that the nationalised sector can have in a revival of economic activity, its more predictable behaviour in relation to directives from the central authority, and the not entirely profit-seeking character of its enterprises could allow for a very powerful, perhaps more efficient, form of intervention.

The fact that this kind of potential remains untapped is not the most worrying feature of the present situation in Portugal. The absence of any measures directed at improving the working conditions of the nationalised industries, this sector's dependence upon restrictive policies such as those dictated by the IMF, the almost total ignorance of its technical capacity, the lack of political will to coordinate, plan, rationalise and make viable its activities have persisted in recent years, preventing the conversion of various nationalised enterprises into the coherent whole necessary for any economic development strategy.

SCENARIOS FOR ENTRY

The Portuguese application to join the EEC is part and parcel of the economic strategy of the past. It is, therefore, legitimate to seek the reasons for considering this policy as a means of resolving the country's basic problems, bearing in mind that important changes have taken place both at the international and national levels.

Customs barriers have not operated for many years, with the exception of 1975 when import surtaxes were imposed. In 1963 the percentage of customs tariffs for total imports (excluding diamonds) reached 12.5 per cent,in 1970 they dropped to 9.4, in 1973 to 6.5 and in 1978 these tariffs were a mere 3.2 per cent (to which 3.7 due to surtaxes must be added). The guidelines 'recommended' by the IMF and World Bank are easily confirmed.

Guidelines for the 'encouragement of exports' were based on the system of taxation in the 'intercalary plan for 1965-67', which gave absolute priority to production growth and chose the exporting industries and tourism as dynamic activites.

There is nothing original in the World Bank's suggestion that the promotion of labour-intensive investment pointing towards exports was a key to growth strategy in Portugal, or in OECD acceptance that 'if the control of internal costs and prices is maintained there is probably more possibility for new export industries of labour intensive types', or that preference to investment in textiles and electronics may come to be more clearly defended than investments in the petro-chemicals, fertilizers and steel.

There is no doubt about the small size of the Portuguese internal market, as well as the poor use of natural resources (even ignorance about them), and it is quite evident that in the long run it is impossible to build a coherent productive set-up from the sectoral point of view with a structure similar to that of the larger industrialised countries.

But if lack of will (political, in the first instance) continues, and no measures are adopted to create and develop the fundamental nucleus of productive machinery on a national basis, with economic, financial and technological autonomy, the strategy which is being planned will result in the development of dispersed industries, highly vulnerable and dependent on foreign capital - the industries in decline - and in the perpetuation of a structure (sectoral and export) typical of that of developing nations.

In such a scenario the evolution of wages would suffer conflicting pressures: on the one hand, the strengthening of trade unions and the influence of the Community could contribute to their being raised in relative terms, but on the other hand the effects of specialisation (and international competition) would be an additional argument for keeping them at their general low level.

Emigration would offer one way out. Nevertheless, it could be impossible given the present structural problems within the EEC. Even with regard to social improvement, the need to maintain duties at levels lower than those for other countries to stimulate foreign investment would not allow sufficient expansion of the social services.

It is against this predictable background that in Portugal and in the EEC countries themselves resistance has been growing against this integrating process whose beneficiaries are well defined social forces, namely the multinationals who, after all, are the ones who have had more benefits from integration and have been able to consolidate their economic and political positions, to reinforce their competitive power and to widen their international influence.

The inadequacy and unworkability of present EEC economic aid, especially the regional and social funds (16) of the EIB to meet requirements after the second enlargement are clearly reflected in the proposals for a 'Marshall Plan for Southern Europe' or for 'a solidarity programme with the partially industrialised countries', or for 'a policy of approximation and a global strategy ... mobilising to the full the Community's potential'.

The task is to define a long-term industrial policy for the Community, and 'to elaborate a plan - necessarily rough to start with - to develop the southern countries which is the result of a concept for intra-European integration and development' (17). It would become necessary to combine the policies of import substitution and export diversification and give examples of 'bunches of projects' which occur in the nationalised sector (for instance, the complete processing of pyrites in Alentejo and the utilisation of iron ore reserves in Moncorvo, expansion of the steel industry and the petrochemical complex in

Sines).

There appears to be no end to the processes to which integration might give rise. However, the power of the Portuguese nationalised sector on the one hand, and the changes occurring in the EEC indicate the need to avoid leaving to market forces the initiative in the structural changes which will take place. There is also a need to act within well-defined and coherent objectives which, in the case of Portugal, implies an additional and qualitatively improved effort in activities and investment policy of the nationalised sector (18).

The priority given to creation of an industrial core based on chosen and inter-connected methods of industrialisation - a priority which assumes the establishment of as coherent an economic structure as possible in which the role played by the nationalised sector is decisive - does not exhaust the list of problems raised by the development strategy adopted for Portugal's entry into the new international economic order (which is not a mere international division of labour).

The present <u>concentration</u> within Portuguese exports, regarding products such as textiles and countries such as those of the EEC and EFTA, together with the deficit in the trade balance, demand the definition of clear guidelines for external trade. These guidelines can only advocate a more advanced structure for exports. On the other hand, it is necessary to reduce the present import elasticity in relation to GDP.

The definition of such guidelines affects the primary sector, agriculture and fishing, the potential of which is still to be explored, and the rational utilisation of the new cooperatives resulting from the agrarian reform, which occupy more than one-sixth of the country's area. It also affects the implementation of large projects in key sectors, which in the long run may stimulate the growth of internal demand, without which it will be impossible to reduce significantly the present level of unemployment.

NOTES

1. Institute for Trade Union Studies of the European Trade Union Confederation, Brussels, 1979.
2. These figures, in the Portuguese case,

reflect the backwardness of the agricultural sector rather than the development of the industrial sector.

3. J.F. Amaral, II Conference on the Portuguese Economy, Lisbon, September 1979.
4. Prepared by the Study and Planning Group of the Ministry for Industry and Technology, Lisbon.
5. According to estimates for 1978 produced by the Central Planning Department, the total of 2.45 million Portuguese wage earners is divided as follows: 386.8 in the primary sector; 773.3 in manufacturing and extractive industries; 271.2 in the building industry; 22.6 in electricity, gas and water services; and 994.1 in the services sector. The textile, clothing and footwear industries, with a total of 254,500 workers, together with the metallurgical, metal products, machine and transport industries, with a total of 208,100 workers, assume an important place within manufacturing industry as a whole.
6. Commission of the European Communities, 'Enlargement of the Community: economic and sectoral aspects', EEC Bulletin, Supplement 3/78, Brussels, 1978.
7. According to the Institute for Trade Union Studies of the European Trade Union Confederation.
8. R. Eckaus, II Conference on the Portuguese Economy, Lisbon, September 1979.
9. Figures are for the period 1969-75 and were supplied by the Ministry for Industry and Technology, Lisbon.
10. In terms of frequency of recourse to foreign technology and of the relative weights of the same sectors in terms of gross production values.
11. The primary role played by State intervention explains that, at one time, the centralisation of capital (that is, the joining of existing capital in the hands of a smaller number of capitalists) was clearly more noticeable than the concentration of capital (the appropriation of surplus value which is created in the process of production by a small number of capitalists).
12. J.M. Rolo, 'Factors of strengthening and

dynamisation of the State owned sector', in Social Analysis, Vol. XIV (55).

13. See Chapter 5, this volume.
14. According to estimates from the Central Department of Planning, in 1978 gross fixed capital formation reached 161,800 million escudos (current prices), that is, 20 per cent of GDP. Of the total, 32,000 million were in housing, 64.8 in the productive private sector, 24 in the non-productive public sector and 41 in the productive public sector.
15. Instituto das Participações do Estado.
16. 'In the EEC, the regional policy is in danger of becoming a non-specified component of the general economic and development policy, and therefore degenerating into an additional policy for stimulating growth. The view may well be readopted that, through the stimulation of growth in industrial centres, the gap between the central and peripheral regions may disappear.' K. Esser, Portugal in the EEC, Berlin, German Development Institute, 1977.
17. Ibid. See also chapters by S. Musto and M. Bienefeld in D. Seers and C.Vaitsos (eds), The Second Enlargement of EEC: The Integration of Unequal Partners, London, Macmillan, 1982.
18. Ideological motivations cause some Portuguese political personalities to argue against the nationalised sector, whose simple existence is deemed 'opposed to Community rules'. They state clearly their intention to use entry into the Community to question the structural changes in the Portuguese economy (similar to the attacks made against the agrarian reform).

Part IV

Spain

8 Characteristics and Motives for Entry

JUAN ANTONIO PAYNO

HISTORICAL NECESSITY OF MEMBERSHIP

For Spain, accession to the EEC has profound historical significance which is unrelated to the short- or medium-term economic costs or benefits (which is not to say that it does not have economic meaning): centuries ago the country was isolated and marginalised by the power structure then, and the same has happened again in the past half-century. Spain's return to the international fold offers the only opportunity - with a fair assurance of success - for Spanish life to take new and definitive orientations. The aim in this chapter is to enquire into the fundamental reasons why the Spanish economy is committed to membership. To do this, we should start with very general questions, such as whether or not the economic growth Spain is experiencing still makes sense; but since the economic authorities do not address themselves to these questions, it would be rhetorical to ask them here. At all events, if there is a change of course one day, it will be in Spain's interest to have a presence in one of the decision-making centres on which it is already dependent economically and politically (primarily the EEC and the United States).

This is not an alternative to dependence on other decision-making centres but rather the consequence of the Spanish economy's high degree of dependent integration with the Community. Spain's future influence will depend on the power structure in the enlarged EEC, but it will certainly have more opportunity to exercise influence there than in isolation.

Nor does the domestic situation in Spain allow any other option: on the one hand, the Government is pursuing economic policies which coincide with those of the EEC, so that it sees accession as a consistent objective; on the other hand, domestic political conditions seem to preclude (for the foreseeable future) any shift in the exercise of power which would be sufficiently significant to bring a substantial change in economic policy (nor does the Portuguese experience justify belief that a radical transformation is viable). In considering the topic of membership, therefore, it is necessary to assume that there will be no change in the existing institutional environment.

Finally, on these assumptions, the internal dynamics of the Spanish economy call for changes which are analogous to those required for accession to the EEC. Consequently, the decisive arguments in favour of membership, from the Spanish viewpoint, are unaffected by quantification of specific costs and benefits (1), although this does not detract from the need to minimise the costs and maximise the benefits.

SPAIN: EUROPEAN SEMI-PERIPHERAL ECONOMY

Spain has a peripheral economy (characterised by political and commercial weakness, lack of technological know-how, dualism, regional under-development, emigration and tourism, cultural colonisation, foreign debt, inflation, dependence on imported defence equipment, etc.)(2) but it has reached a relatively advanced stage of development, comparable with the semi-peripheral European countries (shown in features such as extensive urban development, an almost balanced position on foreign trade, comparable industrial productivity, inflation, foreign debt burden, currency and fiscal system, not to mention degree of cultural autonomy).

The rapid economic growth of the 1960s, with the profound structural transformation of the 1970s, determined the characteristics of the economy as it now is. Today, gross value added per employed person in both industry and services is similar to that in Italy, Britain and Ireland. In terms of GNP per capita, the difference is greater for two reasons: (i) Spanish agriculture is less productive and employs a greater proportion of the overall working population; and (ii) the activity rate is lower, partly because the population is younger (see Table 8.1). In Spain, therefore, per capita income is lower in comparative terms than output per worker, and non-agricultural productivity is better than generally believed.

This dualism affects non-agricultural productivity,

TABLE 8.1 Gross value added per worker in industry and agriculture, and GNP per capita in Spain compared with Italy, Ireland and the United Kingdom, 1964 and 1977

(Spanish productivity as a percentage of each other country)

	1964		1977		
	Gross value added per agricultural worker	Gross value added per industrial worker	Gross value added per agricultural worker	Gross value added per industrial worker	GNP per capita
Italy	54	61	99	127	91
Ireland	55	78	71	98	107
United Kingdom	21	52	39	94	72

SOURCES
INE, _Contabilidad Nacional de España_, Madrid; ILO, _Yearbook of Labour Statistics_; UN, _National Accounts Statistics_ (_seriatim_).

and even if resources for industry and services are used efficiently, total resources are not fully exploited, thus imposing a burden on the economy. For instance, emigration to the EEC and Switzerland reached 10 per cent of the Spanish active population in 1973, reflecting the inadequate level of economic growth achieved. The present high unemployment rate is out of proportion to the fall in domestic economic activity, since it also reflects the fact that the EEC no longer absorbs surplus manpower. This type of economic weakness and dependence condemns the country of emigration to meeting the costs not only of training emigrant labour, but also of adjustment in the economies which benefit from the efforts of such workers. As well as unemployment, there has been a fall in the activity rate, particularly among women (where it was already below the European average), which should be considered in relation to the employment situation.

This maladjustment between employment and population does not happen by chance. The birth rate was kept up by religious pressure and maintained by practical measures, such as prohibition of sales of contraceptives and information about them, in line with the economic thinking of the former regime, which favoured elasticity of labour supply. (The birth rate had fallen during the Republic.)

Some forecasts (3) estimate that Spain will provide 25 per cent of the net total increase in the population of working age in the Twelve up to the year 2000, whereas there will be absolute falls in West Germany and other countries (Spain +4 million, West Germany -2.1 million). Demographic forecasting is, of course, uncertain, and the cultural change in Spain could lead to a fall in the birth rate, but there seems little doubt about the trend, if not the actual figures, foreshadowed in these forecasts. The problem of Spain's net labour supply is, therefore, of vital importance and will remain so for some time to come. With accession in prospect, priority must be given to certain objectives, namely the establishment of more equitable conditions of employment for emigrants, giving them full rights, a more even spread of the costs involved in readjustment by the 'core' European countries (e.g. the problem of exported unemployment), an increase in domestic demand for labour through limited economic expansion, and participation in possible plans for structural reorganisation of a European economy beset by permanent unemployment.

Finally, in relation to recent demographic trends in Spain, internal migration between 1961 and 1970 was estimated at 3.7 million people (over 14 per cent of the average population during the period); there was no regional policy (although there was official raising of personal expectations), so that the pattern of migratory flows which has been traced back to 1900 (4) persisted, accentuating regional imbalances by creating a concentration of population and wealth in a relatively small area. As was forecast (5), the developed area lies within a quadrilateral bounded by the Pyrenees, the Cantabrian and Mediterranean coasts, and an almost straight line running from Oviedo to Valencia by way of Madrid (6). Thus economic growth which lagged behind demographic growth did not allow for full employment and, as balanced economic objectives were not pursued, agriculture remained backward and large population movements were initiated, with increasing regional imbalances and emigration abroad.

PRINCIPLES OF THE FRANCO ECONOMY AND ITS PARTIAL DETERIORATION

The economy had already reached the limits of efficiency before 1975 (when the effects of the international crisis made matters worse), although there had been reluctance, motivated primarily by political considerations, to admit this. Subsequently, the decisive characteristics of the economy under Franco have been modified by political changes and a number of legal changes, and undermined to some extent by a certain willingness to dismantle the apparatus of state intervention. This process has resulted in friction between old and new elements and caused the behaviour of economic operators, accustomed to interventionism, paternalism and corruption, to become badly adjusted to the new situation.

The economy under Franco was designed to accelerate capital accumulation through coercion and domination of the workers by the State. Its aim was not to promote economic growth, but simply to increase the absolute surplus which could be appropriated by certain groups and classes; the logic of accumulation merely induced economic growth as a consequence of the improvement in prospects and the decisive tilting of the scales in favour of the interests of the <u>grande bourgeoisie</u> (which formed alliances with foreign capital) (7). Successive events set up conflicts of interests among various groups and determined the shape of different economic phases (1953, 1959). The last such phase saw the strengthening of economic growth and internationalisation of the Spanish economy.

(a) Direct control of the workers was based on the prohibition of parties and unions, and the existence of the official union. The labour regulations fixed levels of pay. Set against this was the inflexibility of the roll lists, as well as the legal impossibility of dismissing employees. These restrictions did not represent any real burden on production costs for as long as direct control was maintained. The phase beginning in 1959 was characterised by the liberalisation of factors, creating pressures leading to authorisation of collective bargaining and the introduction of a measure of flexibility in the appointment of officers at the official trade union from 1964, resulting in relaxation of direct control. As productivity and surpluses increased, so the struggle for union rights was stepped up, with an increase in the frequency of open disputes which gradually eroded the economic foundations of the regime and were a major factor in the 'deterioration of civil peace' from 1966 (following the high inflation of 1965 and the social reaction to it).

Between 1974 and 1977 the combination of inflation and weak political leadership created the conditions for wage awards which outstripped increases in productivity and therefore cut profit margins. The legalisation of trade unions in 1977/78 created uncertainty and a mood of greater pessimism among employers. Since the Moncloa Pacts of 1977 it has been possible, with control of liquid assets and curbs on the negotiation of wage increases, to restore profit margins to some extent; the restrictive monetary policy has successfully checked inflation and the balance-of-payments deficit (8), but it has been inflexible and has left companies very little scope for increasing net self-financing as a consequence of the net surplus in the external balance and they have been confronted with very grave cash-flow problems.

Social security, which had been a net provider of financial resources to the economy (for instance to the public sector and the electricity generating industry), fell into deficit as a result of the effects of inflation itself and the increase in unemployment. A relaxation of the rules on the use of savings bank resources in 1977 also weakened the financial base of certain sectors. Finally, the 1978 tax reforms, following which the volume of direct taxes rose above that of indirect taxes for the first time, and the psychological impact of the introduction of the wealth tax, also had a negative influence on employers' expectations, despite the fact that the main component of direct taxation is still tax on wages. All these developments helped to produce a right-wing reaction from employers and led to the abandonment of the reforming policies after 1978.

(b) Economic interventionism survived the 1959 liberalisation; the entrepreneur's 'market' was the Government rather than the actual market (9), the logical consequences of this being corruption, speculation and the rise of economic groups connected with the administration, all of which bred habits which were very difficult to change (10). In particular, conditions favoured financial accumulation of capital and its control over industry.

The State was, therefore, paramount in determining the distribution of wealth. There were innumerable specific measures, but the most important were tax exemptions, direct control of prices and an expansionist monetary policy combined with preferential (subsidised) finance facilities for shipbuilding, steel, electricity generation, etc., and in particular the 'concerted action' agreed upon with certain sectors of industry and the State over some target in terms of physical production in exchange for various tax advantages. Not all of these measures have been eliminated, but the new ideology of the right in power since 1977 is moving in this direction.

(c) The foundations of the Franco economy, therefore, have been undermined in such fields as wage control, finance, interventionism, taxation, etc., and the tendency is towards alignment with the EEC. However, this process has been limited by rejection of structural reforms and, at the same time, adjustment of the economy has met with resistance from economic pressure groups. The process leading up to membership of the EEC is helping to neutralise resistance to a liberalising economic policy - which is unavoidable for domestic reasons - or at least to avoid a direct confrontation with the Government. It is doubtful whether it will be possible otherwise for the Government to make fundamental economic changes.

CHANGES IN THE PATTERN OF GROWTH

The crisis in the Spanish economy has been influenced by the international crisis, but it also reflects the inherent limitations in the earlier process of growth. During the autarchic phase (1940-53/59), profit margins were increased, and minimum volumes of products necessary to the performance of the virtually closed economy were maintained. By 1959, when that system's scope for growth in output and intensive appropriation of the proceeds had been exhausted, the Government opted for economic growth, so that the relative surplus could continue growing without any additional pressure on labour, taking advantage of the prospects for a rapid improvement in earnings which the growth rate had led the population to expect, among other factors.

Before 1959 there had already been import substitution; the State had created the basic conditions for production and laid down priorities for industrialisation (in energy, infrastructure, building, mechanical engineering, chemical and textile industries), but aside from the international market. The slight growth in the traditional sectors was not enough to stem the increasing needs for imports and eventually an external bottleneck occurred. The capacity for import substitution had been exhausted in the case of consumer goods and almost in that of intermediate goods; but with capital goods it was still 30 per cent (despite spectacular growth)(11). In 1959 efforts were made to tackle the external bottleneck, inflation and other problems: in a favourable international economic climate, factors of production were liberalised (emigration, imports financed by international borrowing and inflows of foreign capital), so that it was possible to replace obsolete capital equipment, to obtain raw materials and to supplement the supply of foodstuffs (limited by low agricultural productivity), with the additional contribution of foreign capital (12).

The increase in agricultural wages (as an effect of industrial wages) led to mechanisation during the 1960s, increasing surpluses on large holdings and creating a crisis for small farmers, who were proletarianised (13). When confronted with change in the demand pattern for foodstuffs, as a result of improvements in personal income with a tendency towards the more expensive products, such as meat, market garden produce and dairy produce, leading to shortages of the latter and surpluses of traditional products, the State, instead of embarking upon a policy of land reform which would have damaged the interests of the big landowners, chose to pay support prices and buy in surpluses, as a result of which agriculture displayed an increasingly weak trade balance and became a major cause of inflation. The broad influence on the family budget (in which food accounted for 50 per cent) and the other conditions already referred to, explain the brake placed on trade liberalisation from 1963 to 1966, when inflation reached its peak (in 1965), and the general introversion (see above).

From this point on, efforts were made to rationalise the instruments of economic policy in order to contain inflation (e.g. in 1972) and alternately to reactivate the economy (e.g. in 1973/74). However, with pressure building up on costs, the weak regime intensified institutional introversion and protectionism, continuing on the course of reflation (with inflation). The process of adjustment did not begin until 1977, after the first general election.

The increase in productivity between 1962 and 1970 has been estimated at 46.6 per cent in terms of the reduction in manning requirements; labour savings were achieved through investment and, although a larger proportion of the growth in the working population was absorbed, emigration continued to act as the escape valve. Trade liberalisation made for better allocation of resources; in the early stages, more competitive imports replaced domestically manufactured products and subsequently there was an intensive phase of specialisation (see Table 8.2) (14).

The effects of technological change made most impact on intermediate factors, capital goods and transport equipment in general, in spite of which in 1970 there were still manifest shortcomings in the first two of these categories and in the upstream sectors of industry, and production of consumer goods still predominated (15); the extent of the spread of industrial growth had been inversely proportional to the degree of transformation of manufacturing processes.

The most dynamic sectors were the chemical industry, energy, machinery and car manufacture, while traditional industries lost ground (44 per cent of industrial output in 1962, 25.4 per cent in 1972). Some industries (iron and steel, shipbuilding) lost some of their surpluses, but on the whole the net surplus was still being produced by the primary industries, manufacture of consumer goods and credit (16).

TABLE 8.2 Spain: degree of self-sufficiency by sector

Sector	Absolute degree (percentages)	Weighted degree
Agriculture	88.3	96.1
Livestock	98.7	107.4
Fish	96.3	104.8
Raw materials	53.5	58.1
Transport and energy	98.3	107.0
Basic industries	85.8	93.4
Manufactures, first-stage processing (1st group)	81.7	88.9
Manufactures, first-stage processing (2nd group)	94.7	103.1
Intermediate finished goods	88.6	96.4
General services	95.7	104.1
Consumer goods	95.5	103.9
Consumer services	99.7	108.5
Consumables	98.2	106.9
Capital goods	86.5	94.1
Overall average	91.9	100.0
Simple average	89.4	

SOURCE
J.A. Payno, 'Algunos problemas de la Economía español a la luz de las tablas intersectoriales', Estudios Turísticos, No. 49-50, 1976.

TABLE 8.3 Spain: final destinations of domestic output by sector (a)

Sector	Consumption	Investment	Export
	(percentages)		
Agriculture	74	7	18
Livestock	88	3	11
Fish	90	1	8
Raw materials	58	27	17
Transport and energy	72	19	8
Basic industries	61	24	15
Manufactures, first-stage processing (1st group)	82	25	23
Manufactures, first-stage processing (2nd group)	38	48	14
Intermediate finished goods	49	34	17
General services	77	15	8
Consumer goods	87	2	11
Consumer services	89	1	-
Consumables	81	3	8
Capital goods	11	64	5
Total	70	20	10

SOURCE
J. A. Payno, 'Algunos problemas de la Economía española a la luz de las tablas intersectoriales', Estudios Turísticos, No. 49-50, 1976.

NOTE
(a) The value added by any sector is measured for each product, with reference to the sector of origin, not the sector of the final product.

Exports of final products incorporated increasing proportions of the net product of intermediate industries; the import content per unit exported rose during the decade (17), but the statistics do not show up the inverse import substitution during the early years. Increasing specialisation improved competitiveness; in 1962 domestic prices of manufactures had been 68 per cent higher than on the international market, but by 1968 they were only 31 per cent higher (see Table 8.3) (18).

Thus limited liberalisation had enormously positive effects, although there was still a need in 1970 to take the process further, since Spanish capital goods and basic products were less complex than imports, while imported raw materials were incorporated in the more complex production processes; moreover, there were bottlenecks in production of capital goods, consumer durables and intermediate goods (19). The international crisis enhanced competitiveness and the role of foreign trade: whereas between 1962 and 1972 the proportion of the GDP accounted for by exports had been only 22 per cent (20), by 1978 it had risen to 61 per cent (21).

The main drawback of this growth was the fact that it was founded on dependence (emigrants' remittances, tourism and foreign investment, all of which helped the balance of payments, and technology). This left the economy vulnerable to the fall in demand for labour in the EEC and the decline in the general economic situation (which affected tourism). The economy also suffers from the technological control which had accompanied direct foreign investment. This investment had come mainly from the United States, Switzerland and the EEC and concentrated on car manufacture, tourism, the chemical industry and food processing. Payments abroad for technology were $400 million in 1976 (compared with earnings from abroad of $50 million) and corresponded (in 1975) to 0.35 per cent of GNP, 1.3 per cent of gross fixed capital formation and 2.1 per cent of imports of goods; Spain was one of the technologically most dependent countries (see Table 8.4) (22). Against this, expenditure on research was estimated at between 0.2 and 0.4 per cent of GNP.

It has been estimated that 44 per cent of technology contracts contain conditions prohibiting exports, and a further 26 per cent contain other restrictions, in addition to limiting the Spanish companies' access to subsequent technical improvements (23). Almost half of the payments for

TABLE 8.4 Spain: receipts and payments on technology, 1966 and 1977 (millions of pesetas)

Year	Receipts			Payments		
	Fees, trademarks and royalties	Technical assistance	Total	Fees, trademarks and royalties	Technical assistance	Total
1966	212	185	397	3,161	2,656	5,816
1977	1,036	3,445	4,461	8,754	19,974	28,728

SOURCE
Spanish balance of payments, Ministerio de Comercio, Secretaría General Técnica.

technology were made by companies in which foreign interests had majority holdings (and 85 per cent by only 290 companies).

EXTERNAL POSITION OF THE SPANISH ECONOMY

The recession beginning in 1975 led to a fall in imports and acted as a spur to exports, which rose by 32.8 per cent in 1977, 29.2 in 1978, 20.2 in 1979 and 23.9 in 1980 (in pesetas), and increased from 6.9 per cent of GDP in 1976 to 9.5 by 1979 and 10.3 in 1980 (24). Consequently, the cover rate advanced from 50 per cent in 1976 to 68.8 in 1978, 71.3 in 1979 and 60.4 in 1980 - according to unadjusted data. (The 1980 figure is due essentially to the oil bill.)

The trade balance shows large deficits on energy products and raw materials, and a smaller deficit on capital goods; the surpluses are derived from consume goods (both durable and non-durable). Industrialisation has, therefore, reached a relatively advanced stage and, logically, the next phase should be an increase in the volume - and complexity - of exported capital goods.

However, the overall statistics give no indication of the existence of two distinct structures: in its trade with LAFTA countries, Spain is cast in the role of a core country, whereas in its dealings with the EEC, Japan and the United States, it displays characteristics of dependence, as evidenced by its exports of foodstuffs and relatively larger imports of capital goods. Nevertheless, its cover rate on trade with the EEC is close to break-even point.

In the past, exporting (except of agricultural produce) had been the alternative resorted to when the domestic market was depressed, but the recent increase in the export figures - although perhaps achieved by cutting profit margins - gives grounds for hoping that the trend will be consolidated (even allowing for monetary and fiscal factors), building on the change in the pattern during the 1970s and the improvement in competitiveness. The transnationals had doubtless originally been attracted by the high degree of protection, but now they are actively engaged in exporting (especially cars and trucks, rubber and tyres, and processed foods).

The recent liberalisation of trade can create favourable conditions for consolidation; the brief past experience gave a great boost to the economy, but even so, the level of protection remains high. (With the reductions called for in the 1970 Agreement, tariff protection of the Spanish market vis-à-vis the EEC has been estimated at 16.9 per cent, compared with EEC protection of 6.7.)

Imports are structural and technical in character (direct foreign investment during the 1960s made for technological dependence). In 1977, it has been estimated, the elasticity of imports with respect to the GNP was 1.3; however, since imports are more closely bound up with the level of investment, they fell more steeply during the recent years of recession than could have been forecast according to this ratio, and economic reactivation would once again cause serious trade balance problems (apart from the specific case of oil).

The role played by transnationals in trade in semi-manufactures and finished goods alters the real significance of customs protection. Nevertheless, reduction of tariffs can mean an overall reduction in costs and therefore improved competitiveness. With less protection, marginal companies will be eliminated from the market, but this is the price to be paid for better competitiveness, since it is difficult to see how it would be possible to continue to develop exports and lend greater depth to the productive system without achieving a reduction in overall costs.

Greater efficiency in the economy would stimulate domestic investment, which has been stagnant since 1975, in contrast with the intensification of foreign investment and expansion of Spanish capital abroad. Foreign investment increased dramatically in 1978/79, providing evidence of the transnationals' appreciation of the momentum and prospects of the Spanish economy, including the outlook for accession to the EEC. The expansion of Spanish capitalism abroad is partly a corollary of expansion of sales networks, but it includes investment in manufacturing activities and the figures, although modest, are significant for the economy (22,350 million pesetas in 1979). The process of liberalisation is now extending to exports of capital.

To sum up, given the present state of the Spanish economy, there are sound reasons for believing that, overall, tariff dismantling will have a positive effect on the rationalisation of the industrial structure, without which it would seem very difficult for Spain to improve its position on the world market.

THE ROLE OF THE EEC IN THE SPANISH ECONOMY

Against this background, does membership of the EEC make economic sense or is it at least the best of the possible alternatives? What advantages does joining the EEC offer to a fragile, dependent economy with considerable irrationality in its productive structure and great regional disparities, stagnant investment, institutional uncertainties and political weakness? What role can it play in the EEC and what can the EEC bring to it, other than domination by the economically powerful members?

These very questions demonstrate Spain's lack of freedom of choice: even the internal (political and economic) development needed today is more than the weak Government, as at present constituted, could manage (it is incapable of overcoming either internal or external resistance). Moreover, the Spanish economy and society are a conglomeration of realities of different origins which need to be ordered in a coherent manner; procrastination over tackling this task has exacerbated the problems.

Nevertheless, it is an economy which offers productive opportunities, ability to compete and human resources, which commands the confidence of foreign investors and has potential for expansion of its foreign trade. But it is confronted by a crisis which no longer permits a way out by reducing prices of consumer goods; a crisis which it cannot escape on its own, not even by cutting its ties with the world economy. From this viewpoint, the EEC offers institutional compatibility and, moreover, it is the economic bloc with which Spain has the closest ties, being the source of much of its investment, tourism and trade. In particular, the EEC predominates in Spain's foreign trade (although with balanced flows in overall terms). In this trade, Spain specialises in exports of agricultural produce and consumer goods and is a large importer of intermediate goods (two-thirds of its total imports of such goods), capital goods (three-fifths) and consumer goods (two-thirds). Geographically, the main trading partners are Britain, West Germany, France and Italy, which account for almost 40 per cent of Spain's total exports and a similar volume of its imports (excluding oil).

The EEC is absolutely essential for exports of

foodstuffs and as the source of supplies needed to keep industry running. In addition, the volume of exports of capital goods, especially to France and Italy, is substantial (although proportionately lower than in Spain's overall export figures), even in relation to French and Italian imports (cars, for instance).

In recent years Spain has maintained overall trade surpluses with France, Belgium-Luxembourg and the Netherlands, as well as partial surpluses on raw materials with Italy, intermediate goods with France and capital goods with Denmark; apparently, Spain has relatively well balanced trade and has a reasonable ability to compete in the EEC (see Table 8.5).

The degree of specialisation in Spanish exports to the EEC (25) is particularly high in fresh fruits (24 per cent overall and generally above 30, except in the case of Italy, 0.2), edible oils in Italy (15 per cent) and iron (West Germany 3.2 per cent and Denmark 3.8), and to a certain extent in cars (this last due to the activities of the transnationals). Trading strength lies in fruit and vegetables, which have, in fact, lost ground on almost all the EEC markets (see Table 8.6), and the very existence of the EEC is prejudicial to sales of primary products, for which there is virtually no alternative market. On the other hand, the development of the more complex types of mechanical products is to a certain extent independent. Mutual reduction of customs duties with the EEC would tend to reduce industrial costs, to a greater extent than general tariff dismantling with the rest of the world. Industry could benefit on this side and export agriculture would no longer be faced with the discrimination deriving from the CAP and the EEC's agreements with competitor countries which are allowed larger tariff reductions than those granted to Spain under the 1970 agreement (see Table 8.7).

CONCLUDING REMARKS

Would the Spanish economy derive greater benefit from any of the alternatives to the EEC (nationalism, free trade or partial agreements)? Entry into the EEC will require changes and will make market conditions more difficult in some areas, all of which will involve costs, but the state of the Spanish economy does not suggest that a nationalistic course

TABLE 8.5 Percentage shares of imports by EEC countries of selected Spanish products, 1971 and 1977

	Fresh fruit		Edible oils		Iron and Steel		Cars		Total trade	
	1971	1977	1971	1977	1971	1977	1971	1977	1971	1977
West Germany	12.4	12.0	1.6	1.7	1.5	3.1	0.4	2.7	1.1	1
France	22.3	23.2	9.8	2.9	0.9	4.6	1.5	12.0	1.7	2
Italy	6.4	2.7	53.4	11.2	0.6	2.1	0.4	5.5	1.3	1
The Netherlands	14.9	13.8	1.6	1.1	1.0	1.4	2.3	0.7	0.9	1
Belgium-Luxembourg	16.3	13.1	0.5	0.6	0.5	2.6	0.3	0.6	0.6	0
EEC (The Six)	15.0	15.2	16.8	3.9	1.0	3.1	0.9	4.1	1.2	1
United Kingdom	13.5	11.0	4.3	1.1	6.9	2.0	0.3	0.7	1.5	1
Ireland	6.2	5.6	10.4	-	-	1.8	-	1.1	0.7	0
Denmark	15.3	14.5	1.5	-	0.1	1.3	0.3	1.2	0.6	0
EEC (The Nine)	14.6	14.4	14.1	3.4	1.5	2.9	0.8	3.4	1.2	1

SOURCES
OECD, Statistiques du Commerce Extérieur; Trade by Commodities, January-December 1971/77, Paris, and further details from the Servicio de Estudios del BEE.

TABLE 8.6 Penetration of the EEC market by Spanish products, 1977 (a)

	Products		
	Fresh fruit	Edible oils	Iron
SITC	0.51	421-2	671
West Germany	45.9	6.71	3.15
France	30.91	3.76	0.51
Italy	0.21	15.12	-
The Netherlands	39.72	2.98	1.48
Belgium-Luxembourg	50.90	0.92	0.61
The Six	22.62	7.00	2.12
United Kingdom	34.10	3.06	1.35
Ireland	14.34	1.25	-
Denmark	53.15	1.87	3.78
The Nine	23.95	6.49	1.46

SOURCES
Eurostat, Production Végétale, Bulletin Mensuel des Statistiques Générales; OECD, Principaux Indicateurs Economiques, Statistiques du Commerce Extérieur.

NOTE
(a) Method of calculation

$$\frac{\text{Spanish exports of the product/The country's total imports + Output of the product}}{\text{Total Spanish exports/The country's total imports + GDP}}$$

Significance:
- A quotient of one signifies a product of medium weight
- The greater the quotient, the greater the penetration, and vice versa

TABLE 8.7 Comparison of customs tariff reductions granted t
Spain and Morocco by the EEC

Products	Percentage reductio	
	Spain	Morocc
Legumes in the pod or shelled	30	60
Tomatoes	50	60
Sweet peppers	30	40
Dried legumes, shelled, peeled or split	50	60
Dates	50	100
Fresh oranges	40	80
Mandarins and satsumas, fresh; clementines, tangerines and other similar citrus hybrids, fresh	40	80
Fresh lemons	40	80
Apricots	50	60
Peaches, including nectarines	50	50
Pawpaws	50	50
Fruit salads	50	50
Others	50	50
Fruit and vegetables, prepared or preserved in vinegar or acetic acid, with or without salt, spices mustard or sugar	50	100
Fruit and vegetables, prepared or preserved, without vinegar or acetic acid	50	50

SOURCES
El acuerdo Espana-Mercado Común, Asociación para el Progreso de la Dirección, Madrid, and the Official Journal of the European Communities.

would be viable; nor do history, the structure of power groups or current conditions in the world economy seem to favour a free-trade approach; it also seems illusory to hope to be able to negotiate from a position of weakness and gain partial agreements (advantageous to Spain) without concessions in other fields, but it does not seem that Spain has any alternative to membership, not only for political reasons, but also because its own economic structure destines it for similar changes to those confronting the EEC. It is desirable for Spain to have a voice in decisions which are bound to affect it in any event.

This in no sense means that Spain should seek to join on any terms; on the contrary, it must make a very precise calculation of the potential costs and benefits and, above all, a detailed analysis of the effects which entry could have on each area of the economy, at both sectoral and regional levels. In fact, it is implicit in the argument set out here that the EEC is the natural outlet given the structure of the Spanish economy; the corollary of this is that the polarising forces which damage the interests of certain sections of the population, displacing wealth, will continue to operate, perhaps on a greater scale. That it seems impossible to change this tendency by our own devices does not mean that no effort should be made to do so. Clearly, the terms on which Spain joins will be an essential factor here. So too will be the new balance of power in the twelve-member EEC. The most positive factor is the reasonable certainty that entry will provide the opportunity to remove, once and for all, obstacles or habits rooted in the past which are impeding rationalisation of the economy and which would, if Spain were to remain isolated, perhaps not only continue to impede rationalisation but also lead to introversion and chaos (26).

Like any other change, accession to the EEC is a challenge. With any change costs have to be accepted; new openings are turned to advantage only if there is the resourcefulness to identify and exploit them intelligently. Should Spain lack the minimum resources to carry through this innovative action, accession would be suicidal. But this is not the case, and accession will be an opportunity. What is made of it will depend on the Spanish people.

NOTES

1. Chapters 9 and 10 on Spanish agriculture and industry confirm this view.
2. D. Seers, 'The periphery of Europe', in Underdeveloped Europe: Studies in Core-Periphery Relations, Institute of Development Studies, 1979.
3. 'La evolución demográfica de Europa después de la guerra y las perspectivas hasta el año 2000', in Estudio sobre la situación económica de Europa en 1974.
4. A. Garcia Barbancho, Las migraciones interiores españolas: Estudio cuantitativo desde 1900, Madrid, Instituto de Desarrollo Económico, 1967.
5. R. Martinez Cortiña, J.A. Payno, and others, Regionalización de la Economía España, Madrid, Fondo para la Investigación Económica y Social de la Confederación Española de Cajas de Ahorros 1975.
6. Banco de Bilbao, Renta Nacional de España y su distribución provincial 1977, Bilbao, 1980.
7. J. Muñoz, Internationalisacion del Capital en España, Madrid, Edicusa, 1978.
8. The deterioration in the 1980 balance of payments is due to the increase in oil prices. The deficit increased by 441 billion pesetas while the oil bill alone increased by 377.3 billion pesetas.
9. J. Gonzalez, La economía política del franquismo 1940-70: Liberalización y Planificación, Madrid, Tecnos, 1978.
10. J.B. Donges, 'Evolución de los costes de oportunidad de las políticas de comercio exterior de España', Revista de Economía Española, Vol. 1, Madrid, 1971.
11. J.B. Donges, La industrialización en España, Barcelona, Oikos-Tau,1976.
12. F. Estape, Ensayos sobre economía española (reprint of an article written in 1958), Barcelona, Ariel, 1972.
13. J.M. Naredo, La evolución de la agricultura en España, Barcelona, Laia, 1971.
14. O. Fanjul, et al., Cambios en la Estructura Interindustria de la Economía Española 1962-70: una primera aproximación, Madrid, Fundacion del Instituto Nacional de Industria, December 1974.
15. J.A. Payno, 'Algunos problemas de la economía española a la luz de las tablas intersectoriales' Estudios Turísticos No. 49-50, Madrid, 1976.

16. J.A. Payno, 'Distribución sectorial de excedente de la producción española', *Revista de Economía Política*, Madrid, Instituto de Estudios Políticos, Madrid, August 1975.
17. J. Segura and E. Garcia Viñuela, 'El déficit comercial de la economía española', *Información Comercial Española*, No. 536, Madrid, 1978.
18. J.B. Donges, *op.cit.*
19. J.A. Payno, 'El proceso global de producción: tipología técnica', *Revista de Economía Política*, Madrid, Instituto de Estudios Políticos, 1975.
20. J.B. Donges, *op. cit.*
21. Banco de España, *Informe 1978*, Madrid, 1979.
22. It should be made clear that direct investment accounted for only 50 per cent of total foreign investment, while 42 per cent was in real estate and portfolio holdings.
23. V. Parajon, 'La industria española ante las Comunidades Europeas', *Información Comercial Española*, No. 550-551, Madrid, 1979.
24. Banco de España, *Informe 1976* and *Informe 1980*, Direccion General de Aduanas, Avance mensuel de comercio exterior, December 1980.
25. Degree of specialisation:

    $$\frac{\text{Spanish exports of the product/the country's total imports + output}}{\text{Total Spanish exports/the country's total imports + GDP}}$$

26. After the attempted *coup d'état* of 23 February 1981, there have been indications that the Government is recognising pressures for protectionism and State intervention. (This chapter was written first in 1979 and revised in 1980.)

9 The Agricultural Sector

JOSÉ J. ROMERO RODRÍGUEZ

This chapter focuses on the probable effects of full membership of the EEC on Spanish agriculture rather than on implications of Spanish entry for Community agriculture. Analyses of this subject often concentrate on the repercussions of the CAP on Spanish farmers, on the assumption that the policy will remain unchanged (1). We believe that this assumption is wrong. Like any other Community policy, the CAP, despite all institutional momentum, is subject to a dynamism likely to be given further momentum with the enlargement.

THE DIVERSITY OF SPANISH AGRICULTURE

The impact of Spanish entry to the EEC will be determined by the quantitative importance of Spain's agrarian sector, both in absolute and in relative terms vis-à-vis Community agriculture. It employs about 2½ million persons (about 20 per cent of Spain's total active population), distributed in a similar number of farming units (2) and accounts for about 9 per cent of Spain's GDP. Much is expected of the agricultural sector in terms of improving the trade balance and absorbing labour at a time of serious unemployment.

Spain's accession will bring about a 32 per cent rise in the number of people engaged in the agricultural sector in the EEC, a 34 per cent expansion of the farming area of the Community, a 34 per cent increase in the number of farming lots (excluding those smaller than one hectare) and a 15 per cent expansion in total output.

Problems associated with Spanish accession are aggravated by the enormous diversity of Spanish agriculture. The 'dual structure' of Italian agriculture is often referred to (3), but Spain's agrarian sector is even more complex than this, or than the classic 'latifundia-minifundia' division (4). Thus it is appropriate to analyse regional effects rather than to refer to macro-economic implications for the agricultural sector as a whole.

Structural diversity of farming units. Structural diversity is an old and serious problem but liable to be treated too simply from a national or even regional angle, with a small degree of analysis or disaggregation. (Tables 9.1 and 9.2 provide source data.)

From the farming families' standpoint the whole nation suffers from a structural shortcoming that no sectoral therapy can cure. On the other hand, although it is true that large farms predominate in the south (taking area only) the main problem is that of small farmlots, their share being no less than 75 per cent of total farming units. Structural diversity, clearly dualistic in every region, conditions the spatial distribution of Spain's active farming population, with a much larger impact on wage earning farmhands in southern areas. Since only about 300,000 farming units in Spain are larger than twenty hectares, it is these units and the farmhands they employ that will be most affected by Spain's entry to the EEC. On the other hand, smaller farmlots, which are much more numerous, will be more vulnerable to income losses provoked by accession to the EEC (considering their already critical condition) than positively affected by eventual improvements that cannot be quantitatively very important, considering their small output.

Sectoral diversity. The structure of Spain's agrarian output is substantially different from the Nine's average or from that of individual members. The variety in production reflects different climatic and geophysical conditions. But one should not over-simplify and label the whole farming sector as Mediterranean. Sumpsi (5), for instance, has defined which of the Spanish provinces are properly Mediterranean. To assess the likely impact of enlargement on these varying productive systems requires the construction of appropriate typologies adequate to their complexity.

The real problem exists not only at sectoral and structural levels but at the intersection of both. The very same step in a sectoral policy will

TABLE 9.1 Provincial distribution of Spanish agricultural holdings of less than twenty hectares, 1971

Percentages	Provinces	
≥ 95	Alicante	Oviedo
	Avila	Pontevedra
	Castellón	S. C. de Tenerife
	La Coruña	Santander
	Lugo	Valencia
	Orense	
≥ 85 and < 95	Baleares	La Rioja
	Barcelona	León
	Granada	Málaga
	Guipúzcoa	Murcia
	Jaén	Tarragona
	Las Palmas	Vizcaya
≥ 75 and < 85	Albacete	Lérida
	Almería	Madrid
	Badajoz	Navarra
	Cáceres	Sevilla
	Cádiz	Teruel
	Cdad Real	Toledo
	Córdoba	Zamora
	Gerona	Zaragoza
	Huelva	
< 75	Alava	Palencia
	Burgos	Salamanca
	Cuenca	Segovia
	Guadalajara	Soria
	Huesca	Valladolid

SOURCE
Instituto Nacional de Estadística, Censo Agrario, 1972, Madrid

NOTE
National average: 88 per cent.

TABLE 9.2 Percentage of provincial area in Spain occupied by private holdings of 500+ hectares, 1969

Percentages	Provinces	
≤ 7	Alava	Navarra
	Alicante	Oviedo
	Barcelona	Palencia
	Burgos	Pontevedra
	Castellón	S. C. de Tenerife
	La Coruña	Santander
	Guipúzcoa	Segovia
	León	Soria
	Lérida	Tarragona
	La Rioja	Valencia
	Lugo	Vizcaya
	Murcia	Zamora
> 7 and ≤ 14	Almería	Málaga
	Baleares	Orense
	Cuenca	Teruel
	Gerona	Valladolid
	Guadalajara	Zaragoza
	Huesca	
> 14 and ≤ 21	Avila	Madrid
	Córdoba	Las Palmas
	Granada	Salamanca
	Jaén	Toledo
> 21	Albacete	Ciudad Real
	Badajoz	Huelva
	Cáceres	Sevilla
	Cádiz	

SOURCE
Instituto Nacional de Estadistica, Encuesta de Fincas Agrarias Privadas de 500 y más Has, Madrid, 1969.

affect different producers in a widely different manner, because minifundia (on account of their size or due to their productivity or yield levels) will hardly improve their lot. It is to be expected that Community income support policies in the agricultural sector will stimulate further shifts in production emphases in small farms after the enlargement.

Spatial and regional disparities. Surveys on the accession repercussions of enlargement are prone to be 'agrarianist', and frequently ignore spatial and regional aspects. Consideration of the rural world as a comprehensive reality in which peasants live is vitally important (6). Farmers' welfare, in terms of equitable income distribution and comparable living conditions with those enjoyed by the rest of the population, must include consideration of location in relation to other productive sectors and services.

The map of 'marginal Spain', as defined by the 'Inventario' drawn up by the Spanish Ministry of Agriculture (7), serves as an instrument for detecting four large 'poverty pockets', especially depressed areas within Spain. The first is in the north-west (especially in Galicia); the second is in the west-southwest (particularly Extremadura); the third pocket is near the central area in the provinces of Cuenca, Guadalajara, Teruel and Soria); and the fourth is in south-eastern Spain, in Eastern Andalousia. Among the seventy areas at the end of the list (out of a total of 458), nineteen are in Galicia and fifteen in Andalousia.

The magnitude of this problem of poverty pockets makes it essential to consider it in any analysis of integration in the EEC. This implies that special attention should be given to possibilities in the area of European regional policy, particularly for marginal areas and mountain-range farming.

THE IMPACT OF EEC MEMBERSHIP ON FARMING

There is no doubt that the effects of accession on the Spanish economy are bound to be felt in the trade balance. Despite all tariff barriers, 58.5 per cent of Spain's total farming exports (which account for 22.7 per cent of total Spanish export earnings) went to EEC member countries in

1977 (8).

Important changes are also to be expected in the area of employment as a result of the CAP: a rise in productivity for those agrarian outputs which will suffer from competition from other EEC members might provoke increased labour force emigration from the primary sector of the economy - a potentially serious development in view of the serious unemployment situation.

But these macro-economic effects should be considered for the economy as a whole and not only from the angle of the impact that accession is bound to have on the farming sector. We shall, therefore, consider accession from a threefold perspective: structural, sectoral and spatial or regional.

Structural dualism. The large land-holders have always taken advantage of challenges in the agrarian history of Spain. This was the case with the Land Property Disentailment Acts in the nineteenth century which, far from resulting in a fair redistribution of farm land among wage-earning farmhands and small farmers, gave large landlords the lion's share and allowed them to consolidate their latifundia; under Franco agrarian policy defended the rights of these latifundia landowners. Indeed, peasant unrest, mainly in southern areas of Spain, finally contributed to the civil war (9).

It can be asked if the great challenge of the 1980s for Spanish farming will once more turn out to favour the privileged agrarian strata. Even a superficial survey of the effects of the CAP on the present Ten shows that the large landowners in central and northern Europe have imposed the guidelines of an agrarian policy which suits their interests, at the cost of many small and medium-sized farmers, mainly located in southern areas of the Community.

Such a danger might threaten Spanish farmers, especially considering the influence at a national level of the professional agrarian organisations (the heirs of the Francoist 'Hermandades' - brotherhoods or guilds - in which the interests of large farmers are predominant). The budding trade-union movement started by small and medium-sized farmers in Spain, although growing strongly in some regions (the Rioja and Aragon), is still too small to make its weight felt at national level, and it is to be feared that only with unrest (for example, the 'tractors war' in which farmers blocked roads with their tractors, etc.) will their voice be heard in Brussels.

The effects of the EEC structural policy should be the improvement of the farming conditions and of the incomes of small and medium-sized farmers. If, as is clear, no national agrarian policy aimed at reforming structures exists in Spain, one will have to ground all hopes on Community structural steps. But it would be wrong to entertain too many hopes. The comparison, so often made, between the actions in the two sections of the EAGGF is reason enough to show how limited this hope can be. According to latest available figures, total expenditure by the Guarantee Section amounted to 8,677 million EUA in 1978, compared to only 325 million EUA for its Guidance Section (10).

The Community's agricultural policy would have to be changed and, as a prior condition, the relation of forces among the various agrarian interests would have to be profoundly modified for the structural policy to be reinforced by the accession of the South European candidates.

Is solidarity among European small and medium-sized farmers (including the Spanish) to be expected? Or, rather, is a withdrawal within domestic, national quarters by the different European unions and professional movements, running away from the dangers of enlargement, to be feared? Available indications point to the second conclusion.

For instance, in April 1976, the French Young Farmers' National Centre (CNJA) issued a document entitled 'Spain: a shock for Europe' which has been widely welcomed in France and in other EEC member countries (11). Its conclusions are: 'Spain's accession is a mistake for all . . . the conditions that would make the EEC enlargement a benefit for Europe are not present . . . . When a ship sinks, it is better not to take on board more passengers.'

Whatever the outcome of the structural policy the structural consequences of the production policy cannot be ignored. In fact, agrarian policy measures may have more marked effects on some structures or kinds of farm than structural policy. In this sense, it is difficult to reach definite conclusions. It seems that a large number of small farms start the race handicapped by their productive specialisation. That is the case with respect to small northern farms specialising in dairy cattle and products. Also many small farming lots devoted to Mediterranean crops (fruits and vegetables, vineyards, olives) do not start the race with such unfavourable prospects. However, many of the large farms in the southern half of the Spanish peninsula, where cereals are predominant (soft wheat, above all), may encounter sectoral difficulties.

But there is no reason to think that these large farms will not be able to achieve a radical change in view of the possibilities opened up by European markets, especially bearing in mind their technical capacity and substantial advantages of scale. This explains the fear of European experts who visited Andalousian farming areas and foresaw the possibility of a 'Californian-like' boom in that region, with penetration of European capital, under the cloak of the huge commercial expansion that accession might bring for their products. No doubt the development of such a model would be made at the cost of the very Spanish, small lots style of Mediterranean farming.

All this deters us from forecasting the comparative advantages of accession for the different agrarian productive structures in Spain. We think that Botella (12) may be exceedingly optimistic when he considers that due to the 'upward harmonisation' of social conditions, prospects are very favourable for wage-earning farmhands (32 per cent of the total farm labour force) and for family-sized farmlots (66 per cent) but neutral for employers (large landowners) (2 per cent). We believe it is very risky to state such an opinion, given the many possible political interventions and the variety of productive structures.

Productive subsectors. Provided that the CAP remains unchanged, enlargement will produce a favourable net result for agriculture from a sectoral viewpoint (13). Sectoral balance should always be achieved, taking due account of regional and productive structures. Since the overall balance is favourable, taking present EEC conditions, Spain must include agrarian production in the talks agenda from the very beginning. Here a clash is to be expected between Spanish and other EEC negotiators, over the dismantling of tariffs on farm produce and imposition of a longer transitional period than that affecting the rest of the economy, 'so as to avoid the free movement of products provoking disturbances in Community markets during the transitional period' (14).

It is also necessary to consider the likely improvement in inputs for agriculture as a result of Spain's full membership. Since expenditure from the agrarian sector amounts to about 30 per cent of final agrarian product, such an improvement could well spell substantial savings for farms via expenditure.

One fundamental problem which has been noticed by the French Confederation of Young Farmers (CNJA) is whether Spain's incorporation into the EEC will bring about a new solidarity among Spanish and other southern producers of the Community, or whether, on the contrary, a kind of complicity will emerge between Spanish producers and EEC consumers, at the cost of southern Community producers. This could occur via the quoting of lower prices for Spanish products (with the lifting of the duties), the lowering of production costs, or Spain's climatic advantages. As Table 9.1 shows, for a great number of products (except sugarbeet, cows' milk, maize and soft wheat), Spain's lower prices are bound to play against present EEC suppliers.

Furthermore (and this is an idea which is widespread among Community circles) many are wondering if the accession of the Mediterranean countries to the EEC will not spell a radical change in the CAP making the balance of EAGGF funds tip in favour of the Mediterranean products, as against the present massive protection extended to the Northern products (such as milk, cereals and sugar). There is a technical problem here regarding the highly perishable nature of most Mediterranean products and the difficulties in preserving them.

Will it be at all possible to maintain unchanged the present CAP after the accession of the new candidates in view of the financial cost involved? Taking only the case of Spain and mechanically applying the protection systems in force in 1978 and according to that year's budget, the following estimates are reached:

- Full Spanish membership would have increased 1978 expenditure under the Guarantee Section of the EAGGF by 600 million EUA over the actual figure for the Nine of 6,960 million (not taking into account double levies and MCAs).
- Under the EAGGF's Guidance heading, outlays would have increased from 473 million to 673 or 723 million EUA.
- Considering all EEC funds combined, Spain's accession would have raised the Nine's Budget for 1978 by 1,300 million or 1,400 million EUA, over the 12,362 million actually budgeted.

Other experts believe that the accession of three new candidates will lead to disintegration of the entire Community, which, they say, is not sufficiently cohesive. The very existence of the MCAs as a countervailing device, actually implies the *de facto* re-establishment of tariff barriers for farm produce, despite all the efforts exerted by the EEC Commission to dismantle them, patent evidence of a crisis in the intra-Community free-trade, free-market philosophy. Will these gloomy prospects curb the vital development of Spain's farming or is it doomed to the role of a scapegoat for all the ills ailing a world economy in crisis?

We tend to believe that a slow process of *Mediterranisation* will take place, but only modestly without jeopardising the *acquis communautaire* or other established interests in the dominant sectors which benefit from the CAP.

Spatial sub-systems: towards greater regional disequilibria? The impact of accession will vary by regions according to their main products and as a function of the degree of protection that their outputs receive. Some areas, like the Cantabrian corniche and Galicia, highly dependent on milk cattle, as well as a large area in the central plateau (the Meseta), in which soft wheat and sugarbeet by far lead in importance, are bound to be particularly vulnerable to EEC restrictions. On the other hand, Spain's southern and Mediterranean areas, as well as the islands, will benefit as a whole.

As for regional disparities within the EEC, many Spanish regions will be placed at the end of the list (15). Using the concepts employed by dependence theory, widely accepted when tackling the issue of intra-regional disparities, Spain undoubtedly becomes, as regards the majority of her regions, the actual periphery of Europe's great centres. And Spain's least favoured or less developed regions would become the 'periphery of the periphery', thus subject to play a role dependent on the economy of the whole system.

True enough, compensatory steps can be taken, such as those provided by the ERDF, although EEC regional policy has not shown any noticeable effect yet. Regional disparities rooted in dependence can only be overcome by breaking those very ties of dependence. And then the question must remain open as to whether those ties, which already bind Spain's peripheral regions to the present domestic centres, could be broken through Spain's accession to the EEC or whether accession would only further tighten them.

Thus we are not entirely satisfied by the surveys based on estimated effects that sectoral policies will supposedly have on the different regions. Only an all-out, vigorous and urgent effort of a real regional policy (at domestic and Community levels) could redress the situation of dependence between the new 'peripheries' and the 'centres' (16). It remains to be seen if the present autonomic and regionalist process in Spain will become a driving force behind or an impediment to that policy. There is a further question as to whether centrifugal forces working against intra-regional solidarity will actually be stronger than the centripetal pull symbolically represented by the compensatory fund provided by Spain's constitution (17).

Lastly, the accession of the Three to the EEC calls for a re-consideration and re-appraisal of the relation between North and South. As a recent report rightly puts it, this is a 'Mediterranean geo-political problem'(18). On the one hand, the EEC's southern areas can be considered as a semi-periphery of the more industrialised and richer North. So far, so good. But, on the other hand, intra-Mediterranean relations of European countries, especially when seen in the context of enlargement, make up a complex of often conflicting interests.

CONCLUDING REMARKS

The analysis of the impact of accession on Spain's agriculture is a very difficult task, due to the huge diversity of the sector, particularly if one is focusing on the interests of Spanish farmers. The variety of productive structures, sectoral diversity and spatial and regional disparities, make clear: any action aimed at raising the income and improving the welfare of farming families will have to attack on these three fronts at the same time.

If the global effect of accession appears likely to be positive from the sectoral standpoint, one should not forget that changes in the CAP might substantially modify existing conditions. In any case, Spain cannot accept long-term schedules for the dismantling of agricultural tariffs.

It would appear that class and interest group solidarity is not going to work at an international level. The question arises: will an alliance emerge between farmers in the southern new member countries and northern consumers (via lower prices) at the cost of the present EEC producers? Or will a coalescence of interests among farmers (particularly Mediterranean farmers) emerge?

Spanish agriculture is facing a challenge, and to wait for the moment of accession and only then start asking questions and undertaking basic reforms affecting the rural sector would spell disaster for Spanish farmers. From this very moment it is essential to exert a concerted effort at every level, so that the economic policy steps are taken at a national level to redress disequilibria and prepare for the consequences of accession. Such a national effort may well be the greatest benefit obtainable from Spain's accession to the EEC.

NOTES

1. There are some exceptions, for instance, Denis Bergmann, 'La Ampliación hacia el Sur de la

C.E.E.', in *Agricultura y Sociedad*, No. 4, July-September 1977, pp. 119-52.

2. Not 1.7 million farms as stated in 'Avis sur la demande d'adhésion de l'Espagne', by the EEC Commission, which excludes very small farming lots as unworthy of consideration.
3. Cf. Robert Fanfani, 'Política agraria, evolución estructural y productiva de los países y regiones de la CEE: 1962-1975', in *Agricultura y Sociedad*, No. 4, July-September 1977, p.19.
4. This issue has been dealt with by the author previously, for instance, in José J. Romero Rodríguez, 'La crisis de los agricultores andaluces: un enfoque del problema', in *Situación y perspectivas del crecimiento en Andalucia*, Coleccion Estudios y programación, Madrid, Confederación Española de Cajas de Ahorro, 1978.
5. José M. Sumpsi, 'Delimitacion del area de agricultura mediterránea en España', in *Agricultura y Sociedad*, No. 4, July-September 1977, pp. 81-118.
6. See L. Malassis, 'Economie agricole, agro-alimentaire et rurale', in *Economie Rurale*, No. 131, 1979, pp. 3-10 (European Farming Economists II Congress).
7. Ministerio de Agricultura, Secretaria General Tecnica, 'Inventario de Areas en Depresión socioeconomica: Una aplicación del análisis factorial', Working Document No. 10, Madrid, 1977.
8. The data for 1979 are, respectively, 59.87 and 17.48 per cent.
9. See Edward Malefakis, *Reforma Agraria y Revolución Campesina en la España del Siglo XX*, Barcelona, Ariel, 1970.
10. See also Chapters 5 and 11 in D. Seers and C. Vaitsos (eds), *Integration and Unequal Development: The Experience of the EEC*, London, Macmillan, 1980.
11. CNJA, 'Espagne: Un choc pour L'Europe', Paris, 1976, p. 20. On member country views on the enlargement, see also F. Duchêne's chapter in D. Seers and C. Vaitsos, *The Second Enlargement of the EEC: Integration of Unequal Partners*, London, Macmillan, 1982.

12. Francisco Botella, 'La agricultura en el proceso de adhesión a las Comunidades Europeas', Lecture delivered on 22 May 1979 at the ETSIA, Córdoba (mimeo), p. 19.
13. Francisco Botella, 'Situación actual, problematica y consecuencias de la adhesion de Espana a la CEE', in *La incorporación de la agricultura española al Mercado Común Europeo*, edited by A.E.E.S.A., Madrid, 1977.
14. Commission des Communautés Européennes, 'Avis sur la demande d'adhésion de l'Espagne', *EEC Bulletin*, Supplement 9/78, Ref. Nos 56, 58, 60, 62, 80.
15. The problem becomes still much more serious with Portugal's accession; the ratio between Hamburg and Vila Real becomes 17 to 1.
16. See chapter by S. Musto in D. Seers and C. Vaitsos (eds), *op. cit.*
17. Art. 158,2.
18. Institut Agricole Méditerranéen de Montpellier, 'Situation de l'agriculture et de l'approvisionnement alimentaire dans certains pays arabes et méditerranéens et leur développement prévisible', Survey elaborated by the Commission, June 1978, p. 27 (mimeo).

10 The Industrial Sector

LUIS CARLOS CROISSIER

In analysing the implications for Spanish industry of accession to the Community, I shall distinguish between two aspects: (a) the state of preparedness of the main branches of Spanish industry for coping with the consequences of membership; and (b) the main problems which accession poses for industrial policy.

The question whether or not accession is desirable from the viewpoint of Spanish industry is not discussed here, for various reasons, including the fact that the major problems confronting the economy can be solved only at international or regional levels.

A word of caution is in order concerning the analysis of the advantages to be derived from membership by the various sectors of industry. Sector-by-sector comparisons with the Community need to be made at a very detailed level but, at this level, the statistics are extremely incomplete, unreliable and lacking in homogeneity. The variables that are normally analysed (cost structures, productivity, size of companies, customs protection, technology, etc.) are invariably incomplete. Moreover, it would be necessary to add many others, which are very difficult to evaluate, such as company management, degree of market control, capacity for technological innovation and assimilation, strategies of groups of companies, etc. Sectoral analyses on competitiveness and industrial specialisation are also imperfect In addition, the strategies of multinational groups (which dominate many sectors) represent a fundamental variable in any analysis of phenomena determining the location of production facilities; however, a few exceptions apart, the extent of knowledge about these strategies is minimal. Finally, the coordinates conditioning international industry today are subject to rapid and uncertain developments.

SECTORAL ANALYSIS

The review of subsectors will necessarily suffer from lack of uniformity, since many sources of information have been drawn upon and the level of knowledge about the various subsectors is very uneven. The building industry and the energy sector are not covered here, the former because it is mainly confined within the domestic market, the latter because it is basically unaffected by integration.

A preliminary reference to the problem of customs tariffs is required, since the EEC is first and foremost a customs union. Virtually all sectors of Spanish industry face the prospect of substantial tariff reductions compared with the situation established under the Preference Agreement of 1970 and *vis-à-vis* third countries (see Table 10.1).

The effects of these reductions are difficult to forecast but the sectors which will feel the greatest effect in their trade with the Community are: transport equipment, electrical machinery, textiles and made-up goods, foodstuffs, metal products, miscellaneous manufactures, chemicals and non-electrical machinery. Following adoption of the common external tariff (CET), several will also be affected in their trade with third countries; these include transport equipment, electrical machinery, textiles and made-up goods, metal products, miscellaneous manufactures and non-electrical equipment. However, these assessments would no doubt be modified if we had access to figures representing the actual levels of protection, instead of having to rely on the nominal tariffs, and if we took the Community's many agreements with third countries into account.

On the other hand, abolition of certain quotas would have a significant effect on some products (pyrites if the quotas on sulphur disappear, sewing machines, industrial vehicles, paints, cotton textiles, made-up goods and knitwear, and various products of the food-processing industry).

To this must be added the effects of adopting VAT and the consequent reshaping of the Impuesto de Compensación de Gravámenes Interiores (the tax to offset domestic charges) and Desgravación fiscal a la exportación (fiscal relief on exports), which will mean a considerable loss of protection against foreign competition.

TABLE 10.1 The EEC and Spain: comparison of customs tariffs (nominal average rates as percentages, after the reductions introduced under the Preference Agreement)

Sector	Spain	EEC	Reductions required to comply with CET
Mining	2.8	0.8	-2.0
Foodstuffs	20.2	17.1	-3.1
Beverages and tobacco	7.9	27.7	+19.8
Textiles and made-up goods	22.0	8.7	-13.3
Leather and footwear	13.1	6.6	-6.5
Timber and furniture	13.9	6.4	-7.5
Paper and derivatives	13.7	9.1	-4.6
Chemicals	17.3	9.7	-7.6
Basic chemistry	14.9	10.3	-4.6
Coal, petroleum and derivatives	2.8	2.3	-0.5
Non-ferrous minerals	11.5	4.5	-7.0
Basic metals	11.5	6.4	-5.1
Metalworking products	19.6	7.8	-11.8
Non-electrical machinery	14.7	6.1	-8.6
Electrical machinery	21.6	7.9	-13.7
Transport equipment	24.3	10.0	-14.3
Miscellaneous manufactures	17.6	5.8	-11.8
Building	-	-	-
Electricity, water and gas	-	-	-

SOURCE
Economía Industrial, review published for the Ministry for Industry and Energy, Madrid.

Mining Sector
1.2 per cent of GDP, 96,000 employees, tending to decline; EEC, 1.1 per cent of GDP. Of total production and employment in mining, some 55 per cent is accounted for by energy-generating products, the problems of which are not discussed here. Of the remaining products, seven are outstanding in terms of the value of output: limestone, iron, potassium salts, copper, zinc, lead and pyrites. Considered overall, however, the mining sector (including coal) falls very far short of meeting the needs of industry; Spain is 64 per cent dependent on mineral products and the foreign trade cover rate is below 20 per cent. Membership of the EEC will not make any fundamental difference since, in 1977 for instance, only 5.5 per cent of Spain's mineral imports came from the EEC; on the other hand, 40 per cent of exports go to the Community market, where Spain is a leading supplier of mercury and fluorspar.

This industry's problems are rooted in its excessive fragmentation, low productivity (associated with insufficient mechanisation), lack of financial resources and, increasingly, labour shortages. It does not seem that it will be necessary for the series of support measures introduced under the Ley de Fomento de la Minería (Mining Development Act) to be fundamentally revised in order to comply with Community regulations on support.

Turning to specific products, pyrites will be seriously affected by membership, since unrestricted imports of sulphur of petroleum origin pose a threat to this form of mining, in which there has been heavy investment. Iron and fluorite, which are export products, will suffer from the disappearance of the present DFE system. Potassium salts, for which the EEC is an important market, could be affected by the need to disband the cartel which regulates exports of this product. At the other extreme, the products to derive the greatest benefit could be tin and tungsten, in which Spain has a surplus and the EEC a deficit.

Building Materials
The technically and economically disparate group of industries whose products are used by the building industry enjoyed a very strong growth rate until 1975, having undergone radical change. At present it is a mixture of large, highly capital-intensive

companies with a considerable degree of control over their markets and small, technically and commercially obsolete, companies which concentrate on local markets.

(a) Cement industry. This industry is dominated by large companies which are associated with financial groups and have modern production facilities. The location of plants is generally determined by demand since the cost of transporting cement is high and raw materials are readily available in most areas. In theory, this industry is unlikely to be affected by membership (it supplies the domestic market and there is little prospect of exports to Europe). Nevertheless, with the combination of excess capacity resulting from the crisis in demand on the home market and significant demand from various, mainly Arab, less developed countries, Spain has become one of the world's largest exporters in this industry.

In future, the industry might concentrate on the sale of technology and technical assistance, as it has started to do, rather than on exports. It may derive benefit from some of the cooperation agreements which the EEC has signed with less developed countries. However, the EEC legislation on pollution will call for heavy investment (in addition to that necessitated by the energy crisis to reduce the high specific consumption of energy).

(b) Tiles. This export industry is in a position to benefit from easier access to the Community market, despite the likelihood of fierce competition from Italian products. Its efforts to take advantage of these opportunities will be hampered by its structural shortcomings in the areas of production and marketing. Another unfavourable factor will be the disappearance of the present DFE system and the adoption of VAT. Anti-pollution investment does not appear to pose major problems.

(c) Sanitary ware. Although this is an exporting sector with a number of large companies, it does not manage to balance its trade with the EEC. Design and quality are the points to be emphasised by these companies in order to meet competition from the Community and from the less developed countries.

(d) Glass. Flat glass is produced by three companies associated with two French multinationals - Saint Gobain and BSN. Having excess capacity, they have undertaken a major export drive, so that the external balance shows an overall surplus, although there is a deficit with the EEC on account of the low value of exports compared with imports. As regards technology, although this sector has relatively modern plant, substantial investment is required to switch from drawn glass to float glass production. On accession to the EEC, the advantages of protection will be lost and there will be no substantial improvement in conditions of access to the Community market, given the low degree of protection it enjoys and its considerable surplus capacity. In addition, there is the threat implicit in Western Europe's readier access to the Spanish market, and there remains an unknown quantity: the strategy which will be pursued by the multinationals, which have so much control over both Spanish and Community markets.

(e) Refractories. Given its ill-structured productive facilities and technological backwardness, this sector will have enormous difficulties in facing up to competition from the Community, with which there is already a trade deficit.

(f) Other products. Less important products are natural stones and clays, production of which is predominantly by small businesses serving local markets. Gypsum, on the other hand, is a product which is in abundant supply in Spain and in shortage in the EEC, so that it could benefit from membership (there is already evidence of Community investment in this sector).

Iron and Steel

Accession will include membership of the ECSC, in whose domain it is possible to speak in terms of a real common policy. However, there is a state of crisis caused by falling demand, increasing competition from new producer countries, the energy crisis and financial problems. Given these conditions and the highly aggressive marketing activity of the Spanish steel industry (see Table 10.2), this area presents major problems in the negotiations.

At present the Spanish steel industry is made up of three integrated works (two of them state-owned), forty-six non-integrated works producing standard steel and eighteen making special types of steel (workforce: 80,000; productive capacity: 13.8 million tonnes of steel in 1977, of which 55 per cent in integrated plants, 31 in non-integrated plants making standard steel and 14 in plants producing special steel). A particular feature is the higher proportion of electric furnaces in Spain, the only country with a comparable proportion being Italy. The producers with this type of plant are the biggest exporters; they enjoy greater flexibility, but they are highly vulnerable to the price of scrap. A second feature is the low output per man, the historical maximum being the 153 tonnes achieved in 1974, well below the ECSC average (240 tonnes per man). The reasons for this are the excessive level of indirect labour, the obsolescence of some plant and the productive imbalances in various works.

TABLE 10.2 Spanish foreign trade in iron and steel products, 1970, 1975 and 1978 (thousands of tonnes steel equivalent)

Year	Exports (x)	Imports (m)	Balance (x-m)
1970	330	2,535	-2,205
1975	2,054	2,367	-313
1978	5,454	1,013	4,441

SOURCE
Information provided by the Ministry for Industry and Energy, Madrid.

In view of these problems and in order to meet competition from the ECSC and third countries, the Spanish Government has drawn up guidelines for reorganisation over the period to 1985. The aims are to reduce costs by means of heavy investment, to cut consumption of inputs and rectify productive imbalances, to diversify production, concentrating on products with a higher value added, and to rebuild companies' very weak financial structures. The forecas also anticipate the loss of some jobs, closure of the more obsolete works and elimination of the main bottleneck in the industry by building two pre-reducing plants. Various forecasts are made for 1985, on the basis of an undoubtedly high average growth in GDP of 4-5 per cent, as follows: domestic consumption of 14-15 million tonnes, output of 16-18.5 million tonnes with capacity utilisation at 85-100 per cent, a 7 per cent fall in the labour force, investment of 33,800 million pesetas a year until 1980, and a production target of 250 tonnes per man.

The most difficult part of implementing these plans will be the increase in capacity from 13.8 to 18.6 million tonnes. The financial aid systems envisaged and the amounts involved do not seem to depart from the ECSC rules. The DFE problem will be a greater difficulty in the short term.

By way of conclusion, assuming the implementation of these plans, the Spanish steel industry is capable of facing the challenge from the ECSC and is in no worse a position than the ECSC to meet competition from the new producer countries. The greatest difficulties will be finding the necessary investment capacity and supplying the resources essential to the financial health of companies in the industry.

Metals and Metal-working Products

(a) Non-ferrous metals. Production of aluminium, copper and zinc could benefit from shortages in the Community market, but the starting positions of these three products are very different. The aluminium branch is modern, although technologically dependent, and it may be threatened by developments in electricity prices. The two other branches are beset with structural problems, while for lead, heavy investment will be necessary to comply with Community requirements regarding pollution.

(b) Metal-working products. This is a sector in which the EEC is highly competitive. Nevertheless, there are some products which Spanish companies export on a significant scale and they could benefit from enlargement of the market (hand tools, wire, domestic utensils, screws, etc.). They could also benefit from improved and cheaper supplies of raw materials and plant (particularly in wire-drawing, production of nuts, bolts, screws, ferro-alloys etc.).

On the whole, the outcome will depend on a profound structural reorganisation of companies, to increase their size and strengthen their financial and commercial resources. Specialisation in appropriate products is also essential, especially in view of the need in the medium and long term to withstand increasing competition from new producer countries, such as can already be seen in the case of hand tools. A positive factor is the absence of a high degree of international oligopoly, except in the case of certain products.

Mechanical and Electrical Machinery

It is difficult to define the boundaries of this sector, and to break it down into subsectors. Much of its business is accounted for by construction of capital goods for other industries, but it also produces domestic appliances, sewing machines, typewriters and other products.

Manufacturers of capital goods have experienced spectacular growth over the past eight years, during which the value of output rose by 134 per cent (they account for 5 per cent of GDP and 15 of industrial output, and employ a labour force of 350,000). Moreover, although this sector came into existence in order to supply the domestic market, its exports have reached significant levels (160,000 million pesetas in 1977), having risen by over 25 per cent per year from 1970 to 1979. Nevertheless, Spain remains a clear net importer of capital goods (with a cover rate of 37 per cent, despite very sluggish investment in recent years).

The greatest problems confronting producers of machinery for industry are: (i) the small size of companies; (ii) lack of financial resources, especially to launch exports; (iii) the need for greater specialisation and standardisation within this sector's own range; (iv) technological dependence, which is perhaps the crucial problem in the long term (payments for acquisition of technology range between 1 and 2 per cent of sales, while expenditure on research and development is in the region of 0.3 per cent); (v) particularly in the field of electrical machinery, the most competitive firms are subsidiaries of multinationals. The future of this sector will, accordingly, be conditioned by the strategy adopted by multinationals, about which little is known.

There are also favourable factors: (i) the supply of machinery to developing countries is one of the most promising prospects for European industry; (ii) Spain can become a supplier of medium-level technology to certain developing areas where it has some comparative advantage (Latin America, Arab countries); (iii) since the Spanish economy is still insufficiently industrialised in comparison with the EEC, substantial domestic demand can be anticipated; (iv) there are some specialisations, such as textile machinery, in which Spain has developed its own technology and is demonstrating its international competitiveness.

Finally, electrical domestic appliances, a sub-sector which has grown up in a highly protected market, has achieved remarkable development (employing 28,000 workers, with exports worth 8000 million pesetas). Despite the heavy competition characterising this sector in the EEC, there is reason to believe that Spanish companies will be able to cope with the demands of membership, although they will need to regroup in larger units in order to do so.

Other export products, of much less importance, are sewing machines and typewriters. In their case, competition from Japan and certain less developed countries is the greatest risk.

Shipbuilding

As in Europe, this industry, which has been one of the mainstays of the intense process of Spanish industrialisation, is now experiencing a serious structural crisis caused by factors which include: (i) the continuing fall in demand (the requirements forecast for the 1980s are less than half the world-wide installed capacity); (ii) the profound changes in the structure of demand according to types of vessel; (iii) the very strong competition from countries like Japan, Korea and Brazil.

Given the volume of employment generated by this industry (60,000 employees), its geographical concentration and its strategic importance, Spain has no option but to maintain it. Moreover, its productivity (in CGRT per man) is above the Community average and almost double the level in Britain, so that the comparative advantage argument works in Spain's favour. However, if the industry is to survive on a competitive footing, a structural reorganisation plan, which will have to be negotiated with the EEC, will be required. The broad outline of such a plan is as follows: (i) reduction of capacity by some 40 per cent;(ii) specialisation of shipyards and improved flexibility of their installations; (iii) development of their capacity for vessels and equipment involving more advanced technology; (iv) improvement of the supply industry; (v) coordination of shipyards; and (vi) substantial support to restore financial structures and to compete with other countries.

In negotiating this plan, Spain will be handicapped by the enormous delay in implementing the necessary measures. Other problems are the timetable for tariff dismantling, and the customs protection of ships (14 per cent) and the supply industry (20 per cent). Pressures from the Community will be very great, but Spain must not agree to excessive capacity reductions in an industry which holds considerable comparative advantages over other European countries.

Motor and Accessories Industry

This sector, largest in size of workforce, may be broken down as follows.

(a) Private cars. This industry is completely dominated by the multinationals, which are strengthening their positions to prepare for Spain's accession to the EEC and to meet keen worldwide competition. Full liberalisation of trade will not pose problems as a result of European competition, although it will require greater specialisation in the range of models.

(b) Motor accessories. Major transformations will be required in this sector, in line with those in the motor industry itself. Foreign capital can be expected to strengthen its positions (cf. the takeover of FEMSA by Bosch).

(c) Industrial vehicles. This is the only subsector with Spanish capital and technology, which will disappear unless a fundamental reorganisation of company structures is carried out. The most viable solution entails association with foreign capital, preferably European, as the condition for maintaining employment levels.

(d) Motorcycles and mopeds. For all its tradition, this industry could be threatened seriously by European and Japanese competition. Here again, it is necessary to achieve association with foreign capital.

(e) Aeronautical industry. This very small industry's long-term viability is bound up with the development of Community projects and its ability to play a full part in them.

Chemical Industries

Four industries in this broad sector will be seriously affected, given the overcapacity in Europe and competition from industrialising countries: petrochemicals and plastics raw materials, fertilisers, chemical fibres and sodium chloride. Of these, fertilisers have the most uncertain future. The paper industry faces different problems: ill-structured productive facilities and the heavy anti-pollution investment which it will be obliged to undertake.

The industries in a position to derive greatest benefit from access to the wider market which membership will bring are plastics processing, rubber production and manufacture of domestic detergents (the last dominated by multinationals).

Pharmaceutical Industry

A distinction needs to be made between two sets of problems.

(a) Production of raw materials. Except in the case of antibiotics, production is in its infancy, its development having been sheltered by protectionist measures. Its future is conditional upon access to technology which is closely controlled by multinationals.

(b) Proprietary medicines. 450 small laboratories, although 100 of these control 80 per cent of sales. The majority of firms are dependent on foreign companies for capital and technology. It seems unlikely that they will be affected significantly by integration with the European market, given the absence of free movement for proprietary medicines. On the other hand, the obligation to adopt the Community patent system will have significant repercussions.

Textile Industry
This industry should be able to take advantage of free access to the Community market, although it is in a virtually permanent state of crisis. Its plant is modern on the whole, it has a long tradition, good levels of productivity and lower labour costs. However, it will need to raise its standards of management, improve its marketing networks and specialise in quality goods and fashion articles.

Serious problems could be encountered in silk and synthetic fibres, decorative textiles, made-up goods and knitwear. These last two will have to withstand fierce competition from the developing countries, which will oblige them to improve productivity and strengthen the role of fashion and design.

Food Industries
In view of their diversity, all that may be said is that, with their connection with agriculture and their relatively high labour-intensiveness, these are industries on which Spain should be able to depend. Unfavourable factors are the substantial presence of foreign capital (with a high degree of control over marketing) and the excessively small scale of Spanish companies. Nevertheless, free access to the Community market offers clear opportunities to such products as caramels and sweets, preserved fish, preserved vegetables, charcuterie and fruit juices. On the other hand, the sugar sector could suffer serious damage.

Miscellaneous Consumer Goods
The industries in this general field have enjoyed rapid growth rates and have considerable capacity for exporting. They require little capital investment, so that wage costs are a major factor, and small and medium-sized businesses predominate, with design and marketing playing important roles. In order to realise their potential, they need to strengthen their marketing systems and devote particular attention to design problems.

(a) Furniture. For wood and metal furniture, exports could be developed, given greater specialisation making for longer production runs and reduced costs, and strengthening of external marketing networks (to some extent after the examples set by West Germany and Italy).

(b) Board and plywood. Structural reorganisation is required to withstand competition from third countries.

(c) Graphic arts. This sector, which exports a substantial proportion of its output, could benefit from lower machinery and raw materials costs and wider opportunities for cooperation with European industry.

(d) Footwear and leather goods. This subsector should be one of the main beneficiaries of enlargement of the market, although in the short term it will be affected by the discontinuance of the present DFE system.

(e) Glass hollow-ware and ceramics. This subsector could be very sensitive to Community competition for the market in quality products.

(f) Toys. Although the toy industry exports on a substantial scale, it enjoys considerable protection on the domestic market and it would be affected by Community competition at the top end of the market and by price competition from third countries.

SOME REFLECTIONS ON INDUSTRIAL POLICY

In the context of accession to the Community, Spain's industrial policy is confronted with problems of two types, the first concerned with the need to help industry to make a smooth adaptation to the new conditions, and the second with revision of its own machinery for action, in order to bring it into line with the requirements of the Treaty of Rome. Clearly, the two overlap and are affected by other more general problems (energy crisis, new international division of labour, unemployment and reconsideration of the role to be played by economic policy).

Measures to deal with the first series of problems can be inferred from the above analysis, but it will be useful to clarify key points.

(a) There is, as yet, virtually no technological policy for either technological transfer or research and development. It is necessary not only to increase expenditure on research but also to select appropriate fields and to ensure that the results are put to use by industry.

(b) Structural reorganisation of industry, aimed at gearing dimensions and structures in each sector to the new conditions - something more imaginative, flexible and sectorally diversified - is required rather than merely offering incentives for company mergers. An important requirement is definition of criteria on foreign investment, aimed at realising the potential of domestic industry rather than simply selling it off.

(c) A commercial policy is needed in order to establish an image, a marketing network and after-sales service, without which, particularly in the field of consumer goods, Spanish industry will be doomed to competing strictly on price which, with the competition from countries outside the Community, is becoming increasingly difficult.

(d) Financial support is essential, especially long-term support to promote exports, without which it is unlikely that much of the necessary restructuring will take place.

Action in these areas is crucial for the profound structural reorganisation that is needed.

Problems of adaptation in the strict sense are going to arise in at least five specific fields of industrial policy.

(i) Public Aid

As regards state aid to industry distributed according to sectoral or regional criteria, the Commission of the European Communities has drawn up criteria for authorising or refusing such aid. In the light of these, the extent to which the various forms of aid currently granted are compatible or incompatible with the Community rules can be analysed.

(a) Sectoral aids

Concerted action. This instrument does not seem to present major problems, particularly for the types of industries for which it has been used: coal mining, electricity generation and steel.

Priority interest sectors. This type of aid is much more problematical because of its lack of transparency excessive administration discretion and, above all, the sectors which benefit under it, all of which are 'sensitive' in the EEC: motor vehicles and motor accessories, aviation, electronics and data-processing. However, this aid will have lapsed by 1983.

Structural reorganisation plans. Insofar as these plans have been formulated to reduce capacities, they do not raise any problems, especially in the case of the textile industry, whose plans have not been assisted by public funds.

Aid to mining. On the whole, the forms of aid for which the Mining Development Act makes provision seem likely to be acceptable. However, the aid payable in connection with the declaration of a priority substance is more problematical.

DFE (fiscal relief on exports). The present DFE system sometimes contains a hidden element of export subsidies. Adoption of VAT will end this situation, and some sectors which export on a substantial scale could be seriously affected. This applies to certain building materials, steel, aluminium, zinc and lead, machinery in general, typewriters, cars, arms, textiles and some food products.

Exemption certificates. This very powerful instrument for development of domestic industry producing capital goods has been gradually falling into disuse. There is not the slightest doubt that it is incompatible with Community rules.

Other forms of sectoral aid. Mention should be made here of the financial aid granted to the steel and shipbuilding industries; the Community's acceptance or rejection of this aid will be closely bound up with the structural reorganisation plans adopted for these critical industries. There is also the aid granted to users of fertilisers and pesticides, which is very substantial and could meet with Community opposition. On the other hand, it should be perfectly possible to convince the Community authorities of the justification for the aid granted to promote research and technological development, a neglected area in Spain.

(b) Regional aid. The main instruments for promotion of industry in the regions' industrial estates (preferential location zones and large expansion areas) are compatible with Community rules, especially since the systems are sufficiently transparent and the amounts involved are very modest. Moreover, this would be an important card to play on behalf of Spanish industrial policy, since large areas of Spain could be eligible according to the EEC criteria for Community aid of up to 100 per cent, in addition to which other forms of sectoral aid could be payable.

(ii) Maintenance of Competition

One of the most neglected aspects of Spanish industrial policy, promotion and maintenance of competition, should be considerably strengthened by membership of the EEC. At the same time, it will pose problems, especially in regard to monopolies, since the system of commercial monopolies of oil and tobacco is incompatible with Community regulations. Its abolition would involve very serious consequences especially in the case of oil. Spain has a few years in which to build on the CAMPSA monopoly and the public holdings in exploration and refining interests in order to establish a preponderant role for a public corporation in this vital field.

(iii) Industrial Property Law

Spanish legislation on industrial patents does not recognise patents covering products, although it does recognise patents covering processes, in the chemical, pharmaceutical and food industries. Consequently, Spain did not sign the Munich Convention of 1973 on the European Patent, which was the basis for the Community system established under the Luxembourg Convention of 1975. This raises an extremely difficult problem, involving the very survival of large numbers of companies, mainly in the chemical and pharmaceutical industries, which would undoubtedly be unable to absorb the effects of signature of the Convention on the Community Patent over anything other than the very long term. It is, therefore, necessary to negotiate special conditions. A possible solution would be to sign the Munich Convention and make maximum use of the transitional arrangements for which it makes provision.

The food industry, which this problem affects much less seriously than it does the chemical and pharmaceutical industries, would meet with serious difficulties if the regulations on the Community Trade Mark were to be approved. At all events, it is clear that adoption of Community industrial property law will have profound repercussions in a country like Spain, whose industry is so dependent on foreign technology, with further advantages accruing to subsidiaries of multinationals at the expense of genuinely Spanish companies.

(iv) Technical Regulations

Although Community law is not yet sufficiently developed in this field and major non-tariff barriers to free movement of goods still subsist, adoption of Community rules could have serious effects on Spanish industry. However, this is a very complex topic which has not been examined in sufficient depth, so that it would be premature to speculate as to the sectoral effects.

(v) Regulations on Industrial Pollution

Although, broadly speaking, the requirements of Spanish legislation on industrial pollution are not far removed from those of the Community, their application is minimal. Real compliance with Community standards would undoubtedly entail heavy investment in several industries, including steel, cement, oil refining, paper, petrochemicals, electricity generation and textiles. The capital expenditure and continuing costs involved in such investment are going to cause problems in a number of industries which are already insufficiently competitive. A system of aid for anti-pollution investment must, therefore, be set up as a matter of urgency, and it will be necessary to negotiate periods for adaptation to the Community rules.

CONCLUSIONS

A few ideas are offered here by way of final comment. The first is that the extent to which Spain takes advantage of the opportunities offered by membership, and avoids the pitfalls, will depend on industry's capacity to respond and on industrial policy. The second is that, instead of speaking in terms of those sectors which stand to gain or lose, we should be seeking to identify those lines of products which offer prospects for the future and to establish the production conditions which will ensure their success. The third is that the greatest threats to Spanish industry come from countries outside rather than within the Community, and this is further evidence of the fundamentally 'European' characteristics of Spain's economy.

Statistical Appendix

The purpose of this appendix is to give a brief overview of the socioeconomic situation of the countries in the region, emphasising indicators relevant to integration. The tables include basic figures relating to population, development level, economic structure, etc., and also external accounts, centring particularly on the new entrant.

TABLE A.1 Demographic indicators, 1976

	Crude birth rate (per '000)	Crude death rate (per '000)	Population growth (per '000)
West Germany	9.8	11.9	-2.1
France	13.6	10.5	3.1
Italy	14	9.7	4.3
United Kingdom	11.9	12.2	-0.3
Denmark	12.9	10.6	2.3
Belgium	12.3	12.1	0.2
Holland	12.9	8.3	4.6
Ireland	21.6	10.5	11.1
Luxembourg	11	12.6	-1.6
EEC-9	12.4	11	1.4
Spain	18.2	8	10
Greece	15.7	8.2	7.5
Portugal	19.2	10.5	8.7

SOURCE
UN, Demographic Yearbook 1977, 29th edn, New York, 1979

TABLE A.2 European population projections (a)

	Population		Population (% increase p.a.)	Population of working age		Population of working age (% increase p.a.)
	1980 (m.)	2000 (m.)	2000/1980	1980 (m.)	2000 (m.)	2000/1980
West Germany	60.8	58.7	-0.18	37.76	35.58	-0.3
France	53.8	59.6	0.51	32.02	35.69	0.54
Italy	56.6	61.4	0.41	34.3	36.12	0.26
Belgium	9.8	10.0	0.10	5.98	6.02	0.03
Denmark	5.2	5.5	0.28	3.08	3.33	0.39
Holland	14.2	16.1	0.63	8.55	10.00	0.79
United Kingdom	58.0	64.0	0.49	33.33	38.10	0.67
Ireland	3.3	4.0	0.97	1.76	2.27	1.28
Greece	9.0	10.0	0.53	5.23	5.65	0.37
Spain	37.6	45.4	0.95	22.12	26.4	0.89
Portugal	9.7	11.2	0.72	5.84	6.83	0.79
EEC-9	261.7	279.3	0.33	156.78	167.11	0.32
EEC-12	318.0	345.9	0.42	189.97	205.99	0.41

SOURCE
UN 'Evolución demográfica de Europa después de la guerra y las perspectivas hasta el año 2000' in Estudio sobre la situación económica de Europa en 1974, Segunda parte, New York, 1976.

NOTE
(a) Data not available for Luxembourg.

TABLE A.3 Foreign labour force employed in the main EEC countries, by nationalities, 1977 (a)

Country of origin (nationality)	Country of employment (in thousand persons) Belgium (end 1977)	West Germany (30.9)	France	Holland (15.12)	United Kingdom	EEC Total (b)
Belgium		9	25	17	8	68
Denmark	1	3	1	-	2	7
West Germany	11		25	13	71	138
France	39	42		2	17	115
Ireland	1	1	1	-	452	456
Italy	89	203	230	10	72	696
Luxembourg	2	1	2	-	1	6
Holland	18	47	5		11	85
United Kingdom	10	24	11	7		63
Greece	10	155	5	-	50	221
Total EEC	181	565	305	49	684	1,855
Spain	29	97	265	3	37	436
Portugal	6	60	475	2	10	567
Turkey	17	509	25	14	3	574
Yugoslavia	3	374	50	3	4	443
Algeria	3	1	440	-	1	445
Morocco	29	15	130	6	2	183
Tunis	4	10	70	1	-	85
Other countries, not EEC members	35	239	140	11	926	1,396
Total countries, not EEC members	126	1,305	1,595	46	983	4,129
Gross total	307	1,870	1,900	89	1,667	5,984

SOURCE
EEC, Opinion on Spain's Application for membership: Bulletin, Suplemento 9/78, Luxembourg.

NOTES
(a) Foreign labour force employed in Belgium, France and Holland data are estimates from the Commission Services.
(b) Greece not included.

TABLE A.4 Development indicators: countries of Western Europe

Countries	Telephones per 100 people, 1977	Urban population, %, 1980	Infant mortality	GDP pc, %, 1979	Energy consumption kg/pc, 1978	Tourism per 1000 persons, 1977
Belgium	31.5	72	14	11.0	6.1	292
Denmark	49.3	84	8.9	12.9	5.4	271
France	32.9	78	11.4	10.7	4.4	314
West Germany	37.4	85	15.5	12.5	6.0	326
Greece	25	62	20.3	4.1	1.9	66
Ireland	16.1	58	15.7	4.4	3.3	180
Italy	28.5	69	17.6	5.7	3.2	289
Luxembourg	52.3		10.6	11.6		398
Holland	41.8	76	9.5	10.6	5.3	277
Portugal	12	31	38.9 (76)	2.1	1.0	107 (76)
Spain	26.1	74	15.6	5.3	2.4	161
United Kingdom	41.5	91	14	7.2	5.2	255 (76)

SOURCES
Cols. 1, 3, 4 and 6 in OECD, *Etudes Economiques*, 1981; cols. 2 and 5 in World Bank, *World Development Report, 1980*, Washington.

TABLE A.5 GDP by sectors, 1978 (current prices)

	GDP ($m)	Percentage of GDP arising in: Agriculture	Industry	Services
Spain	147.1	8 (a)	36 (a)	55 (a)
Greece	31.6	17	31	52
Portugal	17.8	13	46	41
Belgium	99.0	2	37	61
Denmark	55.9	7 (b)	35 (b)	52 (b)
France	471.5	5	37	58
West Germany	638.9	3	48	49
Ireland	12.4	17 (c)	28 (c)	41 (c)
Italy	259.9	7	42	51
Luxembourg	3.4	3 (a)	42 (a)	21 (a)
Holland	130.8	4 (a)	35 (a)	61 (a)
United Kingdom	309.5	2	36	62

SOURCES
UN, Yearbook of National Accounts Statistics 1977, New York; World Bank, World Development Report, 1980, Washington.

NOTES
(a) 1977
(b) 1976
(c) 1973

TABLE A.6 Agriculture structure, 1978

	Active population in agriculture (thousand)	% of total active population	Agriculture participation in GDP (%)	Mean annual growth of agriculture (1970-8)
West Germany	1,310	4.6	3	1.6
France	2,173	9.5	5	-0.4
Italy	2,649	12.5	7	0.5
United Kingdom	557	2.2	2	0.8
Belgium/ Luxembourg	135	3.4	2	-1.1
Holland	310	5.8	4	3.6
Ireland	271	22.0	n.d.	n.d.
Denmark	189	7.7	n.d.	n.d.
Spain	2,412	18.9	9	1.9
Greece	1,532	38.8	17	-1.9
Portugal	951	27.6	13	-1.9

SOURCES
FAO, Anuario FAO de Producción 1978, Roma, 1979; World Bank, World Development Report, 1980, Washington.

TABLE A.7 Percentage shares of exports (visible and invisible) in GDP (current prices)

	1973	1979
West Germany	23.7	27.4
France	19.3	23.8
Italy	20.7	29.8
Holland	49.3	54.2
Belgium/Luxembourg	53.7	66.8
United Kingdom	27.5	32.8
Denmark	28.4	32.0
Ireland	41.6	54.5
EEC-9	25.9	31.6
Spain	14.7	15.2
Greece	14.7	19.9
Portugal	27.1	26.6

SOURCE
IMF, International Financial Statistics, Washington, April 1980 and 1981.

TABLE A.8 Greece, Portugal and Spain: agricultural trade and total foreign trade, 1979

Absolute values (millions pesos)	Greece	Portugal	Spain
Total imports	7,648	5,142	18,630
Agricultural imports	645	678	2,306
(including imports from EEC-9)	205	92	352
Total exports	3,354	2,426	13,103
Agricultural exports	1,019	350	2,290
(including exports to EEC-9)	466	173	1,371
Total trade balance	-4,294	-2,716	-5,527
Agricultural trade balance	374	-328	-16
Agricultural balance (EEC-9)	261	81	1,019
Percentages			
Agricultural imports/ total imports	8.43	13.19	12.38
Agricultural exports/ total exports	30.38	14.43	17.48
Agricultural imports/ agricultural exports	63.30	193.71	100.70
Agricultural trade deficit/ total trade deficit	n.a.	12.08	0.30
Agricultural imports from EEC-9/ total agricultural imports	31.78	13.57	15.26
Agricultural exports to EEC-9/ total agricultural exports	45.73	49.43	59.87

SOURCES
OECD, Trade by Commodities, 1979, Paris; and calculations by the Servicio de Estudios of BEE.

TABLE A.9 Greece, Portugal and Spain: foreign public debt, 1979

	Total (billions US dollars)	Private credits (%)	Public credits (%)	Reserves/ paid debt (%)	Debt service/ commodities and services exports (%)	Debt service/ GDP (%)	Paid debt/ GDP (%)
Greece	4.7	64.7	35.3	31.9	9.6	1.9	9.4
Spain	11.4	77.1	22.9	159.9	5.7	0.9	4.3
Portugal	4.6	50.1	49.9	52.6	7.7	2.0	18.5

SOURCES
World Bank, *World Debt Tables*, Vol. II, *External Public Debt of 96 Developing Countries*, Washington, 1979; IMF, *International Financial Statistics*, Washington, April 1981.

TABLE A.10 Greece, Portugal and Spain: composition of imports, 1977-9
(% of total imports)

	Greece	Portugal	Spain
Food products, live animals	8.3	13.5	10.4
Beverages and tobacco	0.3	0.6	1.4
Raw materials, excluding fuels	6.5	11.7	14.4
Fuels and mineral lubricants	18.6	17.3	29.3
Animal or vegetable oil and fat	0.2	0.5	0.6
Chemical products	8.1	12.1	9.7
Manufactured articles	12.8	15.6	9.4
Machinery and transportation equipment	41.9	25.1	19.3
Other manufactured articles	3.3	3.3	5.5
Transactions and miscellaneous commodities	0.1	0.1	0.1
Total	100.0	100.0	100.0
Total (million US dollars)	8,024.1	5,454.9	20,549.1

SOURCES
OECD, Trade by Commodities, Paris, several years; and calculations by the Servicio de Estudios of BEE.

TABLE A.11 Greece, Portugal and Spain: composition of exports, 1977–9
(% of total exports)

	Greece	Portugal	Spain
Food products, live animals	23.3	7.4	15.5
Beverages and tobacco	6.9	6.5	2.6
Raw materials, excluding fuels	8.3	10.5	2.8
Fuels and mineral lubricants	9.1	1.0	2.7
Animal or vegetable oil and fat	1.3	0.7	2.2
Chemical products	4.6	5.6	6.9
Manufactured articles	31.6	34.6	29.1
Machinery and transportation equipment	3.8	13.4	25.9
Other manufactured articles	11.1	18.6	12.2
Transactions and miscellaneous commodities	0.1	1.8	0.1
Total	100.0	100.0	100.0
Total (million US dollars)	3,318.0	2,640.7	13,838.5

SOURCES
OECD, Trade by Commodities, Paris, several years; and calculations by the Servicio de Estudios of BEE.

TABLE A.12 Greece, Portugal and Spain: shares of imports from EEC-9 referred to total, 1978

	Spain	Greece	Portugal
West Germany	10.0	15.7	13.9
France	9.1	6.2	9.0
Italy	4.7	9.8	5.5
Belgium/Luxembourg	1.8	2.6	3.2
Holland	2.8	3.4	3.5
United Kingdom	5.2	5.0	10.1
Denmark	0.5	0.9	0.6
Ireland	0.4	0.4	0.1
EEC-9	34.6	43.8	45.8

SOURCES
OECD, Statistics of Foreign Trade, Paris, April 1979; and calculations by the Servicio de Estudios of BEE.

TABLE A.13 Greece, Portugal and Spain: proportion of exports to EEC-9, 1978

	Spain	Greece	Portuga
West Germany	10.7	20.8	13.0
France	16.6	6.7	8.9
Italy	5.0	10.9	5.7
Belgium/Luxembourg	2.9	2.0	3.2
Holland	3.7	5.4	4.0
United Kingdom	6.4	4.4	18.1
Denmark	0.8	0.6	2.1
Ireland	0.3	0.1	0.4
EEC-9	46.3	50.8	55.5

SOURCES
OECD, Statistics of Foreign Trade, Paris, April 1979; and calculations by the Servicio de Estudios of BEE.

.BLE A.14 Greek, Portuguese and Spanish proportions
: imports to EEC, 1978

	Spain	Greece	Portugal
›st Germany	1.4	0.9	0.3
·ance	3.1	0.4	0.3
:aly	1.2	0.6	0.3
›lgium/Luxembourg	0.9	0.2	0.2
›lland	1.0	0.4	0.2
ıited Kingdom	1.4	0.3	0.6
›nmark	0.2	0.2	0.4
·eland	0.8	0.1	0.3
:C-9	1.3	0.4	0.3

)URCES
:CD, <u>Statistics of Foreign Trade, Annual: Tables by</u>
<u>›porting Countries</u>, Paris, 1978; and calculations by the
›rvicio de Estudios of BEE.

TABLE A.15 EEC-9: exports to Greece, Portugal and Spain referred to total, 1978

	Spain	Greece	Portugal
West Germany	1.3	1.1	0.5
France	2.4	0.7	0.6
Italy	1.5	1.7	0.5
Belgium/Luxembourg	0.8	0.5	0.4
Holland	1.3	0.6	0.4
United Kingdom	1.3	0.6	0.8
Denmark	0.7	0.5	0.3
Ireland	1.0	0.3	0.1
EEC-9	1.4	0.7	0.5

SOURCES
OECD, Statistics of Foreign Trade, Annual: Tables by Reporting Countries, Paris, 1978; and calculations by the Servicio de Estudios of BEE.

TABLE A.16 Greece, Portugal and Spain: imports by country of origin (% of total imports)

	Greece		Portugal		Spain	
	1971-3	1977-9	1971-3	1977-9	1971-3	1977-9
Belgium/Luxembourg	3.6	2.5	2.7	3.0	2.4	1.9
Denmark	0.6	0.8	1.0	0.6	0.7	0.5
France	7.7	6.2	6.6	8.4	10.0	9.2
West Germany	19.9	15.6	14.7	12.9	13.0	9.9
Ireland	0.2	0.4	0.1	0.1	0.3	0.4
Italy	9.7	9.3	5.2	5.3	6.0	5.2
Holland	3.6	3.3	2.8	3.4	3.0	2.9
United Kingdom	6.5	5.4	12.4	9.8	7.0	5.0
Total EEC	51.8	43.5	45.5	43.5	42.5	35.0
Greece			0.2	0.2	0.4	0.2
Portugal	0.1	0.7			0.4	0.3
Spain	1.1	1.8	5.1	5.4		
US	7.2	4.7	8.0	11.3	16.0	12.6
Latin America	2.3	2.1	3.9	4.1	8.3	8.8
Africa	3.7	6.4	12.4	4.2	7.3	8.4
Middle East	5.7	10.6	4.4	12.7	8.8	20.5
Others	28.2	30.3	20.6	18.7	16.2	14.3
Total	100.0	100.0	100.0	100.0	100.0	100.0
Total (million US dollars)	2,636	8,052	2,340	5,545	7,038	20,549

SOURCES
OECD, <u>Trade by Commodities</u>, Paris, several years; and calculations by the Servicio de Estudios of BEE.

TABLE A.17 Greece, Portugal and Spain: exports by country of destination (% of total exports)

	Greece		Portugal		Spain	
	1971-3	1977-9	1971-3	1977-9	1971-3	1977-9
Belgium/Luxembourg	3.1	1.8	2.7	3.4	2.5	2.8
Denmark	0.3	0.7	3.0	2.2	0.9	0.8
France	7.7	6.5	5.0	9.1	8.8	16.3
West Germany	21.3	20.4	7.1	12.6	11.8	10.5
Ireland	0.1	0.1	0.5	0.5	0.3	0.3
Italy	9.5	0.4	3.0	5.3	5.6	5.7
Holland	6.5	5.5	2.6	4.0	5.3	4.1
United Kingdom	5.3	4.9	23.1	18.1	8.3	6.7
Total EEC	53.8	49.3	47.0	55.2	43.5	47.0
Greece			0.3	0.5	2.9	1.2
Portugal	0.3	0.2			4.1	1.8
Spain	1.6	0.7	2.1	2.5		
US	8.0	4.9	10.0	6.5	15.0	8.4
Latin America	0.3	0.7	2.0	3.1	9.7	10.4
Africa	4.2	10.2	17.1	8.2	7.1	11.2
Middle East	5.7	13.0	0.7	1.5	2.3	5.7
Others	26.2	21.1	20.8	22.6	18.8	14.2
Total (million US dollars)	992	3,318	1,377	2,640	3,968	13,842

SOURCES
OECD, Trade by Commodities, Paris, several years; and calculations by the Servicio de Estudios of BEE.

Index

Terms which are abbreviated in the text are indexed in the abbreviated forms (see List of Abbreviations, pp. xvi-xvii).